Civil Happiness

Economists have long laboured under the misapprehension that all humans exist as rational beings that find happiness in maximising their personal utility. This volume presents a historical review of the evolution of economic thought, from economic philosophy to contemporary Economics and its critique of how the human and social dimensions of Economics have been lost in this evolutionary process.

This book examines the crucial period in the late eighteenth century when economists such as Smith and Genovesi tried to reconcile the classical tradition of civil humanism emerging in commercial society, and analyses the impact that the hedonist approach to Economics had in removing the ethical conception of happiness as well as focusing on the role that J.S. Mill, Wicksteed and Pareto had in shifting methodological thinking away from an emphasis on Civil Happiness.

Luigino Bruni is Associate Professor of Economics at the Università degli Studi di Milano Bicocca, Italy.

Routledge studies in the history of economics

Civil Happiness

Economics and human flourishing in historical perspective

Luigino Bruni

LONDON AND NEW YORK

First published 2006
by Routledge
2 Park Square, Milton Park, Abingdon, Oxon OX14 4RN

Simultaneously published in the USA and Canada
by Routledge
605 Third Avenue, New York, NY 10017

*Routledge is an imprint of the Taylor & Francis Group, an informa
business*

© 2006 Luigino Bruni

Typeset in Times by Wearset Ltd, Boldon, Tyne and Wear

British Library Cataloguing in Publication Data
A catalogue record for this book is available from the British Library

Library of Congress Cataloging in Publication Data
A catalog record for this book has been requested

ISBN13: 978-0-415-32628-5 (hbk)
ISBN13: 978-0-415-49410-6 (pbk)
ISBN13: 978-0-203-48811-9 (ebk)

To Chiara Lubich

Contents

Acknowledgements

This book is the result of the last seven years of research, which began after my PhD thesis in History of Economics (University of Florence), on "Vilfredo Pareto and the Birth of the Modern Microeconomics". The starting point of this book can be considered the paper, "Moral canals: trust and social capital in the work of Hume Smith and Genovesi", written together with Robert Sugden, published in the year 2000. Through this research, I discovered the issue of "Public Happiness" in the Neapolitan tradition, one of the main research themes developed in the present text.

Work on the second line of research, sociality, began with a paper on the history of the interpersonal dimension in Economics, "Ego facing Alter: how economists have depicted human interactions", also published in the year 2000.

These first two papers were followed by others, on both happiness and sociality.[1] An important phase of development was my part in the organisation, together with Pier Luigi Porta, of two International Conferences in the university of Milano-Bicocca.[2]

During these years I have been very fortunate to meet people who have greatly enriched both me personally and the quality of my research. First of all, I would like to thank Benedetto Gui, Pier Luigi Porta, Robert Sugden, Stefano Zamagni and Giuseppe Maria Zanghì. The friendship of these scholars is the most important outcome of these years of work. My gratitude goes also to Stefano Bartolini, Giacomo Becattini, Nicolò Bellanca, Giovanni Casoli, Piero Coda, Luca Crivelli, Richard Easterlin, Alberto Ferrucci, Luigi Giusso, Shaun Hargreaves-Heap, Maria Intieri, Salvatore Natoli, Vittorio Pelligra, Maurizio Pugno, Alessandra Smerilli, Tommaso Sorgi and Julie Tremblay: from all I have gained something, and from some I have gained a great amount.

I would also like to thank my colleagues in the Dipartimento di Economia Politica of the Università Milano-Bicocca, the members of the "Abbà School" of the Focolare Movement (Rome), and all the participants (scholars, workers and entrepreneurs) of the "Economy of Communion" project, where I have experienced first-hand the deep link between happiness and sociality.

Last, but not least, I would like to thank Kitty Wolf who, though at a difficult time in her life, has been able to find the intellectual and relational resources to help me so much with the English language and in translating some parts of the book originally written in Italian.

Introduction

How vain is Mortals Happiness!

(B. Mandeville, *The Grumbling Hive*)

Underlying most of the past and present philosophical reflections on happiness is the claim that interpersonal relationships and well-being are linked together by an unbreakable chain. *Happiness*, then, is *civil*.[3]

This book aims to offer new elements for understanding a puzzle: why Economics, which was born with strong links with well-being and Public Happiness, has in time completely lost the non-instrumental interpersonal dimension. In fact, in startling contrast to the other social sciences which give a central role to the analysis of sociality, mainstream economists believed – and still believe – it can stay away from the realm of non-instrumental human relationships.

As a consequence, contemporary Economics is the least-equipped discipline for understanding the nexus between happiness and sociality, although, curiously, economists are, together with psychologists, at the forefront in studying happiness.

The intuition that inspired this book is the conviction that, if it accepts to once again consider interpersonal relations, Economics will profit by a rediscovery of its link with the tradition of Civil Economy. In fact, as we shall see, mainstream Political Economy, for reasons that we will analyse, has considered genuine sociality as an extra-economic matter. In the latter's methodological perspective, Economics deals with non-instrumental relationality only in terms of externalities, that is *before*, *after* or *a later* economic analysis. In the Civil Economy perspective, however, the market can also become a place for experiencing genuine interpersonal relationships. The concept of Civil Happiness, therefore, will be key for this research, seeking to understand the interconnections between happiness and sociality in economic thought.

In particular, this book intends:

i to show *how*, *when* and *why* non-instrumental social interactions were overlooked in the tradition of economic science. The crucial period is the late eighteenth century when economists such as Smith and Genovesi tried to reconcile, each in his own way, the classical tradition of Civic Humanism with the emerging commercial society.

ii to show that the hedonist approach to Economics – from Bentham to Jevons – and the reduction of happiness to pleasure, was a further step in rejecting Civil Happiness, and thus removing an ethical conception of happiness.

iii to underline that, parallel to this strand of neoclassic Economics, the Cambridge tradition, and even more so J.S. Mill, followed instead a current methodology closer to the civil tradition, as far as the connection between wealth and happiness is concerned.

iv to show how the subjectivist and hedonist approaches to happiness were also lost, along with the hedonic way of dealing with sociality. Wicksteed and Pareto are the main actors in this shift. They have determined the methodology of twentieth-century Economics, in which the only allowed form of social interaction is instrumental, therefore leaving no room for Civil Happiness.

The historical–methodological analysis, which is the core of the study, is preceded by an overview of the present debate on the paradox of happiness in Economics (Chapter 1), and by the main explanations of it (Chapter 2). The most interesting element that results from this review is how the two classical currents of the happiness–sociality nexus are still at the centre of the contemporary debate: happiness as eudaimonia versus happiness as pleasure. A review of the current economic analysis of the paradox of happiness points to a striking *absence*: the absence of an explanation of the paradox based on genuine sociality.

Chapter 3 basically deals with political philosophy, in a historical perspective. Beginning with Aristotle's idea of Civil Happiness (*eudaimonia*), it passes through Civic Humanism and ends up at the threshold of the birth of classical Political and Civil Economy in the mid-eighteenth century. This chapter also outlines a sketch of the thought of the main protagonists of the "uncivil" political tradition (Machiavelli, Hobbes, Mandeville and Hume), who, in different ways, all broke the nexus between genuine sociality and good life, claiming that a "good society" only needs the right institutions, suited to people "as they are", in order to transform private vices into public virtues.

Both the civil and uncivil traditions entered into the early classical Economics. Thus, Chapters 4 to 6 aim to show how the Italian Public Happiness tradition tried to reconcile these two lines of social thought, seeing markets as a tool for civic virtue, an essential resource for economic development. Neapolitan Enlightenment, Antonio Genovesi in particular, are the focus of this part of the work, while also representing its core.

In Chapter 7, Smith and the British classical tradition are presented as being, at the same time, close to the civic tradition and far away from it.

Chapter 8 is devoted to the post-Smithian English tradition – Malthus, Mill and Marshall in particular. All these economists recognised that wealth *is not* happiness, but only a means that does not always work properly. Economics increasingly became the separate science of wealth (that is, what can be measured by money). This tradition shares Smith's vision that economic interactions are not the realm of genuine sociality.

Chapter 9 deals with the Utilitarian and hedonistic foundation of neoclassical Economics. From Bentham to Jevons and most marginalist neoclassical economists, happiness became synonymous with pleasure. In this approach, however, happiness *can also derive from social interactions*, and thus is not necessarily a matter of only material goods. But any connection to the civil tradition has been lost, and Aristotelian themes have been completely rejected.

Chapter 10 is the last historical chapter, dedicated to Pareto's theory of choice and Wicksteed's non-tuism, the main protagonists of another radical shift in the vision of happiness and sociality within Economics. Having become the realm of instrumental actions, Economics held no place for genuine interpersonal relationships. Pleasure, the main category of earlier neoclassical hedonist Economics, was also removed from mainstream Economics. The chapter ends with a look at the rational choice approach to sociality and Game Theory, in order to claim that both remain within the instrumental approach, where there is no place for Civil Happiness.

In Chapter 11 the work ends by looking at the main "lesson from the past" coming from the Civil Happiness tradition.

This book, therefore, is basically an analysis of how economists currently deal with happiness. If happiness is civil – as I claim on the basis of an ancient and robust tradition and empirical evidence – even the current debate on happiness in Economics, in as much as it has mostly focused on hedonic happiness – is far from entering into the specific domain of Civil Happiness. Thus, the pages that follow hope to offer a contribution for a new collection of studies on happiness and sociality in Economics.

1 Happiness, again

The Easterlin paradox

Not even the most critical observers can convince us that economic variables such as income, wealth or employment are not important objectives in life. Who can deny the evidence that wealthier people usually enjoy better health, longer life spans, lower infant mortality rates, and greater access to goods, services and education? From the enjoyment of such benefits it should take just one short step to affirm that, on average, those who possess more are happier than those who possess less. Yet one of the most important and worrying discoveries of the last decades is that such a step is not that short, nor that certain, and in fact can even take a negative turn.

Studies into the so-called "paradoxes of happiness" have brought the problem out of the closet. The term "paradoxes of happiness" refers, normally, to the empirical evidence, in post-war opulent countries, of long-term increases in wealth accompanied with constant or even decreasing self-reported individual happiness and/or life satisfaction.

Thanks to this paradoxical (contrary to common sense) evidence, happiness is once again of interest of economists, the "professors of the dismal science" (Carlyle 1850: 43).

The process of the rediscovery of happiness in Economics has been mainly a by-product of a process that originated in psychology. In fact, a paper published by Brickman and Campbell in 1971, under the telling title of "Hedonic relativism and planning the good society", can rightly be considered the starting point of the new studies on happiness in relation to the economic domain. In their study, the two psychologists extended the "adaptation level" theory to individual and collective happiness, reaching the conclusion that bettering the objective conditions of life (income or wealth) produces no lasting effects on personal well-being. Such a thesis should have provoked a serious methodological storm about the nature and causes of the wealth of people. Yet it did not; the study remained practically unknown to mainstream Economics for years.

A few years later, two economists, Richard Easterlin (1974) and Tibor

Scitovsky (1976), were persuaded that what was going on in that field of psychology could have something important to say to economic analysis. So, the "paradox of happiness" entered Economics, re-echoing to economic science its classical origins. In fact, the wealth–happiness nexus was central in the classical tradition – as we'll see in Chapters 4–8.[4]

By utilising empirical research on people's happiness, Richard Easterlin managed to open up the debate around the "happiness paradox" – also today called the "Easterlin paradox". He made use of two types of empirical data. The first base was supplied by the responses to an opinion-poll type of survey in which a direct question was asked – a question which is still at the basis of most of the empirical analyses on happiness: "In general, how happy would you say that you are – *very* happy, *fairly* happy or *not very* happy?" (Easterlin 1974: 91). The other set of data Easterlin made use of came from more sophisticated research carried out in 1965 by the humanist psychologist Hadley Cantril (another forerunner of contemporary quantitative studies on happiness), concerning people's fears, hopes and satisfaction in 14 countries. The subjects interviewed were asked to classify their own satisfaction on a scale from 0 to 10[5] – in today's *World Values Survey* questionnaires, happiness is ranked in "qualitative" terms (from "not very happy" to "very happy"), whereas life satisfaction is still measured using a Cantril methodology (a scale from 1 to 10).

Both types of data, then, were based on a *subjective self-evaluation of one's happiness or life-satisfaction* – this subjective definition of happiness is a crucial point in the whole debate, as we shall see.[6] They both produced, in Easterlin's seminal analyses, the same results. Within a single country, at a given moment in time, the correlation between income and happiness *exists and it is robust*: "In every single survey, those in the highest status group were happier, on the average, than those in the lowest status group" (Easterlin 1974: 100). In cross-sectional data among countries, however, the positive association between wealth and happiness, although present, *is neither general nor robust*, and poorer countries do not always appear to be less happy than richer countries. In other words: "if there is a positive association among countries between income and happiness it is not very clear.... The results are ambiguous" (Easterlin 1974: 108).[7] But the most interesting result came from the analysis of time-series at the national level: in 30 surveys over 25 years (from 1946 to 1970 in the US), per capita real income rose by more than 60 per cent, but the proportion of people who rated themselves as "very happy", "fairly happy" or "not too happy" remained almost unmodified.

The main drift of Easterlin's seminal paper came to be developed two years later in Tibor Scitovsky's *Joyless Economy* (1976). Scitovsky – as we will see – added an original contribution, relying more on psychology. Hirsch (1977), Ng (1978), Layard (1980) and Frank (1985) all brought new insights into the explanations of the "Easterlin paradox", which grew slowly but steadily. Today the debate on Economics and happiness is gaining greater and greater attention among economists, psychologists, sociologists and the public.

The theoretical debate about the paradox of happiness is contentious. Almost all scholars, from different backgrounds, agree on the results, that

> over time and across OECD countries rises in aggregate income are not associated with rises in aggregate happiness.... At the aggregate level, there has been no increase in reported happiness over the last 50 years in the US and Japan, nor in Europe since 1973 when the records began.
>
> (Layard 2005: 148)[8]

The relationship between income and happiness within a single country in a given moment in time is not controversial today among economists: almost all agree that a causal correlation running from income to happiness exists and is robust.[9]

Psychologists do not deny this correlation, but, in general, are less optimistic about the importance of income on well-being:

> the effects of wealth are not large, and they are dwarfed by other influences, such as those of personality and social relationships.... [W]hen the sciences of economics and of well-being come face-to-face, they sometimes conflict. If the well-being findings simply mirrored those for income and money – with richer people invariably being much happier than poorer people – one would hardly need to measure well-being, or make policy to enhance it directly. But income, a good surrogate historically when basic needs were unmet, is now a weak surrogate for well-being in wealthy nations. What the divergence of the economics and well-being measures demonstrates is that well-being indicators add important information that is missed by economic indicators. Economic development will remain an important priority, but policies fostering economic development must be supplemented by policies that will have a stronger impact on well-being.
>
> (Diener and Seligman 2003: 10)

Also among economists, however, the cross-country correlation between income and happiness is more controversial.[10] As we have seen, in 1974 Easterlin did not find clear and evident correlation between happiness and income between different countries. Today most economists, using data coming from the *World Values Survey*, agree that a correlation does exist: "Various studies provide evidence that, on average, persons living in rich countries are happier than those living in poor countries" (Frey and Stutzer 2001: 19).

Layard makes an important distinction in the cross-countries analyses:

> if we compare countries, there is no evidence that richer countries are happier than poorer ones – so long as we confine ourselves to coun-

tries with incomes over $15,000 per head. ... At income levels below $15,000 per head things are different, since people are nearer to the absolute breadline. At these income levels richer countries are happier than poorer ones. And in countries like India, Mexico and Philippines, where we have time series data, happiness has grown as income levels have risen.

(2005: 149)[11]

These issues are relevant in economic theory: explaining the happiness paradoxes calls into question some of the basic tenets of contemporary Economics – as we will see.

Before continuing, however, it would be useful to further explore the concept of happiness by comparing it with similar concepts.

Happiness and more

Mainstream economists have only recently begun to be interested in happiness, trapped as they were by the "iron curtain effect" of the hypothesis of rationality. However, social scientists in other fields have been working on the theme for decades. Sociologists were perhaps the first to find "empirical" indicators of the *standard of living*, that went beyond the GDP per capita. Back in the 1920s William Ogburn[12] launched a social research programme on "quality of life" which generated the important "movement of social indicators of the quality of life" that, a few years later, spread from the United States to Europe.[13]

The rise and diffusion of this movement were favoured by the cultural climate of the 1960s which sought to overcome a pure economic conception of the process of economic growth. There were many economists (e.g. Myrdal, Galbraith, Hirschman) who were also working outside of the mainstream of pure economic theory. Their works were sources of inspiration for many social scientists, and fostered research projects on the definition of social indicators. The aim was to find operational solutions capable of effectively quantifying the concept of "quality of life" in order to arrive at a sort of "social accountability".

This "quality of life movement" (Offer 2003) emphasises mainly "objective" and normative (or ethical) ingredients of a good life, while the later "happiness movement" is characterised by a more "subjective" approach, based on self-reported evaluations (questionnaires). In fact, mostly thanks to Sen, the category of *quality of life* tends to encompass new indicators such as democracy, social capital, health, rights, freedom, working conditions and fundamental capabilities. In the 1990s, a "list of fundamental human needs" was drawn up that was mainly based on Sen's and Nussbaum's theory of capabilities. It developed into the United Nation's Human Development Indicators, or HDI.[14]

Thus, Sen widens the vision of well-being in its scope and definition, and emancipates it from the mere absence or scarcity of material goods.[15] For the past few years, Martha Nussbaum has been seeking to wed Sen's approach with the basis of an Aristotelian and Stoic theory of happiness in order to arrive at an *objectivisation* of the "good life".[16] In her search to objectify and operationalise the *capabilities' approach*, she concentrates her analysis on constitutional and political applications.[17]

Thus both the quality of life and the capability approaches consider self-reported happiness as only *one* component of well-being (a capability or a functioning), that has to be anchored on more *objective* bases.

Today happiness studies directly inspire research projects for new national indicators that include essential elements of well-being (on the basis of self-reported data),[18] that are missing in the standard economic indicators such as GDP. The psychologist Ed Diener is one of the leaders in this new field that comes from Social Psychology, while the quality of life movement is a by-product of Sociology and Economics:

> There was a time, when many basic needs were unmet, that economic indicators were a very good first approximation of how well a nation was doing. As nations became wealthier and basic needs were largely met, economic indicators increasingly missed their target. We have argued to this point that national economic indicators alone are now "out of sync" with national well-being in the developed nations. While wealth has trebled over the past 50 years, for example, well-being has been flat, mental illness has increased at an even more rapid rate, and data, not just nostalgic reminiscences, indicate that the social fabric is more frayed than it was in leaner times. These inadequacies lead us to advocate that an ongoing system of indicators be instituted by governments and organizations to track well-being over time.
>
> (Diener and Seligman 2003: 21)

What is happiness?

As Diener and colleagues correctly note:

> A widely presumed component of the good life is happiness. Unfortunately, the nature of happiness has not been defined in a uniform way. Happiness can mean pleasure, life satisfaction, positive emotions, a meaningful life, or a feeling of contentment, among other concepts.
>
> (Diener *et al.* 2003: 188)

Economists do not even like the question, "What is happiness?" To them happiness is not a concept clearly distinct from pleasure, satisfaction or welfare. Ng (1997) defines happiness as "welfare", for Oswald (1997) happiness means "pleasure" or "satisfaction", and Easterlin is even more honest: "I use the terms happiness, subjective well-being, satisfaction, utility, well-being, and welfare interchangeably" (2001: 465). For Frey and Stutzer, "Happiness research in Economics takes reported subjective well-being as a proxy measure for utility" (2005: 116). The sociologist Ruut Veenhoven "use[s] the terms '*happiness*' or '*life satisfaction*' for the comprehensive judgment" (2005: 245). Happiness, for economists, is not generally *defined* but empirically *measured*, on the basis of the answers to questions such as: "How happy are you"? The questionnaires of the *WVS* (*World Values Survey*) ask people about both happiness ("How happy are you?") and life-satisfaction ("How much are you satisfied with your life?"), two data often used also in the academic analyses about people's happiness. The Euro-barometer of the European Commission measures Europeans' self-evaluation of *life-satisfaction*, and these data are often used as synonymous with self-reported happiness in economic analyses (see Oswald 1997). Ingle-hart, the coordinator of the *World Values Survey*, use the Subjective Well-Being (SWB*)* Index which is a combination of the responses to "happiness" and the responses to "life-satisfaction" questions.[19]

Some economists (Frank 1997, 2005; Layard 2005) use the category of SWB simply as a synonym for happiness, relying on psychologists for the definition. Actually, in psychological studies the story is more complex. In psychology, in fact, experimental studies on happiness began in the 1950s, and, in general, psychologists use the expression "happiness" with more precision than economists. Psychologists distinguish between: (a) "Life satisfaction", which is a cognitive element; (b) "Affect", the affective component; (c) SWB, defined as a "state of general well-being, synthetic, of long duration, which includes both the affective and cognitive component" (Ahuvia and Friedman 1998: 153).

Ed Diener, for example, proposes on the basis of abundant empirical evidence a hierarchical model of SWB where the four components are: (1) pleasant emotions (joy, contentment, happiness, etc.), (2) unpleasant emotions (sadness, anger, worry, stress, etc.), (3) global life judgement (life evaluation, fulfilment, meaning, success, etc.), and (4) domain satisfaction (marriage, work, health, leisure, etc.).[20] In this approach the SWB is made of all these components, and therefore, happiness is considered to be a *narrower* concept than SWB, and different from life satisfaction: life satis-faction and happiness are both considered *components* of SWB – as in the Senian capability approach where happiness is just *a* component of a "good life". In particular, life satisfaction reflects individuals' perceived distance from their aspirations (Campbell *et al.* 1976). Happiness results from a balance between positive affect and negative affect (Bradburg 1969).[21] SWB is instead defined as "a general evaluation of a person's life" (Diener *et al.* 2003: 191). In general,

> the term subjective well-being emphasizes an individual's own assess-ment of his or her own life – not the judgment of "experts" – and

includes satisfaction (both in general and satisfaction with specific domains), pleasant affect, and low negative affect.

(Diener *et al.* 2003: 189)

For this reason, "SWB is not a unitary dimension, and there is no single index that can capture what it means to be happy" (Diener *et al.* 2003: 213).

In this approach to SBW, to "be" happy is considered to be different from to "feel" happy: SWB is a synonym of "being happy", a concept close to the Aristotelian approach to happiness as *eudaimonia*, whereas the concepts of "satisfaction" and "happiness" belong to "feeling" happiness.

I would stress that in psychological studies of happiness we find a tension between a "hedonic" idea of happiness and a "eudaimonic" one. In the "hedonic" approach, happiness is the result of avoiding pain and seeking pleasure; according to the contrary "eudaimonic" approach, happiness arises as people function and interact within society, an approach that places emphasis on non-material pursuits such as genuine interpersonal relationships and intrinsic motivation (Deci and Ryan 2001).

More precisely, "hedonism" (Kahneman *et al.* 1999, 2003) reflects the view that *well-being consists of pleasure or happiness*: "Hedonism, as a view of well-being, has thus been expressed in many forms and has varied from a relatively narrow focus on bodily pleasures to a broad focus on appetites and self-interests" (Deci and Ryan 2001: 144). In 1999, Kahneman *et al.* announced the existence of a new field of Psychology. The title of their work, *Well-being: the Foundations of Hedonic Psychology*, clearly suggests that, within this paradigm, the terms "well-being" and "hedonism" are essentially equivalent.[22]

The second view (Eudaimonism), both in its ancient and current forms, claims that well-being consists of more than just hedonic or subjective happiness: "Despite the currency of the hedonic view, many philosophers, religious masters, and visionaries, from both the East and West, have denigrated happiness per se as a principal criterion of well-being" (Deci and Ryan 2001: 145). It lies instead in the actualisation of human potentials. Due to a close continuity with the Aristotelian ethics, this view has been called *eudaimonism*, conveying the belief that

well-being consists of fulfilling or realizing one's *daimon* or true nature. The two traditions – hedonism and eudaimonism – are founded on distinct views of human nature and of what constitutes a good society. Accordingly, they ask different questions concerning how developmental and social processes relate to well-being, and they implicitly or explicitly prescribe different approaches to the enterprise of living.

(Deci and Ryan 2001: 143)

Carol Ryff and other psychologists (see, among others, Ryff and Singer 1998, 2000), also drawing from Aristotle, describe well-being not in terms of attaining pleasure, but as "the striving for perfection that represents the realization of one's true potential" (Ryff 1995: 100). This school has even proposed to speak of Psychological Well-Being (PWB) as distinct from Subjective Well-Being (SWB): "Whereas the SWB tradition formulates well-being in terms of overall life satisfaction and happiness, the PWB tradition draws heavily on formulation of human development and existential challenges of life" (Keyes *et al.* 2002: 1008).[23] Another, complementary, way of presenting this tension is to distinguish between an *ethical* approach to happiness (the Aristotelian) and a purely *subjectivist* one based on psychological experience (the hedonic). In fact, the philosophical reference point for the hedonistic approach is Bentham (or Epicurus), while Aristotle is the father of the eudaimonic/ethical one. Given the importance of Aristotle's *eudaimonia* in the context of my research, it would be worthwhile to go a bit deeper into his theory of *eudaimonia*. This is done in Chapter 3 where I begin my historical analysis. In the next chapter, I present the main current explanations offered for the "Easterlin paradox".

2 Explanations of the Easterlin paradox

Truth, virtue and happiness are bound together by an unbreakable chain.

(Marquis de Condorcet)

The hedonic treadmill and set-point theory

I want to stress right from the beginning that economists working today on the "happiness paradox" are normally far from the eudaimonistic tradition. An economist who is moving along a line of research very similar to the Aristotelian one is Amartya Sen. Although he cannot be considered a "scholar of happiness",[24] on the whole his work reminds economists that happiness, in order to be a proxy of a good life, must be translatable into human flourishing, in terms of capabilities and functionings, human rights and freedom:

> If we have reasons to want more wealth, we have to ask: What precisely are these reasons, how do they work, on what are they contingent and what are the things we can "do" with more wealth? In fact, we generally have excellent reasons for wanting more income or wealth. This is not because income and wealth are desirable for their own sake, but because typically, they are admirable general-purpose means for having more freedom to lead the kind of lives we have reasons to value. The usefulness of wealth lies in the things that it allows us to do – the substantive freedom it helps us to achieve. But this relation is neither exclusive (since there are significant influences on our lives other than wealth) nor uniform (since the impact of wealth on our lives varies with other influences). It is as important to recognize the crucial role of wealth in determining living conditions and the quality of life as it is to understand the qualified and contingent nature of this relationship.
>
> (Sen 2000: 14)

As far as sociality is concerned, apart from very few exceptions (Gui and Sugden 2005) interpersonal relations, or sociality-as-relationality, is absent among the *key ingredients* of happiness as it is represented in Economics. Sociality-as-positionality is very central, but such an idea of sociality is anything but Aristotle's *philia*. In fact in the explanations of the paradox of "more income and less (or constant) happiness over time" there is an important missing link: the role of sociality seen as a direct source of happiness. The idea is that, by concentrating on such crucial variables as income, wealth or consumption, economic science *neglects something relevant in the interpersonal domain*, which affects happiness or well-being. The following review, therefore, is oriented to spot an *absence* – the lack in Economics of a deep analysis of sociality for explaining the paradox of happiness – a review that is basically an introduction to analyses that will follow.

The first economist who attempted to explain the "Easterlin paradox" was Richard Easterlin himself, in his seminal 1974 paper. His explanation was based on Duesenberry's (1949) "relative income" assumption. Many authors working on Economics and happiness today still base their analyses on the relative income hypothesis: among them Robert Frank (1997, 1999), Yew K. Ng (1997), Heinz Höllander (2001) and Richard Layard (2005).

Before entering into an analysis of the most common explanations of the Easterlin paradox, grounded in the relative consumption hypothesis, it is important to consider other explanations, based on individual "treadmills".

While the relative consumption hypothesis can be considered an internal evolution of the *economic* tradition, the explanations of the paradox that makes use of the treadmill effects have a clear origin in psychological researches. Such psychological theories are based on the *hedonic adaptation* or *set-point* theory. According to set-point theories, there is a level of happiness that remains practically constant during the lifecycle, because personality and temperament variables seem to play a strong role in determining the level of happiness of individuals. Such characteristics are basically innate to individuals. In other words, in the long run, we are fixed at hedonic neutrality, and our efforts to make ourselves happier by gaining good life circumstances are only short-term solutions. Therefore, life circumstances including health or income often account for a very small percentage of variance in SWB: people initially do react to events, but then they return to baseline levels of well-being that are determined by personality factors (Argyle 2001; Lucas *et al.* 2002). Empirical research (Lykken and Tellegen 1996 among others), concluded that more than 80 per cent of the variance in long-term stable levels of SWB could be attributed to inborn temperament. On this basis, these psychologists have claimed that people have inborn SWB "set-points".[25] The various shocks that hit people over a lifetime affect happiness only temporarily. We inevitably return to our set-point after a brief period. As Daniel Kahneman writes:

individuals exposed to life-altering events ultimately return to a level of well-being that is characteristic of their personality, sometimes by generating good or bad outcomes that restore this characteristic level.

(1999: 14)

Many psychologists and economists today maintain that there is a *hedonic treadmill* operating in the area of economic goods. The *hedonic treadmill*, a metaphor coined by Brickman and Campbell (1971), comes from the "set-point theory": one is running constantly and yet remains at the same place because the treadmill runs at the same pace – or even faster, in the opposite direction.

Today, set-point theory is also popular among economists (Easterlin 2005; Frey and Stutzer 2005). According to this theory, in effect, happiness is essentially a congenital matter that mostly depends on subjective elements such as character, genes or the inherited capacity to live with and overcome life's hardships. In other words, there is a given level of happiness, around which the various experiences of life gravitate. It is an approach not far from the thesis of Herrnstein and Murray (1994) who, in their *The Bell Curve*, claimed social programmes were useless on the basis of the innate level of intelligence that cannot be permanently changed by education.

Although in a quite different methodological line, Ruut Veenhoven (2005)[26] rejects the common stereotypes that sees misery, handicaps and inequality in income distribution as the principal causes of people's unhappiness, reaching the conclusion that there is no "paradox" of happiness (in Easterlin's meaning). In his *World Database of Happiness*[27] Ghana and Colombia take the highest ranks among all the nations classified according to their happiness level. France and Italy take a back seat to Guatemala.

Satisfaction treadmill

More recently, Kahneman made a distinction between two types of *treadmill effects*, namely, the *hedonic treadmill* and the *satisfaction treadmill*. Whilst the *hedonic treadmill* depends on *adaptation*, the *satisfaction treadmill* depends on *aspiration* "which marks the boundaries between satisfactory and unsatisfactory results" (1999: 14).

As their incomes increase, people are induced to seek continuous and ever more intense pleasures in order to maintain the same level of satisfaction. The *satisfaction treadmill* works in such a way that one's *subjective* happiness (self-evaluation) remains constant even when one's *objective* happiness improves. In this case, while people may get a boost in their objective well-being, or happiness, because they have bought a new car, the fact that they have had a rise in income has also made their aspirations about the ideal car to own rise, so that their *subjective satisfaction* level remains the same. This is true even though they may be *objectively* more comfortable in their new car.[28]

Easterlin carried out an interesting experiment over a period of 16 years in which he periodically asked the same group of people the following question:

1   We often hear people talk about what they want out of life. Here are a number of different things. [The respondent is handed a card with a list of 24 items.] When you think of the good life – the life you'd like to have, which of the things on this list, if any, are part of that good life as far as you personally are concerned?
2   Now would you go down that list and call off all the things you now have?

(Easterlin 2005: 45)[29]

The first question aims at measuring the aspirations, while the second measures the means (income). The results showed that, with an increase in material means (indicated by the first list), the things that were considered necessary for a happy life change (the second list). Thus, in the first phases of the lifecycle, a summer home at the sea-side and a second car were not indicated as being important for a good life, while they did enter the list as income increased. The ratio between possessed goods and desired goods remains practically constant over a life span, much as in a treadmill where means and aspiration run, more or less, at the same pace. Layard calls this effect the "effect of habit":

> The process at work here is the basic human process of adaptation, whereby people adjust to a change in circumstances, be it upwards or downwards. This is for example the mechanism that explains the famous endowment effect, whereby people suffer more from losing something than they would gain from obtaining it.
>
> (Layard 2005: 152)

This mechanism is also very close to one of the most important ideas in modern behavioural Economics, the idea that preferences are *reference-dependent* (Tversky and Kahneman 1991).

This idea is not completely new in the tradition of Economics – as we shall see in Chapter 9.

The "social treadmill": relative consumption and positional competition

Explanations based on the relative consumption hypothesis can be rightly considered as a development of the satisfaction treadmill. The hedonic treadmill based on adaptation is essentially individual and a-social. The satisfaction treadmill is instead associated with social comparisons, although the satisfaction treadmill can apply even in isolation – i.e. it can even occur on Robinson Crusoe's island, when he tries to overcome his standards (in cultivation, fishing, etc.). In other words, while the hedonic treadmill doesn't necessarily require society for it to function, the satisfaction *normally* occurs in society; but neither the hedonic nor the satisfaction treadmill *needs sociality by necessity*. A *pure* social treadmill is instead the "positional" one.

Even the relative consumption hypothesis is not a new one. In making use of his "relative income" theory, we have already mentioned that Duesenberry was the first to explicitly introduce relative consumption theory in 1949. Duesenberry claimed that a person draws utility, or satisfaction, from his or her own level of consumption in relation or in comparison to the level of other people's consumption (1949: 32).

In other words, he basically said that we are constantly comparing ourselves to some group of people, and that what they buy influences the choices about what we want to buy. It is the old "keeping up with the Joneses'" scenario, where the consumption function is constructed upon the hypothesis that our consumption choices are influenced by the difference between our level of income and the level of income of the others, instead of the absolute level. Therefore, the utility of a person's level of consumption also depends on the *relative* level, and not only on the *absolute* one.

Without going back to eighteenth-century authors, where considerations about the social dimensions of consumption were prominent (we shall consider later Smith and Genovesi), at the end of the nineteenth century, Veblen (1899) treated consuming as a social issue, because of the simple fact that the most significant acts of consumption are normally carried out in public, under the gaze of others. In recent times, Scitovsky (1976, chapter 6) dealt with the relationship between consumption and status, and Fred Hirsch (1977) coined the term "positional good". The basic element of the contemporary positional theory is the concept of *externality*: conspicuous commodities share some characteristics of the "demerit goods" (private goods generating negative externalities), with the typical consequence of Pareto inefficiency:

> That many purchases become more attractive to us when others make them means that consumption spending has much in common with a military arms race. A family can choose how much of its own money to spend, but it cannot choose how much others spend. Buying a smaller-than-average vehicle means greater risk of dying in an accident. Spending less on an interview suit means a greater risk of not landing the best job. Yet when all spend more on heavier cars or more finely tailored suits, the results tend to be mutually offsetting, just as

when all nations spend more on armaments. Spending less – on bombs or on personal consumption – frees up money for other pressing uses, but only if everyone does it.

(Frank 2005: 83–84)[30]

Thus, the relative consumption theory can also be described by using the image of a treadmill: together with our income or consumption, *something else is running along*: the income of the others.

Summary

The theories reviewed above, that are the main explanations of the paradox of happiness in contemporary literature, take sociality into consideration mainly as a public good problem: increases in aspirations or positional competition generate negative externalities in consumption that affect or "pollute" individual utility – consistently from this comes Layard's and Frank's recipe: Pigouvian taxes. In other words, these theories do not deal with the *direct* relationship between individual well-being and sociality-as-relationality. Coherently, the economic explanations of the "Easterlin paradox" do not refer to sociality as a source of happiness per se.

Mainstream economic literature, in fact, finds it hard to do this kind of analysis: this book can be read as a study for comprehending *why it is so hard*, and to identify the methodological bases for a theory of happiness where relationality plays a key role.

3 From the "civil" to the "uncivil" animal

Man is a civil animal.

(Leonardo Bruni)

Aristotle's eudaimonia

A multidimensional reality

The roots of modern Political Economy are very deep-rooted, let alone the roots of the philosophical reflection on happiness. Where can the starting point for such a historical analysis be fixed? I choose to begin with Aristotle because his theory of happiness-eudaimonia sets the course for the discussion on happiness in western culture. In that theory of happiness, enclosed in the term "*eudaimonia*",[31] we find the fundamental coordinates that will mark the route for the research we will carry out in the following chapters. Socrates, Plato and Aristotle, as well as all the classical schools of philosophy (i.e. Stoicism)[32] explored the diverse dimensions of happiness. The fundamental ideas they shared on happiness were:

a   happiness is the final, or ultimate, end of life: is the "highest good" for the human being;
b   happiness is self-sufficient, because there is nothing that, added to it, would increase its value;
c   there is an inseparable bond between happiness and the practice of virtues;
d   because virtues bear fruits regardless of self-interest, happiness can be reached only as a by-product if it is sought in non-instrumental ways, seeking to be virtuous.

On the other hand, differences between Aristotle and the other classical Greek philosophers arose around such questions as the connection between the active and contemplative life, and then over the role of sociality and civil virtues in order to reach the *good life*.

The Aristotelian meaning of the eudaimonia is semantically impoverished when translated into the English word *happiness*: the Greek expression meant the highest end that humans can realise: "what is the highest of all goods achievable by action" (Aristotle, *Nicomachean Ethics* (NE), I, 4, 1095a).

As a consequence, eudaimonia is an end "which is in itself worthy of pursuit more final than that which is worthy of pursuit for the sake of something else ... for this we choose always for self and never for the sake of something else" (NE, I, 7, 1097a). That makes happiness "the best, noblest, and most pleasant thing in the world" (NE, I, 8, 1099a). All the other good things, including wealth, are only means for reaching happiness. Happiness, therefore, *is never a means*; on the contrary, it is the only goal which is impossible to instrumentalise, because of its very nature. For this reason it is the "final" end: being final cannot be an "instrument" for something else (there is nothing to be reached beyond it). Out of this comes the thesis that neither wealth, nor health can ever be ultimate ends. They can only be important means (instruments) for living a good life. As the philosopher Martha Nussbaum writes: "happiness is something like flourishing human living, a kind of living that is active, inclusive of all that has intrinsic value, and complete, meaning lacking in nothing that would make it richer or better" (2005: 171).

Furthermore, eudaimonia is a multidimensional and diverse reality. First, one of the primary objectives of Aristotle was to distinguish eudaimonia from the hedonism of Aristippus and his school: "To judge from the lives that men lead, most men, and men of the most vulgar type, seem (not without some ground) to identify the good, or happiness, with pleasure" (NE, I, 5, 1095b). Eudaimonia, then, cannot be identified with pleasure, but neither with honour nor money.

This is why the neo-Aristotelian philosophers in the Anglo-Saxon world preferred to translate eudaimonia with "human flourishing" rather than happiness, because in common language today happiness also indicates momentary euphoria, carefree content, a pleasurable sensation or *tout court* pleasure.[33]

To Aristotle, pleasure is not the *end* of action, then, but only a *sign* that the action is intrinsically good. Pleasure, instead, can signal the value of an activity, not its scope, "virtuous actions must be in themselves pleasant" (I, 8, 1099a).[34]

Second, *eudaimonia* is the end of politics. This idea can be rightly considered the synthesis of the fourth section of the first part of the *Nicomachean Ethics:* "what it is that we say political science aims at and what is the highest of all goods achievable by action ... for both the general run of men and people of superior refinement say that it is happiness" (I, 4, 1095a). The aim of politics is happiness because politics "gives utmost attention in forming citizens in a certain way, that is to make them good and committed to carrying out beautiful actions" (I, 9, 1099b). What is more, political life is the only place in which happiness can be fully experienced: "It is natural, then, that we call neither ox nor horse nor any other of the animals happy; for none of them is capable of sharing in such activity" (I, 9, 1099b).[35]

As a third (and very crucial) element, eudaimonia is the indirect result, a by-product, of the practice of virtues. Let us see why.

The word *eudaimonia*, in fact, originally derived from the phrase "good demon" (*eu daimon*), which meant that only those who have a good demon or good fortune on their side can reach eudaimonia. So happiness and good fortune were used as synonymous words.[36] Socrates, but above all Plato and Aristotle, invested the word eudaimonia with new meaning. The idea that even a person with bad luck could *become* happy by means of virtuous actions began to enter into the philosophical imagination.

Aristotle defines eudaimonia as "a virtuous activity of soul" (NE, I, 9, 1099b). It also requires material goods such as health, beauty, contemplation (*theoria*), and "there are some things the lack of which takes the lustre from happiness" (I, 8, 1099b). And, as has been sufficiently emphasised by many interpreters, happiness is tied to a right and balanced combination of various ingredients. Therefore, it is plural and multidimensional because it is composed of diverse things. While such things as beauty, friendship and virtues are intrinsic, other things, like material goods, are merely instrumental. Then, Aristotle specifies, "happiness seems to need this sort of prosperity in addition; for which reason some identify happiness with good fortune" (I, 8, 1099b).[37]

Linked with the key connection between virtues and eudaimonia, we find a fundamental tension regarding the whole Aristotelian theory of happiness-eudaimonia: although the virtuous life is a way to happiness, virtues bear their fruit (happiness) only if sought *not instrumentally*, only if internalised as being *intrinsically good*. In fact, as soon as virtue is used as a means, it ceases to be a virtue. So happiness is the indirect result of practising virtues, which makes them, at the same time, means and ends, part of eudaimonia.

MacIntyre proposes an inspiring reading of this tension between virtues/happiness, means/end in Aristotle:

> The virtues are precisely those qualities the possession of which will enable an individual to achieve *eudaimonia* and the lack of which will frustrate his movement toward that *telos*. But although it would not be incorrect to describe the exercise of virtues as a mere means to the end of achieving the good for man, that description is ambiguous. Aristotle in his writings does not explicitly distinguish between two different types of means–end relationship. When we speak of any happening or state or activity as a means to some other, we may on the one hand mean that the world is as a matter of contingent fact so ordered that if you are able to bring about a happening or state or

activity of the first kind, an event or state or activity of the second kind will ensue.... But the exercise of the virtues is not in this sense *a* means to the end of the good for man [eudaimonia]. For what constitutes the good for man is a complete human life lived at its best, and the exercise of virtues is a necessary and central part of such a life, not a mere preparatory exercise to secure such a life.

(1984: 148–149)

Virtues are means to happiness only if they are *not only* a means: this represents the basic "Aristotle's happiness paradox", or "teleological paradox" (see Brennan and Pettit 2004), that leans in the association of virtues to gratuitousness and genuineness: virtues lead to happiness only if practised genuinely for their *intrinsic value* (the virtuous action has in itself its reward).[38]

Only if we keep in mind this fundamental tension in Aristotle's vision of eudaimonia is it possible to properly understand the Aristotelian approach to the relationality–happiness nexus. As we are about to see, interpersonal relations lead to happiness only if they are genuine expressions of the practice of virtues. Every relational theory of happiness, ancient and modern, is also related to this key idea. And, finally, we find this Aristotelian paradox any time we deal with a genuinely civil approach to happiness.

Eudaimonia and relational goods

The above analysis of Aristotle's eudaimonia has shown that his vision of happiness is basically *Civil* Happiness. Following this idea, we find in the *Nicomachean Ethics* that there is a strong point of attraction, perhaps the strongest of the entire Aristotelian ethics. It is the *civil* or *political* nature of a good life, of happiness – notice that Aristotle, like all classical thought, did not distinguish between the *civil*, *social* and *political* spheres, that is a typically modern distinction.[1] This focus is one of Aristotle's most quoted passages:

Surely it is strange, too, to make the supremely happy man a solitary; for no one would choose the whole world on condition of being alone, since man is a political creature and one whose nature is to live with others. Therefore even the happy man lives with others; for he has the things that are by nature good. And plainly it is better to spend his days with friends and good men than with strangers or any chance persons. Therefore the happy man needs friends.

(IX, 9, 1169b)

In its highest expression, friendship is a virtue, and for this reason having (virtue) friends, being part of eudaimonia, is more important than wealth, which is only a means to the end of the good life:

For without friends no one would choose to live, though he had all other goods;... for what is the use of such prosperity without the opportunity of beneficence, which is exercised chiefly and in its most laudable form towards friends? Or how can prosperity be guarded and preserved without friends? The greater it is, the more exposed is it to risk. And in poverty and in other misfortunes men think friends are the only refuge.

(VIII, 1, 1155a)[39]

Like Aristotle, Plato advised the wise to be detached from external circumstances. Together with Epicurus, Pliny and other classical philosophers, Plato put relationships-with-others in the category of external circumstances, because one's happiness is potentially dependent on other people's choices. Plato's aim, as Aristotle's, was to make happiness self-sufficient: coherently, Plato's suggestion was to be dependent as little as possible on external circumstances, interpersonal relationships included. In fact, if such an operation would be possible, happiness will be separated from fortune, "goodness without fragility", as Nussbaum (1986) summarises Plato's vision of the good life.

Aristotle, instead, thinks that the operation of separating happiness from fortune is not possible: "goodness without fragility" is not an achievable goal for the human life, perhaps, for a "god or a beast". This impossibility emerges clearly from his theory of the relationality–happiness nexus.

For Aristotle, and in the whole western civil tradition, there is an intrinsic value in relational and civil life, without which human life does not fully flourish. Though human life must be able to flourish autonomously, in the sense that it cannot be totally jeopardised by bad fortune, it is also true that in the Aristotelian line of thought some of the essential components of the good life are tied to interpersonal relationships. Participation in civil life, having friends, loving and being loved are essential parts of a happy life.[40]

By definition, we have said, eudaimonia cannot be reached instrumentally: it is the *indirect* result of virtuous actions, carried out for their intrinsic value. Nussbaum calls "friendship, love and political commitment" the three basic *relational goods* in Aristotle's *Ethics*.[41] Therefore, they have intrinsic value, are part of eudaimonia, and cannot be used as just a means. This has been a common point of agreement for many philosophers throughout history, and still today, despite other differences between their schools of thought.[42]

The peculiarity of Aristotle's theory of the happiness–relationality nexus emerges from his analysis of the diverse forms of friendships found in the eighth book of the *Nicomachean Ethics*. Friendship, for Aristotle, "is besides most necessary with a view to living" (VIII, 1, 1155a). Thus, to him, true friendship is virtue-friendship. It is that which remains in the virtuous and happy person even after he has reached contemplation. It is not friendship "For the sake of pleasure" or "For the sake of utility"(VIII, 1, 1155a), but desired for the good of the friend: "Aristotle insists that virtue-friendship supplies the 'focal meaning' of friendship" (Brink 1999: 260).

Because they are *made of* relationships, "relational goods" can be enjoyed only in reciprocity. This concept is well expressed by Martha Nussbaum:

> Mutual activity, feeling, and awareness are such a deep part of what love and friendship *are* that Aristotle is unwilling to say that there is anything worthy of the name of love or friendship left, when the shared activities and the forms of communication that express it are taken away. The other person enters in not just as an object who receives the good activities, but as an intrinsic part of the love itself. But if this is so, then the components of the good life are going to be minimally self-sufficient. And they will be vulnerable in an especially deep and dangerous way.
>
> (Nussbaum 1986: 344)

So, by affirming the importance of relational goods in a happy life ("The happy man needs friends"), Aristotle brings happiness back under the influence of fortune.[43]

This internal tension in the Aristotelian eudaimonia, that has to be at the same time the final end, self-sufficient[44] *and* fragile (because it depends on others), marks the deepest difference between the two approaches of the happiness–sociality nexus (i.e. the Aristotelian and the Platonic) that have characterised the whole western cultural trajectory until now.[45] Though Aristotle agrees with Plato that the contemplative life is superior to the active life, *at the same time* he affirms the necessity of friends *for every stage of life*. In an Aristotelian approach, happiness, the good life, is, *at the same time*, constitutionally civil and *therefore* fragile.[46] To renounce its fragility would mean we would have to renounce the good life itself.

This is the basic stress on which the happiness–sociality nexus completely leans on. In the following chapters we shall see that an awareness of the civic life's fragility accompanied the entire trajectory of western thought up to modern times. We shall see how modern political philosophy wanted to resolve the paradox of civic life by renouncing, *de facto*, a *fully* civic life, hoping to avoid its fragility. In particular, the invention of the market economy is positioned at the centre of this trajectory and its tension. More than any other modern invention, the market emancipates us from *dependence* on other people. It frees us from the benevolence of our fellow citizens. The market emancipates from the dependence, but, in doing so, it may remove the locus of genuine sociality. Finding new loci may be very difficult because – if what we have said is true – happiness cannot be sought instrumentally.

This tension will be one *fil rouge* of the work.

Civic Humanism

The Aristotelian vision of happiness remained marginalised in the first millennium of the Christian era. Neo-Platonism, instead, was the prevailing culture of the Middle Ages. After the collapse of the Roman empire, civic life and civil virtues (those of Aristotle or Cicero) disappeared from the conception of the good life, that became identified with contemplation and solitude, also thanks to the first mediation of Christianity characterised by neo-platonic categories.[47]

A new spring-time of civic life in Europe has been "Civic Humanism", a period of the history of Europe – of Italy in particular – that is more and more re-evaluated in view of the understanding of the cultural origins of both Scottish and Italian Enlightenments. Civic Humanism constitutes the first, and central, important episode of our story in search of Civil Happiness.

The historians Hans Baron and Eugenio Garin have coined the expression "Civic Humanism", to identify that period of return of the Aristotelian and republican idea of *polis* and *civitas* in Tuscany, after the "un-civic" Scholasticism of the *Trecento*, and before Machiavelli in the *Cinquecento*. This interpretation makes the *florentina libertas* Civic Humanism's reference point; that is, the period of the republic of Florence, that began in 1402 with the Medici victory over the Visconti of Milan. A moment of "crisis" that originated the new civic and participative culture in Florence.

This thesis has been developed, and partially revised, by the so-called "Historic School of Cambridge" of Pocock (1975) and Skinner (1978) and their followers, who reinterpreted Civic Humanism or "classical republicanism" as an important and lasting tradition in the western political thought:[48]

> According to Pocock, Civil Humanism constituted a distinct political discourse which (via a "Machiavellian moment") had passed from Renaissance Florence to Oliver Cromwell's England, and thence to colonial America, where it formed the ideological matrix of the American Revolution.
>
> (Hankins 2000: 2)[49]

The historiography tradition of Civil Humanism, from Baron to Skinner and Pocock, locates Machiavelli within this same civic flow: Aristotle, Cicero, Bruni, Machiavelli and Jefferson are heroes of an unbroken tradition that today – according to them – has a new offspring in the modern communitarian thought.

In fact, the reading of the Medieval period as the dawn of Humanism and Modernity is gaining momentum today. After the pioneering work of Sombart (1967 [1902]) and Fanfani (1968), many historians are nowadays moving back in this direction: "It is now well established that many of the republican ideas Baron claimed had emerged around 1400 in the writings of Italian humanists had, in fact, a long prehistory in the Medieval scholastic and rhetorical traditions" (Hankins 2000: 8).

In this and the following chapters, although supporting the idea of a civic tradition that crosses all western civilisations, I don't endorse either of the interpretations (Baron's or that of the Cambridge School) I refer to above. In particular, following most of the very recent literature, I do not see Machiavelli as being part of the same tradition: "Bruni is still very much within the Aristotelian tradition from which Machiavelli has definitely and intentionally departed" (Mansfield 2000: 228). In my reading, Machiavelli will be presented as the breaking point in the classical (Aristotelian) civic tradition, and as the main starting point of the modern individualistic political philosophy.

Nevertheless, apart the differences in historiography interpretations, today all historians agree that the "golden age" of Civic Humanism was Tuscany of the first half of the *Quattrocento:* "especially in the *Quattrocento* studies, the Baronian model of Renaissance republicanism remains virtually unchallenged" (Hankins 2000: 7).[50] The main protagonists were Coluccio Salutati, Poggio Bracciolini, Leonardo Bruni, Leon Battista Alberti, San Bernardino from Siena, Matteo Palmieri, among many. It was the time when the city of Florence was enjoying the extraordinary talents of such artists as Brunelleschi, Masaccio, Donatello, Botticelli, Luca Della Robbia and Beato Angelico – mentioning only the major names.[51]

The basic element characterising Civic Humanism is the *reawakening to the necessity of a civic or political life for a fully happy human life:*

> Without love for the *humanitas* of the ancients, and the readiness to be educated by it, there can be no Humanism; and without minds opened in sympathy to the values and ideals of the *vita activa et politica* of Greek and Roman citizens, civic Humanism could not come into being.
>
> (Baron 1955: 92)

In Baron's and Garin's interpretation, Civic Humanism begins with Coluccio Salutati and had its peak with the *Aretino* chancellor Leonardo Bruni. In such a periodisation, Civic Humanism is just the opening season of the entire period of humanism up to mid-*Quattrocento*. It merits the adjective "civic" because of its Aristotelian roots and social thrust. The curtains fell on the first act of humanism in the second half of the *Quattrocento* and *Cinquecento*, with the onslaught of the Platonic, individualist, contemplative, solitary and esoteric soul (like that of Pico della Mirandola and Marsilio Ficino). By distinguishing between two humanisms (the first "civic" and the second "un-civic"),[52] Baron and Garin placed themselves at a distance from the classic work of Jacob Burckhardt (1869) who said

Italian humanism in general was the origin of modern individualism – to Baron and Garin, only the second humanism (after the 1450s) was individualistic.

Thus, the same two distinct souls that had accompanied the western trajectory from the radiance of its Greek dawn found their way into the period of Humanism, namely, the active–civic–Aristotelian–Ciceronian, and the individualist–contemplative–Neo-platonist–Epicurean.[53] They are the same souls that were to give life to the two diverse traditions in modern social sciences, which we will analyse in later chapters. The individualistic soul was to grow into hedonism between the 1600s and the 1700s, while the civic soul was to develop into the tradition represented by Hutcheson or Genovesi.

The Humanism movement took forward the re-evaluation, which had begun already in the last Middle Age, of the horizontal and relational dimensions of the human being, from the family to the city to the state:

> The two sweetest things on earth are the homeland and friends ... Providing, serving, caring for the family, the children, relatives, friends and the homeland which embraces all, you cannot fail to lift your heart to heaven and be pleasing to God.[54]

Coluccio Salutati is an important civic humanist, disciple of Petrarca, and teacher of Leonardo Bruni, the key figure in Civic Humanism according to Baron. Baron writes of Salutati:

> In his early years, he had planned a treatise *De Vita Associabili et Operative*. He had begun work on it in 1372. To judge by its title, the work must have been intended to be a counter-piece to Petrarch's *De Vita Solitaria*, and to be written from a point of view of a citizen. If Salutati's work had been completed, it would have occupied the place in the history of Civic Humanism which was to be filled, two generations later, by the *Della Vita Civile* of Matteo Palmieri, a disciple of Bruni.
>
> (1955: 89)

The attitude of the civic humanists towards the role of the culture "is crossed by this need for a philosophy that is a school of life, a serious and profound meditation on the problems of life" (Garin 1994: 37), which is precisely how it became nearly four centuries later with Genovesi and his "Civil Economy". Matteo Palmieri wrote in his *Vita Civile:*

> Philosophy governs all things and is the utmost principle of all human doctrines and acts. It has two very worthy parts. The first is placed in the investigation of nature's secrets, which is certainly sublime and excellent, yet which is much less useful for our life than the second

part, which administers the customs and approved way of life of virtuous men ... This other part of philosophy is entirely ours, guide of
men, master of virtues, crusher of vice, friend of the good life.

(Palmieri 1981 [1440]: 29)

"Well-living" was to become one of the distinctive traits of the civil
economy tradition of the 1700s and 1800s, as we will see later. "In Florence", writes the historian Franco Cardini,

> the first humanists, those of the Civil Humanism, are, like Coluccio
> Salutati, Chancellors of the Republic. In the service of their homeland,
> they offer the resources of their style, as well as their philological and
> literary cognitions which are not felt as exhortatory, but as an integral
> part of their political and moral mission. The humanist-chancellor
> does not study during the time he is free from work. On the contrary,
> he studies precisely in order to improve the way in which he carries
> out his work.
>
> (Cardini 1986: 200)

It shouldn't be surprising then that Bruni, Alberti, Bernardino of Siena
or Poggio Bracciolini brought to maturation the Medieval thesis on the
social value of wealth, anticipating intuitions which only became common
in the eighteenth century. For example, let us take Poggio Bracciolini and
his treatise, *De Avaritia* (1429),[55] in which he praises the spirit of initiative,
the development of commerce and even the love of money, because
without these,

> every splendour would disappear from the city, every beauty, every
> ornament; no more temples, monuments, arts...; our entire life and
> that of the State would be overthrown if everyone only procured that
> which is necessary ... Money is the backbone of the State, and the
> greedy must be considered its basis and foundation.
>
> (Quoted in Garin 1994: 55)

Even within monastic culture, human work was no longer seen as
having less value than contemplation. It is given new worth and raised to
the realm of participation in God's own creative activity. Also in reaction
against a certain abstract form of Scholasticism, the civic humanists
strongly affirmed that the only *true* virtue is *civic* virtue, and that the only
truly human life was – using Hannah Arendt's famous expression[56] – *active*
life. Therefore, there is no virtue in solitary life, but only in the city. Man,
a "weak animal, insufficient by himself, only reaches his perfection in civic
society".[57]

Salutati was the teacher of both Bernadino of Siena and Leonardi
Bruni, authors who made praise of civic life and the importance of human

affairs the pillars of their vision of economic and social life.[58] Bruni took the same interpretation of *studia humanitatis*, from which humanism takes its name, and rechannelled it into the orbit of civic life, "they are called *studia humanitatis* because they form the complete man" (quoted in Garin 1994: 48). He defined the human person as a "civil animal" (*animal civile*), clearly inspired by Aristotle, a definition that well encapsulates Civic Humanism's anthropology.

Bruni, who for Baron is the archetype of the civic humanist, saw perfect assonance between the Christian vision and that of Plato and Aristotle:[59] "The part of philosophy which deals with customs, the governing of states and the best way of living is almost the same in both the pagan philosophers and ours" (quoted in Garin 1994: 54).[60]

Finally, the civic humanists' reflections surrounding the theme of happiness also tie into these civic themes because, following Aristotle (and Cicero), happiness is seen as the outcome of civil virtues and therefore as a constitutionally social reality: "if it is an excellent thing to give happiness to one alone, how much better will it be to conquer it for an entire state?" (Leonardo Bruni, quoted in Garin 1994: 52). Such are the roots for Public Happiness which will become the dominant theme of the Latin, especially, Italian economic tradition in the eighteenth century.

The sunset of the civil

The civil soul of the Middle Ages flowed, then, into Civic Humanism, a period as rich as it was short. In fact, the brief oasis of republican freedom and a citizens' culture ceded to the *Signorie*, despotic monarchies which gave life to an authoritarian epoch all over Italy. It was a far cry from the *florentina libertas* of which Bruni sang in the first half of the *Quattrocento*. It is no coincidence that reflection on civil life came to a shrieking halt at the end of the fifteenth century. Neither is it by chance that the humanists stepped out of the *universitas* and city life, shed their political garb and civil commitments and took on the guise of solitary individuals who roamed from one European court to another (Trinkaus 1965, chapter 3).

In this context, happiness too became an individual, neo-Platonic and Epicurean affair. Life-in-common was berated in various treatises by Marsilio Ficino, Filippo Beroaldo, Piero Valeriano, Lorenzo de' Medici or Pico della Mirandola for being the source of pain and suffering. They advised that happiness is to be found by fleeing the city and its creatures. At the end of the Middle Ages and the dawn of humanism, men like Bruni and Palmieri had opened perspectives and set the stage for peace and civil life, but the process never reached its maturity. In the words of Henry de Lubac (1977), Humanism was an "unfulfilled dawn".

Instead, the sun, whose rays burst over the *Cinquecento* and early *Seicentos*, ignited "utopian" dreams, and plans for the "perfect state". Under the influence of Plato, utopian writings flowed from the pens of philosophers like Thomas More, Doni, Patrizi, Campanella and Bacon, while authors like Agostini Lolini and Paruta architected the "perfect state" under Aristotle's direction. Their literature assumed a particular importance after the disintegration of the first humanism, up until the birth of Political and Civil Economy in the second half of the eighteenth century. Marked by disappointment and pessimism, the period of the "second humanism" or Renaissance, set people dreaming about ideal societies as a means of escaping the sad, political reality and the asocial, individualistic thoughts of their times. Botticelli's mythological pictures took the place of Lorenzetti's *Buon Governo*: art was no longer a tool for signifying to the people the ideal city and government, but a decoration for private chapels and bedrooms with mythological gods far from civil and real life.

Although the expression "The Happy City" (*la città felice*) appeared in the titles of the treatises of such authors as Doni (1552) and Patrizi (1553), it was, by then, just a nostalgic echo of a concrete attempt to construct "*Civil Happiness*", which had lost its appointment with history a century earlier.[61]

"At the same point" – Garin writes – "where the sense of a human society divided and tormented becomes more severe and hard, higher becomes also the need of a city finally peaceful and serene" (1988: 93).

Thus, a hiatus was created between Civic Humanism and Modernity. The dynamics set into motion by the Protestant Reformation and Catholic counter-reformation helped sweep the broken dawn of Civic Humanism off the horizons of history. Reacting against the valorisation that Protestantism (Calvinism in particular, as highlighted by Max Weber) gave to individual enterprise and freedom,[62] the Catholic Church after the Council of Trent (1563) condemned commercial and economic activity once again, although during the period of humanism the first economic revolution in the city was nurtured by "saints" such as Bernardino of Siena or Bernardino of Feltre. Such a reaction was well on its way to finding a resolution in the first humanist period.

The Italian cities' experiments with civil life did not light the way for Renaissance culture, which, instead, succumbed to bitter factional wars. Yet, when we realise that the humanist thinkers failed to explore the anthropological foundations of the *animal civile*, it should come as no surprise. In fact, the civil life of Florence showed itself to be just as fragile as in the Athens of Pericles, which had so inspired Aristotle. None of the humanist thinkers went beyond a naïve repetition of the classical thesis of the human animal's sociability. Nor did they attempt to philosophise on the anthropological themes that were begun by Augustine, Aquinas and the great Scholasticism in order to integrate them with the new civil demands. Thus, there is no trace of the first humanism's civil experience in the anthropological reflections of the *Cinquecento*. The reality of the individual self, masterly depicted by Pico della Mirandola's *De homini dignitate*, had taken its place. Renaissance's anthropological reflection took off from the individual who rose from the ashes of Civic Humanism. And, in the eyes of Machiavelli and Hobbes, what an individual he was: villainous, uncivil, fearful, and cunning – the modern adjectives for the "new" human being.

Life-in-common took on a double nature in the modern era. While it was the only place for the human social animal, it was also the place where he or she risked drifting towards depravity. Kant's definition of the human condition as characterised by an "unsociable sociability", grasps western modern thought on the modern human being.[63]

The "uncivil animal" tradition: Machiavelli, Hobbes, Mandeville and Hume

Machiavelli's political virtue

It would be impossible to understand how the foundation of Political or Civil Economy faced the paradox of the "unsociable-sociability" without first coming to terms with some key figures of the political thought that paved the way. Given the outline of this work, I choose to deal with only four thinkers: Machiavelli, Hobbes, Mandeville and Hume, because they are ideal mediators for understanding the intellectual project of the first economists.

The Florentine Niccolò Machiavelli lived in an era of great moral and political upheaval. Instead of Republics, the civil hopes of the first human-ists for liberty and political participation had produced *Signorie*, the dominion of authoritarian elites. From the land of *comuni*, the *Signorie* turned Italy into a land ravaged by continuous wars and mercenary armies. With an atmosphere of fear and malaise looming over the peninsula, philosophers took refuge in neo-Platonism, magical esoterism and utopian literature. Personally outraged by the incivility of his times, Machiavelli gave politics autonomy, founded on new anthropological bases far from the Aristotelian and civic traditions. Because civil virtues had proved to be incapable of creating a national consciousness and maintaining peace, a different basis to justify the possibility for peaceful cohabitation was needed.

Far from the first humanists' view of the individual as naturally soci-able, Machiavelli's anthropological view was tainted by the particularly nasty historical circumstances in which he lived. The atmosphere of his age, permeated his entire works with a radically pessimistic anthropology:

> For it is a good general rule about men, that they are ungrateful, fickle, liars and deceivers, fearful of danger and greedy for gain. While you serve their welfare, they are all yours, offering their blood, their belongings, their lives, and their children's lives ... so long as the danger is remote. But when the danger is close at hand, they turn

against you ... friendships that are bought at a price, and not with greatness and nobility of soul.

(1513, chapter 17: 46)

If this is the actual nature of the human being, then the basis of life-in-common cannot be reciprocal *love* but rather reciprocal *fear*:

> People are less concerned with offending a man who makes himself loved than one who makes himself feared: the reason is that love is a link of obligation which men, because they are rotten, will break any time they think doing so serves their advantage; but fear involves a dread of punishment, from which they can never escape
>
> (1513, chapter 17: 46)[64]

Thanks to his political virtue, therefore, the prince is he who frees his subjects (*sudditi*) – citizens no longer – from the destructive conflicts that are unleashed by the *uncivil animal* when he is left free to act in the city. Machiavelli's revolution was essentially anthropological and was the basis for his political theories.

His version of the classical theme of the relation between fortune and virtue is also meaningful. Over the course of 15 centuries, Christianity, along with other monotheistic religions, had sought philosophical foundations for the idea that history is entrusted to the loving "hand" of Providence rather than to chance and circumstance under the guidance of the blindfolded goddess. Machiavelli felt Christian anthropology's preoccupation with the city of God had rendered the human being incapable of constructing the city of men, and he broke with the Christian and Aristotelian humanism, starting a new era. To Machiavelli, the Renaissance is not so different from medieval scholasticism: both remain within the classical tradition, and both remain Christian due to their common reliance on "imagined republics and principalities that have never been seen or known to exist in truth" (1513: xv).[65]

Furthermore, the idea of Providence operating in social matters was removed, putting history under the dominion of Fortune[66] once again. He gave the Prince suggestions on how to defend against, mitigate with or "attract"[67] Fortune. The Prince makes the blind goddess pour the gifts of her cornucopia over him. Fortune's favours are not shed on civil virtue, but on the heroic, exceptional and solitary man.

This theme of "fortune", central, as has been shown, in Greek philosophy, was developed and partially transformed by Latin philosophy (the Roman *virtus* of Cicero and Seneca was not distant from Neo-Platonism) which was gaining popularity in the second humanism. We mentioned the different conceptions of the fortune/virtue relationships held by Aristotle and Plato. The re-emergence of Neoplatonism of the late *Quattrocento* put the emphasis back on the individual virtues (courage, prudence...), and in flight from the civil. Machiavelli aligns himself with this tradition. In the last chapter of *The Prince*, he advises the prince on how to establish an alliance with fortune. He says, "Fortune is a woman, and the man who wants to hold her down must beat and bully her.... We see that she yields more often to men of this stripe than to those who come coldly towards her" (chapter 25: 69).[68]

Machiavelli occupies an important role in the context of the history of Civil Happiness, because he created the template of a new way of looking at society: after his criticism of the classical vision of the human being, the link between virtuous citizens–virtuous State broke down: honest and good people were no longer considered the tool for building a good society. A bridge between individual virtue and public virtue collapsed: Hobbes', Hume's or Mandeville's theories were created to find new explanations of the mechanisms that make life in common possible, wealthy and growing, and, more importantly, new explanations for justifying how a society made of definitively selfish and asocial members would work, without falling into permanent self-destructive wars and endemic conflicts.

Hobbes' political revolution

More than 100 years after Machiavelli, Hobbes elaborated a response to the crisis of the civil that was partially similar (although in some aspects deeply different) to Machiavelli's. In Hobbes' fundamental treatises, the way in which he broke away from the classical conception of the civil by adopting a new anthropology closely recalls Machiavelli's approach.

The change of the political situation in Italy had a great importance for understanding the "uncivil" political theory of Machiavelli, as the wars of religions were an important element in the formation of Hobbes' philosophy. History's real events played an important part in the formulation of Hobbes' political and anthropological pessimism, just as they had in Machiavelli's case. Those theories required the *Prince* or the *Leviathan* to recompose the unity in a civil life that had proved itself to be too immature to manage the dynamics of the life-in-common announced with enthusiasm by civic humanists. There is, therefore, an analogy between Machiavelli's *Prince* and Hobbes' *Leviathan*.[69]

Hobbes, it is known, found the common denominator between human beings to be their vulnerability to being killed: *reciprocal fear*. Anyone can be killed by anyone else. Conflict, the struggle to oppress the other and gain power, are men's ordinary condition. Peace and concord are temporary in the state of nature. Fear, therefore, became the new foundation for life-in-common. Far from Civic Humanism and the classical tradition, and close to Machiavelli, are the emblematic first pages of *On the Citizen* (1642):

The majority of previous writers on public Affairs either assume or seek to prove or simply assert that Man is an animal born fit for society, – in the Greek phrase, Ζῷου πολιτικόυ. . . . This axiom, though very widely accepted, is nevertheless false;. . . By nature, then, we are not looking for friends but to honour or advantage from them. This is what we are primarily after; friends are secondary.[70]

Hobbes' theory is therefore based on a "psychological egoism" (that is, a theory of human nature that claims that humans are necessarily and exclusively self-interested), and ends up in an "authoritarian individualism". All men pursue only what they perceive to be in their own, individually considered, best interests. Everything people do is motivated solely by the desire to better their own situations, and satisfy as many of our own, individually considered, desires as possible. We are infinitely appetitive and only genuinely concerned with our own selves: this is the basic anthropology coming from the *Leviathan*.

From this micro-assumption comes his macro-theory of social contract. According to Hobbes, the justification for political obligation is a consequence of the fact that men are naturally self-interested but *rational*; thus they will choose to submit to the authority of a Sovereign – the Leviathan – in order to be able to live in a civil society, which is conducive to their own interests. To Hobbes, the *sommum bonum* is not happiness (Aristotle) but the conservation of life. At the opposite end of the spectrum from Aristotle and Thomas Aquinas, Hobbes therefore excludes the possibility of a civil society born from a dynamic between persons who are naturally sociable or civil, and replaces it with a state that can exist only if it is created by an artificial pact and forcefully maintained by an impersonal Leviathan.

The whole of Hobbes' project must be considered, however, in order to make a correct evaluation of his theoretical system: his idea of an artificial pact among equal and free human beings, a "social compact", was also conceived as a tool for discarding the *natural* but *unequal* traditional society. In fact, since Aristotle, the normal way of conceiving society was the "natural aggregation" of individuals into families, families into villages, villages into cities and finally cities form – with or without a social contract – the civil society. The blueprint of this classical vision is Aristotle's *Politics*:

> when several families are united, and the association aims at something more than the supply of daily needs, the first society to be formed is the village. And the most natural form of the village appears to be that of a colony from the family, composed of the children and grandchildren, who are said to be suckled "with the same milk." . . . When several villages are united in a single complete community, large enough to be nearly or quite self-sufficing, the state comes into

existence, originating in the bare needs of life, and continuing in existence for the sake of a good life. And therefore, if the earlier forms of
society are natural, so is the state, for it is the end of them, and the
nature of a thing is its end.

(Chapter 1)[71]

All this system leans on the hypothesis that "man is by nature a political
animal" (Aristotle chapter 1). "It is surprising" – Bobbio affirms – "how
lasting, permanent, stable, and vital this way of conceiving the origin of the
state has been over the centuries" (1993: 6). This Aristotelian vision of
society imbued, in various forms, Scholasticism's natural law theory, Civic
Humanism, and, in modern times, was championed by philosophers such
as Bodin and Althusius; this vision was surely dominant before Hobbes.[72]
This tradition – this is the point I would stress – brings about *two fundamental implications*: first, society is the result of the natural sociality of
people; second, the inequality of society is *natural* as it is natural in the
family, where men, women and children are *social but unequal*. The classical vision of society was, therefore, *naturally unequal*:

> Since individuals live in families from the time of their birth, the pre-
> political condition is not one of freedom and equality. It is rather a
> condition in which fundamental relationships existing in a hierarchical
> society, such as the family is, are between superiors and inferiors. Such
> are the relationships between father (and mother) and child, or
> between master and servant.
>
> (Bobbio 1993: 8–9)

In this context, Hobbes' theory, by recommending an artificial pact
among individuals *before* society, born "as mushrooms", wanted to create
the possibility of a new society constituted by *free* and *equal* people
(although not naturally social). The price of this invention was, however,
the creation of a distance from Civic Humanism, and from a civil anthropology: it was the substitution of the "ethics of the person" with the
"ethics of the individual" (Bobbio 1993: 152).

In summary, Hobbes was surely influenced by the contradictions of religious wars and the violent birth pangs of the national states. Classical
sociability of man, or Grotius' *appetitus societatis*, collapsed in front of a
scenario of incivility better explained by the uncivil individual hypothe-
sised by Hobbes. Hobbes' solution for avoiding the war of all against all
(*bellum omnium contra omnia*), for keeping the peace and making possible the life in common, was to "frame" and "contain" interpersonal relationships and delegate the mediation of the inter-subjective dimension of
human beings to the Leviathan-State.

As Machiavelli sacrificed the "civic" for the sake of power, Hobbes sacrificed the "civil" for the sake of the political. In other words, Machiavelli

seems ready to pay the price of sacrificing the *fraternity* of the citizens for the liberty of the state, whereas Hobbes gives up the liberty of the individuals for the security and equality[73] of the subjects under an authoritarian ruler.

Mandeville's vices and virtues

Mandeville's *Fable of the Bees* – originally published as "The Grumbling Hive", in 1705 (last edition 1729) – is another important step along the uncivil or individualistic tradition. Although between Mandeville's and Hobbes' philosophies there are important differences, they share the criticism of both the classical vision of man as social animal and of the necessity of civil virtues for a good society.

In other words, Hobbes and Mandeville share the idea that, in the big society – the commercial society – individual virtues are no more the proper tool for building the wealth or the happiness of nations. In this context Mandeville's contribution to the theory of the interplay between public and private sphere is particularly radical and relevant.

On the other hand, Mandeville's continuity with Machiavelli is also evident. His famous Introduction to the *An Inquiry on the Origin of Moral Virtue* opens as it follows: "One of the greatest Reasons why so few People understand themselves, is, that most Writers are always teaching Men what they should be, and hardly ever trouble their Heads with telling them what they really are" (Opening). And not by chance F.B. Kaye, the editor of *Fable*'s critical edition (1923), in commenting on this passage, inserts in a note an extract from Machiavelli's *Principe*:

> Ma, sendo l'intento mio scrivere cosa utile a chi l'intende, mi è parso più conveniente andare dietro alla verità effettuale della cosa, che all' immaginazione di essa;... perché egli è tanto discosto da come si vive a come si dovrebbe vivere, che colui che lascia quello che si fa per quello che si dovrebbe fare, impara piuttosto la rovina che la preservazione sua...
>
> (*Il Principe*, chapter 15)

In respect to Hobbes, the attack against civil virtues comes from a different perspective. Not only is it against the factual evidence to consider the human being a "civil animal" who by nature seeks relationships with others, Mandeville maintains that if it were ever to be true, or if the human being became so by way of education, he should rein in his virtues because they are not conducive to the good of society. Vice – not virtue – brings about the good-life of society:

> So Vice is beneficial found, When it's by Justice lopt, and bound; Nay, where the People would be great, As necessary to the State, At

Hunger is to make 'em eat. Bare Vertue can't make Nations live In Splendour; they, that would revive A Golden Age, must be as free, For Acorns, as for Honesty.

(1923 [1729], §§425–430)

According to Mandeville, the role of virtues changes radically in passing from small to big societies: in small communities, such as a family or village, private virtues are immediately related to public virtues, as private happiness is connected to Public Happiness. In big societies, however, not only is there no guarantee that private virtues of citizens will bring public benefits, but, according to Mandeville, private virtues bring no economic growth and felicity: "A Golden Age, must be as free, For Acorns, as for Honesty." This is more than a critique of Shaftsbury's theory of virtues: Mandeville's theory of commercial society represents a real rejection of the civil tradition anchored on the pivotal idea that *a good society is the natural outcome of actions of good citizens*, or that a wealthy and happy people is the direct consequence of virtuous and public-oriented persons. Then, in commercial societies, cooperation does not spring from civil virtues, is not an expression of the natural sociability of the humans beings, but is just a matter of mutual advantages among self-interested, "self-liking" and egoistic individuals.

In the *Fourth Dialogue between Horatio and Cleomenes*,[74] we find a discourse useful for understanding both Mandeville's "humanism" and his consequent vision of happiness:

HORATIO: "But is there in the Mind of Man a natural Affection, that prompts him to love his Species, beyond what other Animals have for theirs; or are we born with Hatred and Aversion, that makes us Wolves and Bears, to one another?"

CLEOMENES: "I believe neither. From what appears to us in human Affairs, and the Works of Nature, we have more Reason to imagine that the Desire as well as Aptness of Man to associate, do not proceed from his Love to others, than we have to believe that a mutual Affection of the Planets to one another, superiour to what they feel to Stars more remote, is not the true Cause why they keep always moving together in the same solar System."

HORATIO: "You don't believe that the Stars have any Love for one another, I am sure: Then why, *more Reason?*"

CLEOMENES: "Because there are no *Phænomena*, plainly to contradict this Love of the Planets; and we meet with Thousands every Day to convince us, that man centers every thing in himself, and neither loves nor hates, but for his own Sake. Every Individual is a little World by itself, and all Creatures, as far as their Understanding and Abilities will let them, endeavour to make that Self happy: This in all of them is the continual Labour, and seems to be the whole Design of Life. Hence it follows, that in the Choice of Things Men must be determin'd by the Perception they have of Happiness."

(Mandeville 1929 [1725], Vol. 2: 178)

The cultural revolution carried out a few decades later by the founders of Political and Civil Economy was an attempt to overcome this humanism, but, at the same time, to save the civil and civilising role of self-interest and commerce, and to describe the behaviour of individuals "as they really are".

Hume's cooperation without benevolence

Society, commercial society, does not come from mutual benevolence of relational persons, but from the awareness of mutual advantages of self-liking people: this is the post-Civic Humanism main line of thought. This is an approach in line with Hume who, in his *Treatise of Human Nature* (1978 [1740]) explained how civil society can be, and actually is, based on a *cooperation without benevolence*. As Mandeville limits the positive role of virtues to small communities, Hume claims that benevolence can be effective in creating cooperation only in small societies. In fact, according to Hume, although benevolence is part of human nature, it springs from sympathy, and the force of sympathy depends on the closeness of the relationship between the people in question ("intimacy"): we are benevolent to our family and friends, and to those whose happiness or misery is "brought near to us, and represented in lively colours" (Hume 1978) [1740]: 481).[75] Commercial society needs cooperation to bring all of its advantages; cooperation requires justice, but according to Hume, "self-interest is the original motive to the establishment of justice" (1978 [1740]: 499). He tries to show that justice, in *de facto* form, would emerge spontaneously out of the repeated interaction of self-interested individuals. In particular, the reason for following the rules of justice, which, for Hume, is an *artificial* virtue, comes from an interest for our reputation:

> There is nothing, which touches us more nearly than our reputation, and nothing on which our reputation more depends than our conduct, with relation to the property of others. For this reason, every one, who has any regard to his character, or who intends to live on good terms with mankind, must fix an inviolable law to himself, never, by any temptation, to be induc'd to violate those principles, which are essential to a man of probity and honour.
>
> (1978 [1740]: 501)

Accordingly, Hume explains cooperation as a practice that evolves out of bilateral practices of mutual assistance, based on reciprocal self-interest. This concept of cooperation-without-benevolence – still central in modern economic theory – is masterfully expressed in a classical passage on the explanations of how selfish cooperation is generated and reproduced:

> Men being naturally selfish, or endowed only with a confined generosity, they are not easily induced to perform any action for the interest of strangers, except with a view to some reciprocal advantage, which they had no hope of obtaining but by such a performance. Now as it frequently happens, that these mutual performances cannot be finished at the same instant, it is necessary, that one party be contented to remain in uncertainty, and depend upon the gratitude of the other for a return of kindness. But so much corruption is there among men, that, generally speaking, this becomes but a slender security; and as the benefactor is here supposed to bestow his favours with a view to self-interest, this both takes off from the obligation, and sets an example to selfishness, which is the true mother of ingratitude. Were we, therefore, to follow the natural course of our passions and inclinations, we should perform but few actions for the advantage of others, from disinterested views; because we are naturally very limited in our kindness and affection: And we should perform as few of that kind, out of a regard to interest; because we cannot depend upon their gratitude.

Then the famous examples of the two egoist (but rational) farmers:

> Your corn is ripe to-day; mine will be so tomorrow. It is profitable for us both, that I should labour with you to-day, and that you should aid me to-morrow. I have no kindness for you, and know you have as little for me. I will not, therefore, take any pains upon your account; and should I labour with you upon my own account, in expectation of a return, I know I should be disappointed, and that I should in vain depend upon your gratitude. Here then I leave you to labour alone: You treat me in the same manner. The seasons change; and both of us lose our harvests for want of mutual confidence and security.

From that "egoism failure", rational and self-interested cooperation could come:

> Hence I learn to do a service to another, without bearing him any real kindness; because I forsee, that he will return my service, in expectation of another of the same kind, and in order to maintain the same correspondence of good offices with me or with others. And accordingly, after I have served him, and he is in possession of the advantage arising from my action, he is induced to perform his part, as foreseeing the consequences of his refusal.

(1978 [1740]: 520–521)

Machiavelli, Hobbes, Mandeville and Hume – all these authors, although very different in their overall philosophical systems – nevertheless have a theory of civil society no longer based on civil virtues: the common denominator among their theories is represented by an asocial and selfish anthropology. After the collapse of the *Christianitas*, also due to the religion wars, rational cooperation self-interest-based sprung as the new "bond of society" of the new commercial society. The spread of the markets, therefore, was considered the way to make this logic of new cooperation fully workable.

In this sense I agree with the philosopher T. Todorov, according to whom "in studying the vast currents of European philosophical thought regarding the definition of what is human, one reaches an unexpected conclusion: the social dimension, the element of life in common, is not generally considered necessary to man" (Todorov 1998: 15). In the modern philosophical mainstream, he claims, from Montaigne to La Rochefoucauld, from Hobbes to Helvetius or Pascal, one common denominator is the idea that a human being's true nature is egotistical and, above all, "solitary" (1998: 15).

In the next chapters, I intend to show in that sense the birth of the Political and Civil Economy represented, although in different ways, exceptions with respect to the "individualistic" and asocial cultural mainstream of Modern Europe.

4   Public Happiness

Wealth, however, is a means not the end of the society.

(G. Palmieri)

Towards a new foundation of civil life

The founders of modern economic science were fascinated by the cold analysis of the individualistic authors, without, however, sharing their deep pessimism about humankind and their distrust towards civil virtues. What more fascinated the first economists – from Smith to Genovesi – was the realism of the founders of the political science in describing society: the social scientist shouldn't imagine the "ideal" man, but must describe and predict the actions of the man "as he is" (in Machiavelli's or Mandeville's words). These "uncivil" authors had grasped some aspects of the real dynamics of modern societies, and their realistic approach left their mark on the first modern scholars of the new market economy.

More basically, the first economists had to address the objections raised by those radical critiques before they could attempt to found an economic science that could be called "civil" or "political". The same would have had to be done before they could have dared to cite Civic Humanism, the Greek *polis* or the Roman *civitas* as examples of the civilising role of the economy and commerce. Actually, they did more than simply looking again at Civic Humanism. The "uncivil" philosophers had described a society regulated simply by the working of interests and just laws, where there is no place and no role for civil virtues or, more generally, for genuine and not fully instrumental relations. But – and this is the key point – deeper was the conviction, shared by most classical eighteenth-century economists, that *without civil virtues there is no room for a market economy*: the market can work properly (so bringing wealth and welfare) only among people capable of cooperation and trust – cooperation and trust that, perhaps, require more that self-interest.

In what follows we shall see that the first economists began their work by *laying down a new anthropological and ethical foundation for a new commercial society.* Keeping in mind the critiques of the individualist authors, they delivered well-founded new arguments for the role of the civil society and civil virtues.

For this reason, it is incorrect to say that modern Political Economy was born by emancipating itself from ethics, because modern social science was born incorporating a very clear (individualistic and anti-social) ethics. For this reason, as we'll see later, it is not by chance that both Smith and Genovesi, the leaders of two important schools of modern economic science, before writing their economic treatises, wrote on moral philosophy and anthropology. In other words, modern economic science was born in the attempt to lay the foundations for a *new ethics* which allowed market relationships, intended as a particular civil relationship, to be civil in spite of the radical criticism perpetrated by the first modern political individualistic theories. We'll see that the content of the new ethics was different in Naples and in Glasgow, but the need for an anthropological novelty was present in these founders of modern economic science.

Furthermore, and at a different epistemological level (that of economic and social history), it is not by coincidence that this re-foundation came about during the age of peace and political reforms of the mid-eighteenth century which could till the ground of credibility for a new rational reflection on the *civil animal*. In Naples, Charles III of the Bourbons opened a new era of civil reforms, and Glasgow in Scotland, at the beginning of the eighteenth century, experienced an economic and civil spring-time, with houses and palaces adorned in a Renaissance fashion.[76]

In this chapter we shall see how the founders of modern Political and Civil Economy grasped the significance of the uncivil criticism and how they went beyond it by bringing the discussion to a different level: civil society was conceived as a network of actions, rules and institutions that were made to insure that man's ambivalent nature, his "unsociable-sociality", was oriented to the common good (national wealth or Public Happiness). Thus, they recognised that the "great society", the modern commercial society, cannot put too much trust in man's benevolence, because the "real man" mostly tends to look after his own personal interests. Yet, from within the perspective of the civil society put forward by the first classical economists, personal interests are not vices because they are tied by an unbreakable chain to the interests of the others, to the common good.[77]

Modern Political (Anglo-Saxon) or Civil (Italian) Economy was born in the midst of rich and complex reflections on the nature of the human person and society that was, *at the same time*, in line and in rupture with the individualistic modern tradition. Those reflections sought ways of making personal interest compatible with the interest of others, although in different ways, as we shall see in the central part of the work. Benevolence was considered not in opposition to self-interest; self-interest, instead, was one side of the coin, the interest of others was the other side, as one of the leaders of the Neapolitan School of Civil Economy, Giuseppe Palmieri, wrote in his book on "Pubblica felicità":

> Utility is the great motivator of human action. The well-being to which everyone aspires, makes all men run to where utility and the good come forth best and where they best meet.... All may be persuaded, however, that in order to bring about one's own good, one must seek it by procuring the good of his fellows.
>
> (1788: 24)

A similar thesis can be found also in the work of Adam Smith:

> To feel much for others and little for ourselves ... constitutes the perfection of human nature ... As to love our neighbour as we love ourselves is the great law of Christianity, so it is the great precept of nature to love ourselves only as we love our neighbour.
>
> (*TMS*, I, 1, 5)

Next, we start our analysis of the foundations of modern Economics, with respect to happiness and sociality, by introducing a key phrase for the entire research project, namely *Public Happiness*.

Della Pubblica Felicità

There is no happiness outside society and there is no society without civil virtues and intentional love for the public good: this is a central element of the Italian tradition, so important that the Italian economist Achille Loria, at the end of the eighteenth century, wrote, "All our [Italian] economists, from whatever regional background, are dealing not so much, like Adam Smith, with the wealth of nations, but with Public Happiness" (1904: 85).

Historians of the nineteenth century commonly tended to contrast the classical "happy" Italian Civil Economy with the "wealthy" English Political Economy. Although we will observe that the positions were more shaded than that, that general view will be our departure point for analysing the Italian and Scottish traditions' ideas on wealth and happiness.

The Neapolitan philosopher Paolo Mattia Doria's book, *Della vita civile* (1710), (a clear "civic humanist" heading) had an influence on Genovesi's thought and that of the Neapolitan School in general. The book begins with the following words: "Without a doubt, the first object of our desire is human happiness."

The word "happiness" appears in various titles of treatises by economists, not only in the Kingdom of Naples (as we'll see), but also in the book of Tuscan physiocratic economist Ferdinando Paoletti (*I veri mezzi di render felici le società*), and in the many economic treatises in Milan. The Public Happiness tradition found a warm welcome in Milan, soon becoming the central theme of the emerging Lombard School. Men like Pietro Verri, Cesare Beccaria and, in the nineteenth century, Gian Domenico Romagnosi and Carlo Cattaneo, made Milan one of the capitals of the European Enlightenment and of the economic civil tradition.[78] According to the founder and leader of Milan's economic school, Pietro Verri, the civil society held the central place in social and economic dynamics. Civil society is an "industrious reunion of conspiring forces" that makes it possible to reach "the well-being of each one, and which is resolved in Public Happiness, or at least the greatest happiness possible shared with the greatest equality possible. Every human law must tend to such an aim" (1964 [1763–1781]: 100).[79]

More generally, the economy–happiness link is a key characteristic of the whole eighteenth-century Italian tradition, beyond regional difference: "the discussion *on happiness* has as its object a very common argument upon which many have written" (Verri 1963 [1763]: 3).[80] Nevertheless, Naples occupies a special place in the tradition of Public Happiness – as the next two chapters will show.

Della Pubblica Felicità (*On Public Happiness*) was extremely important to civil tradition in the eighteenth century. Previously, we saw that happiness, after Civic Humanism, under the influence of acivil philosophies, became an individual and subjective matter, identified with pleasure or considered, for instance by Kant, to be inadequate from the ethical point of view.[81] Reflection on happiness broke away from the classical tradition which had always considered happiness as a matter connected with civil virtues and distinguished from pleasure.[82]

The tradition of Public Happiness is a core topic of this research. The historians of economic ideas don't give particular attention to "Public Happiness", which they consider as the "poor sister" of the "wealth of nations". Although the reflections on *pubblica felicità* only endured the morning hours of the Latin tradition, it is an important chapter in this research dealing with the relationships between happiness, sociality and Economics. By looking at it from within the civil tradition, and by connecting it to the contemporary discussion, we immediately see important issues under that romantic-sounding expression.

Which is the genesis of the *Pubblica Felicità* tradition? It is usually considered a by-product of the Latin Enlightenment's philosophers, who on the eve of the French revolution began to think that happiness could be increased by working on the social order. Hirschman shows this in the following passage:

Saint-Just's famous phrase: "The idea of happiness is new in Europe" – it was then novel to think that happiness could be *engineered* by changing the social order, a task he and his Jacobin companions had so confidently undertaken. Let us note in passing that the idea of a perfectible social order arose at about the same time as that of unintended effects of human action and decisions. The latter idea was in principle tailor-made to neutralise the former: it permitted one to argue that the best unintentional institutional changes may lead, by those unforeseen consequences or "perverse effects", to all kinds of disastrous results. But the two ideas were not matched up for this purpose. In the first place, the idea of the perfectibility of the social order arose primarily in the course of the French Enlightenment, while that of the unintended consequences was a principal contribution of the contemporary Scottish moralists.

(1982: 1463)

I indulged in the quotation above because it is particularly suitable for sketching the coordinates of the "Public Happiness" tradition that we are buckling up to face. In fact the Public Happiness theme was already entrenched in Europe by the mid-1700s, well before the French Enlightenment; and, as seen, the Italian humanists were already discussing the problem of *unintended results of actions*, which will also become an innermost issue of the Civil Economy tradition.

In particular, Muratori's *Pubblica Felicità* came out a few years prior to the economic items in the *Encylopédie* which launched, in France and then in the rest of the world, the theme of Public Happiness as the great cultural and social programme of the Enlightenment – for example, the "pursuit of happiness" in the USA's Declaration of Independence in 1776 is particularly well-known.[83] Consequently, we may consider the Public Happiness theme as an outcome of the process that began in Civic Humanism, passed on through utopian literature and the crisis of the civil, before flowing into Public Happiness in the eighteenth century. Therefore, Public Happiness was not a by-product of French Enlightenment and then exported to Italy and the rest of the world. The expression first appeared in a title of a book in 1749, *Della Pubblica Felicità*, written by the Italian philosopher and historian Ludovico Antonio Muratori:

> The master desire in us, and father of many others, is OUR OWN PRIVATE GOOD, OR OUR PARTICULAR HAPPINESS ... Of a more sublime sphere, and more noble origin is another Desire, that of the Good of the Society, of the Public Good that is Public Happiness. The first is born of nature, the second has virtue for a mother.
>
> (Foreword)

From this simple sentence, we have three elements that are central in the tradition of Public Happiness:

a   the transformation of "individual" into "public" happiness is not immediate, because Public Happiness is neither an aggregation nor just an unintentional result of the private interest;

b   "*Public* Happiness" is strictly connected with the "*public* good", that comes directly from the natural law tradition of Scholasticism and Civic Humanism;

c   there is a direct link between Public Happiness and civil virtues: happiness, both private and public, springs from virtues.

Della Pubblica Felicità was Muratori's last book (he died in 1750), and was a synthesis of his reflections on society. In 1743, Muratori wrote a book entitled "Happy Christianity" [*Cristianesimo Felice*], in which he described the story of the Jesuit father, Cattaneo, who lived for a few years in Paraguay as part of the Jesuits' *reductiones* experiment. Through his narration, Muratori presents the ideal of a happy city that would inspire his more mature work on happiness: "Well-regulated liberty, sufficient provisions of food, clothing, lodging, public peace and the soul's tranquillity, in my opinion, are the true and only ingredients, which form the happiness of a people" (1824 [1743]: 175).

It has to be noted, however, that Muratori's *pubblica felicità* is a treatise addressed to the "prince", to the Administrator, as also the complete title of the book recites: "On Public Happiness, object of good princes" ("*Sulla pubblica felicità, oggetto dei buoni principi*"). Public Happiness, according to Muratori, is the scope of the action of the "good prince". It is the Aristotelian idea that happiness is also the end of the politics, but without the analysis of the role of the civil virtues of citizens, following the emphasis of Muratori put on the virtue and on the activity of the king or, better, of the ministers of the republic:

> We therefore with public happiness intend nothing but that Peace and Tranquillity, that a wise and lovely Prince, or Minister, tries to ensure to his people, as much as he can.
>
> (1749: 4)

Of course, Muratori's Prince is not Machiavelli's: here we are close to the Republican idea of governors. But, also in this approach, civil society's proper role is missing.

Between tradition and modernity

Muratori's reference point for such a happy society is the Salomon's kingdom, or the Roman emperors such as Titus and Traianus, who stamped on their coins "felicitas pubblica", "temporum felicitas" or "Felicia tempora". So the Roman republic, and the thoughts of Cicero, Livy or Seneca, were very much present in Muratori's conception of *Pubblica Felicità* – and, in some sense, in the whole Italian school.

Behind this vision of Public Happiness there is the traditional vision of the society as a body: the happiness of the body is the happiness of each member, and vice versa. The Prince is the head of the body, and there is no conflict between the happiness of the Prince, the happiness of the State, and the happiness of each component of society. The whole Christian vision of society, from which Muratori's social philosophy comes, was based on this harmonic or *organic* vision of the society as a whole.[84] Such a vision was dominant in western civilisation from Plato up to the French Revolution, when this organic and harmonious conception of society collapsed due to a "conflict of interests" between the bourgeoisie and the aristocracy within the same society and State, the same "body".

This organic vision is still present, although contaminated, in the founders of modern Political Economy, Smith and Genovesi included.[85] Smith, in the famous (and much discussed[86]) *incipit* of Book IV of *Wealth of the Nations* wrote: "Political oeconomy, considered as a branch of the science of a statesman or legislator,... proposes to enrich both the people and the sovereign." A vivid example of that vision is given by Smith's famous eulogy (following Hume) of the high-wage economy in the *Wealth of Nations*. Commenting on the improvements of the labouring classes, Smith poses the problem as follows:

> Is this improvement in the circumstances of the lower ranks of the people to be regarded as an advantage or as an inconveniency to the society? The answer seems at first sight abundantly plain. Servants, labourers and workmen of different kinds, make up the far greater part of every great political society. But what improves the circumstances of the greater part can never be regarded as an inconveniency to the whole. No society can surely be flourishing and happy, of which the far greater part of the members are poor and miserable.
>
> (*WN*, I, chapter 8, §36)[87]

It is to this passage that Marx retorted (in the first of his *Manuscripts* of 1844) that, since Political Economy does encourage the pursuit of wealth and that goes along with this "suffering of the majority", it follows that the goal of "the economic system is the *unhappiness* of society".[88]

Genovesi too is in line with this traditional vision of "Pubblica Felicità". In fact, in Genovesi's words, Public Happiness must become the sovereign's ideal of good government, because "he is the supreme and independent moderator for the Public Happiness, that is, for the happiness of the entire body and for each member" (*Lezioni*, I, chapter 1, §2, p. 3). In chapter 6, he writes: "The State is a great family" (§1, p. 83). Public Happiness is the happiness of the social body, of both the sovereign and the people.[89] But for Genovesi (as it is for Smith), there is also *something more and different* that puts him on the side of modernity, as we shall see in the following chapters. He was a true Enlightenment thinker and social reformer, very critical towards the old regime and its idea of society.

The Enlightenment, in fact, represented a radical criticism towards the organic vision of society, but, it has to be noted, the criticism was essentially addressed towards the lack of *freedom* and *equality* typical of the organicistic societies, not mainly towards the idea of society as a body. In fact, after Civic Humanism had affirmed the equality of citizens and the importance of freedom, including economic freedom, social and political theories typical of unequal societies returned with great strength between the seventeenth and eighteenth centuries. Also, under the influence of the Catholic counter-reformation, the vision of society that emerged after the *Cinquecento* was that of an unequal society, hierarchical and pyramidal.[90] Social harmony in such feudal societies is founded on organic and holistic analogies where harmony and the unity of the body are achieved because every social class carries out its duty. But there is also an *ontological* inequality between the classes which was theologically justified. *Il Principe Cristiano pratico* (*The Practical Christian Prince*) by De Luca (1680) is typical of this period (seventeenth to eighteenth century) of re-feudalisation and theorisation of inequality as the physiologic state of society. Utilising the Biblical metaphor of the Statue of Baruch, the book describes the perfect society: "The nobility ... which, however, he describes as silver, ... after the gold, of which the head is formed. ... The vilest plebes, these last, like the feet of a statue, are presented as mud or earth."[91] The French Revolution's violent reaction was against this "uncivil" inequality and not against Humanism's civil virtues. The principle of fraternity, proclaimed together with liberty and equality, was the way of expressing, at the same time, a criticism towards a non-fraternal social life, typical of the feudal system, and the acknowledgement of the necessity of a new bond for a new horizontally structured society. We shall see that both traditions, the Scottish and the Neapolitan, found a strict connection between the market economy and fraternity, but in different ways.

In this context, Political Economy came as a novelty with respect to the organic vision, but not because classical economists (Smith included) refused the harmonic vision of the interplay of different interests, but because of the real innovation of pointing out a *new mechanism* that allows commercial, large and conflicting societies to harmonise private and public good, namely the "invisible hand" mechanism. An innovation, however, that was already present in the Neapolitan School – as we shall see.

In the next chapter, dedicated to the Neapolitan School, we shall analyse the various dimensions and meanings of Public Happiness and Civil Economy, and we shall see how the top-down conception of Public Happiness of Ludovico Muratori will become, in Genovesi and his school, more and more balanced with a bottom-up theory of society based on civil virtues, on citizens' actions.

5 Genovesi and the Neapolitan School of Civil Economy

I don't write for loners, nor for obscure misanthropes. I write for those who live in the midst of the city.

(G. Filangieri)

The bright lights of Naples

The motto "*Deliciae regis felicitas populi*" upheld the reign of the Bourbon King of Two Sicilies, Charles III. In 1752, he had the phrase stamped on the coin placed under the first stone of his royal palace in Caserta. Two years later in Naples, the Tuscan Bartolomeo Intieri instituted history's first chair in economic matters "Cattedra di commercio e meccanica" (chair on commerce and mechanics).[92] Antonio Genovesi was asked to take up this position so that economic studies could be oriented towards the building of that *felicitas populi* which was to become the emblem of the Italian economic tradition.

Neapolitan Enlightenment is a crucial chapter in this research. The season of civilisation that Charles III inaugurated during his reign, from 1734 to 1759, matured into a civil, economic and cultural rebirth under Ferdinand IV which brought about economic reforms and development (see Venturi 1969). Although it was brief, it was such a bright spring that humanist ideals and civil hopes began to bud once again, and the tradition of Neapolitan Civil Economy, in particular, flourished.[93] The Civil Economy tradition must be understood within the context of Neapolitan culture in general, which was one of Europe's most vibrant and important centres in the first decades of the eighteenth century. Scarlatti and Pergolesi, Alfonso Maria dei Liguori, Pietro Giannone and Vico were making Naples a European capital of music, ethics, law and philosophy.

Antonio Genovesi (1713–1769)[94] was the leader of the Neapolitan School of Civil Economy, and, in a certain sense, leader of the entire Italian school, as well as a few other Latin countries.[95] For more than a century, writers like Doria, Filangeri, Pagano, Bianchini and many others wrote pages that compare very favourably with their northern European contemporaries, while they remain inspiring even to this day in the specific theme of happiness and sociality.

Genovesi does not occupy any place in the official history of economic thought. The *New Palgrave* (II: 514) disqualifies him for lacking "any systematic order", and labels him as a late mercantilist.[96] This is not the only possible interpretation of him, and perhaps not the fairest.

During the long sojourn in Naples, Genovesi will help us to chart the characteristics of Public Happiness and Civil Economy, while the other figures will help us map some of its streams so that we may see the larger picture of this economic approach.

In what follows, I am interested in reconstructing the original theory of Public Happiness in the Neapolitan School. To comprehend "Civil Happiness" in Genovesi and his school, however, it is absolutely necessary to analyse it within the theory of Civil Economy.

Genovesi used the expression "Civil Economy" for his main economic treatise (*Lezioni di commercio o sia di economia civile*, 1765–1767). Few other economists shared his liking for this term; others preferred, instead, expressions like "social", "political", or "public" economy. Genovesi himself coined the expression "Civil Economy" only at the end of his career, in the printed version of his *Lezioni*, in 1765.[97] In fact, in his manuscript lectures, *Elementi di Commercio* (1757–1758), the second volume is called "Degli Elementi del Commerci o sia della Pubblica Economia" – "On the elements of commerce"– that is, on public economy – as Beccaria did a few years later in Milan.

Why this shift? And what does it mean?

A plausible interpretation relies on the growing importance in Genovesi's theory of the dimension of the civic, urban life in relation to the rural one: to the Neapolitan economists, the countryside meant feudalism. In fact, as M.L. Perna, the editor of the *Lezioni*'s critical edition, also recognises (p. 910), one of the main differences between the *Elementi* and the *Lezioni* was the intensification of Genovesi's anti-feudal polemics. One of the consequences of the eclipse of the culture of Civic Humanism in the sixteenth and seventeenth centuries was, in Italy, a return to land and a discrediting of the urban life and activities. *Vita civile* in the late sixteenth century, became, in southern Europe in particular, synonymous with barren and vicious (luxurious) life; only rural life was considered the place for virtue. The citizen was no longer the person committed to economic and civil activity but "who does not make any mechanical arts, but lives on rent".[98] The "nobility of land" became an essential requisite for occupying public functions, and furthered the "divide between merchant activity and the exercising of public appointments that was underway during the *Cinquecento*" (Frigo 1988: 90).

As nobility is inherited by blood and lineage, the new "political" virtues mustn't have anything to do with vile economic arts. This emphasis on urban life and on commerce, in opposition to rural life and agriculture, is a common denominator between Naples' and Glasgow's visions of economy – that in this respect was different than French Physiocracy, still anchored on land as the centre of the economic system.

In a process that some have called *re-feudalisation* in the seventeenth century, the Southern European society began to gravitate around land once again. Possessing land was praised and became the way to enter the nobility and thus to government duties.[99]

Notwithstanding the lexical difference (public or civil), the conception of an economy as an area of civilisation, and as a means of civilising, for bettering the "good living" of people, was continuously present in the Italian economic tradition, at least up until the mid-nineteenth century.[100]

Genovesi attended Vico's lectures in Naples and considered "The illustrious Giambastica Vico" one of his "masters, man of everlasting fame" (*Lezioni*, II, chapter 1, §5, footnote "e"), and decisively influenced Filangieri and Pagano.[101] He studied the works of Descartes, Montesquieu, Locke and the Cambridge Platonists and taught Metaphysics and Ethics in Naples, the city of Thomas Aquinas. The daring theological theses he put forward in an attempt to draw a synthesis between these diverse perspectives placed Genovesi under a high degree of ecclesiastical pressure. The authorities accused him of bringing forth unorthodox (materialistic and pantheist) theology because of his familiarity with the "northern" philosophers. Yet, from a methodological perspective, he held Aquinas and classical Christian philosophy as his points of reference. In fact, he did more than many of his contemporaries to bring about a confluence between the new stream of Enlightenment solicitations and the classical Greek and Latin civil traditions.

Genovesi's emphasis on "public faith" (*fede pubblica*) and civil virtues, and the mere fact he quotes Aristotle more than any other author in his works, leaves no doubt about the classical construction of his thought. Neither can there be any doubt about the modernity of his ideas. His writings are full of Galilean and Newtonian themes, Cambridge Platonism, French Illuminists, English and all modern philosophers. Genovesi's thought, therefore, is basically characterised by the *mediation* between *veteres* and *novatores*.

In synthesis, Genovesi's Civil Economy can be defined as a modern version of the Italian civil tradition that began in the Middle Ages, while also influenced by modern philosophies.

Civil virtues, Public Happiness

To enter into the various aspects of the Neapolitan vision of Civil Happiness,[102] the following quotation by Genovesi is particularly suitable as starting point:

> Every person has a natural and inherent obligation to study how to procure his/her happiness; but the political body is made of persons;

therefore, the entire political body and each of its members is obligated to do his/her part, i.e. all that he/she knows and can do for common prosperity, as long as that which is done does not offend the rights of the other civil bodies. This obligation, from the civil body, with beautiful and divine ties, returns to each family and each person for the common pacts of the society. Each family and every person are under two obligations to do that which they can to procure public happiness: one comes from within nature, and the other comes from the subsequent pacts of communities. A third obligation can be added, that of one's own utility. That which Shaftesbury (*Inquiry of Virtue and Merit*) said will be eternally true: he said that the true utility is the daughter of virtue; because it is eternally true that the great depth of every man is the love for those with whom he lives. This is the love that is the daughter of virtue.

(*Lezioni*, I, chapter 1, §39)

This passage captures the elements carrying the nexus between civil life and Public Happiness, which is the foundation for the entire edifice of the tradition of Civil Happiness.

First of all, from this quotation we deduce a strong continuity with the classical tradition (i.e. happiness is the *sommum bonum*). Second, the classical vision of "happy citizens = happy society" is already acknowledged. Third, although Genovesi recognises that Public Happiness comes from a natural obligation, at the same time he acknowledges that Public Happiness also "comes from the subsequent original pacts of community living". This is a clear reference to the contractualist tradition, which is not seen in opposition to the "natural law" vision: in Genovesi the two approaches go hand-in-hand, reinforcing each other. Finally – and again in both Hobbes' and Grotius' thinking – "a third obligation can be added, that of one's own utility".

In what follows we shall see Genovesi as a *mediator* between the classical tradition ("virtues versus interest" and "common good versus private good") and the modern view of society based on private interests and individual utility. This mediation is the content of his vision of both Public Happiness and Civil Economy: an economy is civil if based on civil virtues and then contributes to Public Happiness; at the same time, civil virtues are the tools for reaching private interest and individual happiness. In Genovesi, thus, there is no *structural* contrast between economic growth and happiness, or between civil virtue and private interest: they are two sides of the same coin.

Nevertheless, the transformation of wealth into happiness and the harmony between common good and private interests are never simple, direct or natural: it is a common thesis in the whole Neapolitan tradition that the transformation works *only* within the civil dynamics of the *polis*. But, it has to be repeated, Genovesi's general argument does not deny wealth for the sake of happiness, nor private interest for civil virtues. His was an attempt to keep all these contrasting elements *together*: in this dwells the originality of his thought. Reading Genovesi's economic theory outside of this perspective leads to the conclusion of the non-originality of his thought.

The civil and doux *commerce*

In line with Montesquieu (whose "doux commerce" was very well-known during the Enlightenment) and with the Scottish School, the Neapolitan tradition considers economic activity as an expression of civil life. It sees commerce as a *civilising factor*. Like the civic humanists, Genovesi and the Neapolitans see commercial activity as an expression of civic virtue, and civil life as the place where virtues could be expressed to their fullest. Montesquieu's theses are common in Genovesi's writings. Genovesi translated the French philosopher's works in Naples (and commented on the *Eprit des lois*). In Naples, Montesquieu was very influential, his ideas nourished the entire Enlightenment movement. This can be seen clearly, for example, from the political and legal thought of Gaetano Filangieri, Genovesi's follower: "Every form of government has a different engine principle: *fear in the despotic states, honour in the monarchies, and virtue in the republics*" (Filangieri 2003 [1780]: 32).[103]

The vision of the economy as a sign of civilisation runs through all Neapolitan writings. The complete title of Genovesi's *Lezioni* makes that very clear – *Lezioni di commercio o sia di economia civile* (*Lectures of Commerce, or Else of Civil Economy*) – in which the term "or else" underlines his view that commerce *is* a civil matter:

> I heard it said amongst us that we do not have commerce. This either means that the 800,000 families of this kingdom do not form a civil body, or else he who says this is without a head.
>
> (*Lezioni*, I, chapter 16, §6, footnote "a")

Expressing a thought in the tradition from Montesquieu to Verri to Kant, Genovesi even wrote that one of the fruits of commerce "is to bring the trading nations to peace.... War and commerce are as opposite as motion and quiet" (*Lezioni*, I, chapter 19, §7). And again: "The *spirit* of commerce is not that of the conquests. Barbarous people conquest people and lands; trading people conquest riches" (I, chapter 17, §2).

Genovesi's disciple, Mario Francesco Pagano, shared the same positive attitude towards commerce: "Happy are the peoples where freedom of commerce is untouched and inviolable; wise are the laws that found it, blessed and adored the princes' hands which vigorously guarantee this freedom" (Pagano 1962 [1789]: 844). And Giuseppe Palmieri: "There is no society without commerce; even more, we can say that society has been born for the need of the commerce.... It is then evident that commerce leads to happiness" (1788: 147).

From this civilising vision of commerce and the market comes also the liberal vision of most of the leaders of the Neapolitan School. These are the ideas of Filangieri: "The administration should adopt that great principle to regulate its own behaviour: enter in as little as possible, let things work as much as they can" (Filangieri 2003 [1780]: 68). In particular, laws must sustain competition and remove situations of rent seeking: "Thus, laws that destroy or limit the required competition are a calamity for art and manufacturing" (2003 [1780]: 80). He also expressed an intuition about internal and external[104] commerce as being a "positive sum game" (to use contemporary Game Theory language):

> we will find the private interest of each and every nation closely united to universal interests, and *vice versa*, universal interests closely united to the particular [in such a way] that a nation cannot lose without the others losing, and cannot gain without the others gaining.
>
> (2003 [1780]: 86)

The depth and originality of Filangieri's writing fascinates. His theory of law was very influential and should be placed in the same category as Montesquieu, and above that of Beccaria, at least in terms of its systemisation. Although he died in 1788, when only 35 years old, his law theory made an enormous impact on the entire Enlightenment movement, and inspired many reforms in the post-1789 period of the French Revolution.

Finally, Filangieri was also the most effective in highlighting the relationship between commerce and civil life, the cornerstone of the *pubblica felicità* tradition, as is clear from the following passage:

> When [wealth] is nothing but the fruit of conquest, when it is not the sweat of the farmer, the artisan, the merchant, that brings it together, wealth corrupts people, foments hatred, and accelerates the ruin of nations.... But the present state of things is entirely different. There is no booty today, no tributes by subjugated peoples, nor betrayed alliances, nor huge taxes for the king, which Cesar, Pompey, and the Roman Patricians sold for the highest offer. I say, today these are not the means by which States bring riches together.... Today the wealthiest nations are those where the citizens are the most free and the hardest working. Today riches are no longer to be feared, but on the contrary are to be desired; and the principal object of laws should be to call for them, since these are the sustenance of peoples' happiness, of political freedom beyond the States, and of civil freedom within the States.
>
> (2003 [1780]: 66–67)[105]

Although the writers of the Neapolitan School praise commerce and civil wealth, they still do not say that wealth and growth simply and naturally bring Civil Happiness: "one can be rich for an accumulation of many goods, without being civil" (Bianchini 1855: 11).

Luxury, vice or virtue?

Genovesi's *Lezioni di Economia Civile* ends by referring to another central issue in his and the classical economists' theories, *the role of luxury for Public Happiness*, "a great matter of contrasts" among philosophers (*Lezioni*, I, chapter 10, §1).

Luxury – with respect to economic development and morality – was a very popular eighteenth-century issue.[106] The positions of Smith and Hume on luxury deserve to be mentioned in order to frame Genovesi's own vision.

A growing taste for luxury commodities played – according to Hume's *History of England* – a key role for both England's economic development and for the fall of the feudal landlords, aristocracy and clergy. Luxury was, according to both Hume and Smith, the main tool for a "secret revolution" (Hume, *History of England*, IV), a "revolution of the greatest important for the Public Happiness" (*WN*, III, chapter 4, §17) – note here the very rare use of the expression "Public Happiness" in Smith's work. The unequal and hierarchical feudal society collapsed thanks to an unintended consequence – an application of the "invisible hand" mechanism – of the desire for luxury from the upper classes. In Hume's philosophy of history, luxury played this providential role:

> The new methods of expenses gave subsistence to mechanics and merchants, who lived in an independent manner on the fruits of their own industry. . . . By all these means the cities increased; the middle rank of men began to become rich and powerful.
>
> (Hume 1983 [1778], IV: 384)

Smith's theory of luxury drew mostly on Hume, and, in spite of a change (discussed in literature) in the passage from the *Lectures on Jurisprudence* to the *Wealth of Nations*, Smith's position on luxury remained very much anchored to Hume's.

In his historical analysis of Europe, Smith claims that feudal societies began to decay when, motivated by individual self-interest, the landed proprietors diverted their surplus from the maintenance of retainers to the purchase of luxuries that were manufactured in the towns. As an unintended consequence, the proprietors lost the basis of their former power and authority. Because of the division of labour in the market economy, purchasing power does not translate into political power as it does under feudalism.

The following is a key passage of the *Wealth of Nations* that acknowledges Hume's paternity of Smith's attitude towards luxury:

> commerce and manufactures gradually introduced order and good government, and with them, the liberty and security of individuals, among the inhabitants of the country, who had before lived almost in a continual state of war with their neighbours and of servile dependency upon their superiors. This, though it has been the least observed, is by far the most important of all their effects. Mr. Hume is the only writer who, so far as I know, has hitherto taken notice of it.
>
> (*WN*, III, chapter 4, §4, p. 383)

A few pages later:

> A revolution of the greatest importance to the public happiness was in this manner brought about by two different orders of people who had not the least intention to serve the public. To gratify the most childish vanity was the sole motive of the great proprietors. The merchants and artificers, much less ridiculous, acted merely from a view to their own interest, and in pursuit of their own pedlar principle of turning a penny wherever a penny was to be got. Neither of them had either knowledge or foresight of that great revolution which the folly of the one, and the industry of the other, was gradually bringing about.
>
> (*WN*, III, chapter 4, §4, pp. 389–390)

Genovesi most probably did not know any of Smith's writings, but he quotes many times, in his *Lezioni*, from Hume's *History of England*: in fact, in Genovesi's theory of luxury we find an extraordinary similarity to Hume – but also something more.

In the analysis of the role of luxury, Genovesi's starting point is Mandeville's *Fable of the Bees*, who "seems to be the apology of all vices". On the other hand, other philosophers (such as Shaftsbury or Rousseau) "have decided to fight against it" (*Lezioni*, I, chapter 10, §2).

Genovesi's vision of luxury is between these two poles: "Personally I don't think that there can be vices which are good for the civil society" (*Lezioni*, I, chapter 10, §2). At the same time, however, he considered the luxury produced by the increased commerce an inevitable consequence of a civilisation's progress, because civilisation itself progresses with the increase in the desire to distinguish from our fellow citizens, and by emulative competition. Furthermore, he holds that a certain degree of luxury

> not only is useful but also necessary to culture, diligence, politeness and virtue of nations; necessary for fostering some arts that are essential for not being uncivil or indebted to foreigners. For that I can

conclude that a certain degree of luxury not only is not a vice, but is actually a virtue.

(*Lezioni*, I, chapter 10, §3)

As noted by Venturi (1962: 191, footnote 1), Genovesi's attitude towards luxury became more and more positive through the years. In the *Elementi di commercio* (1757–1758), the evaluation of luxury is still more influenced by moralistic considerations, which disappeared in the first and, even more so, in the second-printed Neapolitan editions of the *Lezioni* years later.[107]

In particular, to Genovesi, luxury is essential for driving demand, therefore it is "very useful to the State,... because [it] increases the consumption of our commodities, and then, through the money of those who can spend and love to spend, luxury animates the labour and spread it" (*Lezioni*, I, chapter 10, §24). Thus, he criticises those who were nostalgic for the primitive community (Rousseau in particular: see §2), and stresses the importance of governing, rather than repressing, "the instinct of distinction" (*Lezioni*, I, chapter 10). For Genovesi, in fact, the "instinct of distinction" is a providential tool for both social mobility and national wealth:

> The engine spirit of luxury is the natural instinct of distinction. Such an instinct is even in the savages, but it comes out only thanks to natural or civil occasions.... When the occasions for awaking the instinct of distinction are the various civil elements composing the civil body, and when the tools are the representative (not natural) riches, then the true luxury are the manners and the qualities for distinction.... The reasons that push a person to distinguish himself from another, or to emulate a superior one, push also the superior classes to find new ways for distinguishing themselves from the inferior ones.... This play, where the arts are protected and the trade is free, produces three effects: (i) undermines the feudal slavery, (ii) releases that part of humankind that suffers for the pressure of the dominating part, (iii) ruins the great and old families and rouses new ones. One cannot fool nature for long. Luxury comes in order to compel rich people to restore the poorer of what they took dishonestly from the common wealth: and in order to make slave free, and the free slaves.
>
> (*Lezioni*, I, chapter 10, §§16–18)[108]

This is one of the more beautiful of Genovesi's pages, that reveal the presence in his system of the unintended consequences mechanism as clearer than in Hume or in Smith. Let us deconstruct the passage into its key elements:

a   The "positional consumption" (consuming for "distinction") is not a typically modern phenomenon. It can also be found "among the savages". Genovesi does not tell us whether or not this kind of consumption has changed substantially in modern society (as Veblen will say much later, in 1899). He only says that this "instinct of distinction" has to be "awaken" by "natural or civil occasions". When this instinct is activated by natural elements then power (Hercules), cunning (Odysseus), ingenuity (Archimedes) come to play: "these are almost the only things able to distinguish the republicans in rudeness times" (§17).

b   In civilised societies, a significant tool for distinction is luxury. To say that does not at all mean that luxury is a modern phenomenon, but only that luxury is particularly linked to civil life; it flourishes in cities, where it plays a providential (although not intentional) role.

c   Luxury, in fact, is a powerful engine of social change and of social circulation – an analysis very close indeed to that of Hume in *History of England* and Smith in *Wealth of Nations*. The want for luxury generates unrestrained expenses, division of labour and, again in the civil context ("where the arts are protected and the trade is free"), this brings the fall and rise of elites: "like the wheel of Fortune, the lowest classes rise to the middle stage; the middle ones go to the top; those of the top fall first to the middle, then to the bottom" (§19).[109] Genovesi's goal, however, was to use this argument for fostering the Neapolitan idea of a providential and just order that inspires social dynamics: the richest, by living a luxurious life, themselves *unintentionally* create the conditions of both their decline and the rise of the inferior classes.

Genovesi is prudent in praising the luxury addressed to foreign commodities, because it "weakens domestic manufactures" (§22), and impoverishes the nation. At the same time, if "this luxury of foreign things is moderate and concerns only few classes, instead of harming it can help because it awakes the spirit of emulation and thus improve the arts". This spirit of emulation "recreates both the intelligence and the body: makes people more sociable, namely more virtuous; and the states wealthier" (§23). It comes back to Genovesi's *leit motif* that commerce is a civilising activity, which fosters civil society. In fact, he specifies that, to the *economic* positive fruits of the "moderate luxury" (§26), we must add the

> moral ones. The first is the politeness of the manners … The second the humanity, a greater sociality, the civil conversation, and a cheerful and brilliant spirit. … The third are the sciences and the belles arts that go hand in hand with humanity and the propriety of life.
>
> (§26)

At the end of chapter 10, entirely dedicated to luxury, he summaries his vision as follows:

Let us reduce this matter to few aphorisms. I say:

1   Luxury, generalised and crazy, hurts every State: but this is not actually possible. . . .
2   Luxury not generalised, but fostered by only foreign commodities, is a certain ruin of every political body, and cannot last long.
3   Foreign luxury very moderated helps in awaking intelligences and emulation of peoples in the arts and in the commerce.
4   Without any sort of luxury, or **magnificence**,[110] a nation is ferocious and wild. . .
5   This moderated luxury has to be called not luxury but, more correctly, propriety, **decency** and kindness of an educated people: **then, more than a vice luxury is a virtue, being an average between the rude and sordid parsimony, and the fool and vain prodigality**.
6   Finally, if the luxury arts serve to foster foreign trade, they are a great source of wealth. . . .
7   Therefore to pretend to eradicate or depress all arts of luxury would be a wrong way of thinking. **It would be to say to many persons and families: kick your heels (*state colle mani nella cintola*)**.

> (*Lezioni*, I, chapter 10, §61)[111]

After this short analysis of Genovesi's thought on consumption and luxury, we have more elements for stating that Genovesi, along with other founders of modern political thought, looked at society in a modern way: far from being only or mainly a moralistic or normative appeal to an "ideal" but non-existent person, his analysis aims at describing human beings *as they really act in society*. Rather than dream about a world of imaginary people, he thought that the social or civil scientist must indicate the mechanisms of the real behaviour of people (*l'uomo quale è*). Often such behaviour does not spring from the consideration of civil virtues; however, if such behaviour arises within adequate civil institutions, it too can, in fact, contribute to the common good: this was Genovesi's main line of thought. When he lists the means for increasing the kingdom's opulence and therefore its happiness, he writes the following as a synthesis of his thought on this issue:

> Nothing has greater or more ample force than commerce. When public value is assigned to the human heart's natural covetousness, this strong impulse can be well regulated and produce all our civil goods.
>
> (*Lezioni*, I, chapter 16, §1)

This thesis is in line with the theories of the so-called *heterogenesis of ends* or non-intended consequences of intentional actions. What are the Neapolitan peculiarities in dealing with such a central matter in modern social thought?

On the other hand: private interests and common good in Civil Economy tradition

Genovesi's point of departure is the philosopher Giambattista Vico (1668–1744), the outstanding personality of the Neapolitan Enlightenment. To Vico, only the analysis of the historical facts is true knowledge. Science is important in view of its practical applications for improving civil life and welfare. His main interest, however, lay in the philosophical reflection upon civic life. *Verum est factum*, the hallmark of his philosophical system, expresses the idea that true knowledge ought to be based on *facere* (as opposed to the Cartesian *cogito*), which includes both conceptual elaboration (metaphysics) and experimenting (physics). Vico was essentially receptive to, though not uncritical of, the Galileo–Newtonian tradition, which also explains why Mechanics acquired a central role in Naples at the time.[112] Vico's thought is based on sociality: to Vico, civilisation means sociality, and he used the adjectives "uncivil" and "solitary" interchangeably. In Vico's thinking, only in civil life or civil society do individual and self-directed passions become social and produce "*Civil* Happiness".

Coming more directly to the topic of heterogenesis of ends or unintended results (or consequences) of actions, what is normally overlooked when telling the story of "invisible hands" – even in excellent studies such as Rothschild (2003) – is that, well before Smith, Vico in his *Scienza Nuova* (*New Science*), first published in 1725 (third edition: 1744), had written one of the most acute accounts on the heterogenesis of ends. Vico moved the field of civil legislation away from metaphysics because it considers the human person "as he or she should be" and therefore "cannot help but those very few who want to live in Plato's Republic rather than grovel in Romolo's riff-raff" (1948 [1744], chapter II, §7) – a common element in the Italian tradition after Civic Humanism.

Vico, therefore, seems to link his thought to authors such as Machiavelli or Mandeville, who contrasted their descriptive philosophies to the normative metaphysics. But Vico's philosophy is, in fact, original.

To him, civil legislation must consider

> man as he is in order to serve human society well; like ferociousness, avarice and ambition are the three vices that run through human kind and become the militia, the commerce, and the court, and so the strength, the opulence and the wisdom of the republics; and thus civil legislation can transform these three great vices, that would otherwise destroy the human generation on earth, into *civil happiness*. This dignity proves to be divine providence who is a divine legislative mind and takes man's passions, which tend to private utility and so would cause him to live as a wild beast in solitude, and turns them into civil orders by which they live in human society.
>
> (Chapter II, §7, my italics)

Thus, according to Vico, Providence – not fate nor fortune: here a first difference with respect to authors such as Machiavelli or Mandeville – has designed the world, putting in civil dynamics mechanisms that convert ferociousness into the army and strength, avarice into commerce and opulence, and ambition into politics and the art of good government. In this way the various passions of people "as they are" unintentionally all contribute to "Civil Happiness" – an expression that well summarises the nexus between happiness and Civil Economy. Immediately afterwards, however, Vico adds another consideration that reveals an added dimension of his vision of the "heterogenesis of ends": "Man has free will, though it be weak, to turn passions into virtue; but is helped by God with divine Providence and supernaturally with divine grace" (chapter II, §7). In other words, while Vico recognises the existence of an unintentional or "objective" mechanism which transforms asocial passions into "Civil Happiness", at the same time, and in continuity with Civic Humanism, he does not neglect the essential role of virtues for a good and civil society.[113]

In Vico's approach, is clear that the heterogenesis of ends mechanism is *subsidiary* – not in *opposition*, as it is in Mandeville – *to civil virtues*: given human failure in searching intentionally and directly for the common good, God's providence helps us by sketching into human nature and civil cohabitation a providential social dynamic that orients our self-interested passions towards the common good – a sort of "canning of reason".[114] Thus, the strong accent Vico gives to the role of civil life and virtues is, at the same time, modern *and* in strict continuation with the Civic Humanist tradition.[115]

Within civil life, thanks to institutions, laws and education, private interests *may be* guided by "hand"s providence towards the common good, Public Happiness. Individual utility becomes (private and public) happiness *only in civil society*.

Vico's position inspired the entire Neapolitan School.[116] We find his thesis again in one of Naples' most universally recognised economists, Ferdinando Galiani, who wrote *Della Moneta* in 1750. In what is one of the most brilliant books in classical economic thought, he praises mysterious mechanisms that "balance everything" in the markets and society, and adds:

> this equilibrium marvellously suits the right abundance of life's comforts and earthly happiness, although it does not derive from human prudence or virtue, but rather from the vile stimulus for blind profit: Providence, with Her infinite love for humankind, conceived of the order of everything so well that those vile passions of ours, often as if to spite us, are ordered towards the good of all.

(1803 [1750]: 89–90)

A few lines later, we find the metaphor of the "hand" explicitly referred to as Providence:

> I bless the Supreme hand every time I contemplate the order with which everything is constituted to our utility.
>
> (1803 [1750]: 92)

In Genovesi's *Lezioni* the "invisible hand mechanism" is fully developed, in a fashion surprisingly similar to Smith's most famous theory. In his analysis of free trade (*la libertà di trafficare*), in arguing why the freedom of commerce is desirable for the common good, Genovesi wrote:

> Because, the profit and the comfort that people nearly foresee, and that may be actually reaped, makes people feel a great wish of working, trading and enriching. And notwithstanding when people endeavouring to enrich they aim only at their own self interest, it is no less true that enriching they promote the public advantage by enriching the whole nation.
>
> (*Lezioni*, I, chapter 17, §12, p. 264)

It is interesting to observe the analogy between this passage and Smith's "invisible hand" argument, both in his *Theory of Moral Sentiments* (1759) and the *Wealth of Nations* (1776). In fact, in 1759, Smith's invisible hand came into play for describing landlords' unintended consequences: although they are motivated by "their own vain and insatiable desires ... they are led by an invisible hand to ... without intending it, without knowing it, advance the interest of society" (*TMS*, IV, 1, 10). In the *Wealth of Nations* the invisible-hand metaphor is used only once, in the context of the criticism of the mercantilist system. In this context – that is, the same of Genovesi's passage quoted above – he wrote:

> Every individual is continuously exerting himself to find out the most advantageous employment for whatever capital he can command.... He generally, indeed, neither intends to promote the public interest ... he intends only his own security ... he intends only his own gain, and he is in this, as in many other cases, led by an invisible hand to promote an end which was no part of his intention.... By pursing his own interest he frequently promotes that of the society more effectively than when he really intends to promote it.
>
> (*WN*, 4, chapter II, pp. 419, 421)

Genovesi thus recognises the role of "the invisible hand"; nevertheless, he gives more weight to the *visible* fabric of civil virtues for Public Happiness:

To repeat it here again, whence it is intended that virtue is not an invention of philosophers, spread and fixed in the soul with education and with laws, as the author of the "Fable of the Bees" [Mandeville] pretends; but is a consequence of the nature of the world and of man.

(*Lezioni*, II, chapter 10, §12, p. 142)

Economia Civile and *Fede Pubblica*[117]

The implications of Genovesi's civil account of economy become clear in his discussion of trust (*fiducia*). In his "Discorso sopra il vero fine delle lettere e delle scienze" (1754), a manifesto for the Neapolitan Enlightenment and for his own research programme, Genovesi was asking why Naples is not a developed nation like other States in Italy or in northern Europe. Naples, he says, is well populated; it is "a seminary of noble and gifted people"; it has one of the best climates in Europe; having good access to the sea, it is well-placed for the development of commerce (*Scritti*, p. 246). What has gone wrong?

Genovesi's answer, which comes at the end of his "Discorso", is that Naples lacks *buon costume*, "the most efficacious ... cause of the wealth, power and happiness of a people" (Scritti, p. 268).[118] For Genovesi, then, trust is *the* civil virtue, and is an essential economic resource:

it is my opinion that nothing can be more certain than virtue, and only the virtue of citizens, is the greatest means for sovereigns to use in order to make the arts flourish, and multiply the productive action of goods and riches and increase the industry and income of the nations. (*Lezioni*, I, chapter 14, §15). ... Nothing is more true: good habits and virtues are the primary forces driving the arts, opulence, and the happiness of every nation.

(*Lezioni*, I, chapter 14, §19)

In his economic writing, Genovesi explains in detail how virtues promote economic development.

We have seen how much emphasis Genovesi placed on emphasising that trade is mutually beneficial, and the source of the wealth of nations. To understand how nations become rich, therefore, we must understand what prompts commerce. Genovesi argues that the most important precondition for commerce is trust. For the economic and social development of a nation,

nothing is more necessary than public trust [*fede publica*] in a wide and easy circulation. ... Trust is for civil bodies what the law of gravity is for natural bodies. ... From the life of primitive people it is possible to realise how important it is to keep increasing trade. There, because of lack of trust, there is no reciprocal reliability, no society, no industry and no trade among peoples.

(*Lezioni*, II, chapter 10, §1)

In the footnote ("a"), Genovesi adds an interesting point: "The [Latin] word *fides* means rope that ties and unites. Public faith (*fede pubblica*) is therefore the bond of families united in companionship."

Genovesi devotes the entire chapter 10 of the second volume of the *Lezioni* to public trust. He subdivides public trust into *ethical trust, economic trust* and *political trust*. Ethical trust is "the reciprocal confidence that every citizen has in the probity and justice of the other, that is, simple conventions and promises". *Economic* trust is "the security which springs from the certainty of funds on which to ground debts". Then "finally [there is the trust which] comes from conventions and promises sustained by the civil law ... [and] by the wisdom and strength of the state; it is called *political*" (*Lezioni*, II, chapter 10, §3). All three components of *fede pubblica* are essential for the development of commerce and, hence, for the creation of wealth. However, Genovesi states several times that ethical trust is the *foundation*, the grounding of all kinds of public trust:

All these forms of trust have to be cultivated ... as fundamental for civic society, for the arts, industry and the spirit of the nation, for commerce, public peace and opulence. [But most importantly] the ethical form, since it is the basis of both [i.e. of economic and political trust].

(II, chapter 10, §3)

Similarly, in the *Ragionamento sulla fede publica* (*Reasoning on Public Trust*), a first draft of part of chapter 10 (Vol. II) of *Lezioni*, published in 1757, Genovesi wrote: "when the reciprocal love of families and peoples composing a state is extinguished, and in its place diffidence, distrust and reciprocal fear are born, there is no power that can sustain it" (*Scritti Economici*, p. 499).

Given his diagnosis of the causes of the Neapolitan disease, what cure can Genovesi recommend? Naturally, the solution has to be the cultivation of all forms of trust, but especially of *ethical* trust. The main tool for this task is the civil and religious education of the people, adults as well as children, by the Church and in public schools (*Lezioni*, II, chapter 10, §7). As a true Enlightenment thinker, Genovesi believes that true virtue is recommended by correct reason. Thus, the way to make people virtuous is to give them a rational education.

To complete this argument, Genovesi has to show *how* reason endorses ethical trust. He does this by way of what he calls the "little catechism of natural law" (*Lezioni*, II, chapter 10, §10). The first presentation of this catechism in the *Ragionamento sulla fede pubblica* (*Scritti Economici*, p. 857[119]) is as the following sequence of 11 propositions:

1   Nature and reason both push us to seek happiness.
2   No human condition is more unhappy than to be alone, separated from any relations with other people.
3   Thus, we must try to be sociable with one another and to cultivate the virtues which enable us to live companionable and friendly lives.
4   But sociability is not enough for human society; there is human society only when men are united by the will to be useful to one another.
5   The peculiarity of human society is that it is based on rationality, not reciprocal pleasure.
6   This kind of rational society cannot be achieved unless the people who compose it are reciprocally and sincerely friendly with one another.
7   Men cannot be sincerely friendly with each other unless they have sincere confidence in one another.
8   Only where everyone is persuaded of each other's virtue and piety can there be this sincere confidence.
9   As soon as any member of society is known to be ready to offend and deceive people, everyone sees him as one with whom it is impossible to deal or to communicate.
10 Such a person is excluded from all social relationships, and can get none of the comforts that make life pleasurable.
11 It is impossible that such a situation can last for long; the community will soon send that person away from civil and natural society.

One significant feature of this catechism is the close association it makes between *friendship* and *trust*. For a reader who is more familiar with modern Economics, this association comes as a surprise. Friendship, one might think, is a private relationship among specific individuals who are linked by ties of affection, while trust – or at least, the kind of trust which underpins the market – is impersonal, and based on interest rather than affection. Genovesi does not accept this distinction. As the first three propositions in the catechism make clear, he postulates a universal human desire for social relationships and takes this to be the primary motivation for social cooperation. Ethical trust (which, for Genovesi, is the foundation of economic and political cooperation) is rational in the same sense that friendship is: it is a precondition for social relationships. Thus, for Genovesi, trust is embedded in social relations in a much deeper sense than it is for modern theorists of social capital (or, as we shall see, for Smith).

The catechism also reveals that, for Genovesi, rationality is a property of dispositions and not of actions. Notice that Genovesi is recommending us to cultivate *sincere* friendship with one another, and the *will* to be useful to one another.[120]

What exactly is a disposition towards *friendship*? The logic of Genovesi's argument suggests that we should identify friendship with reciprocal assistance, reciprocity being understood in an individually not fully instrumental way. A person with this disposition does not simply act in a way that is useful to others, expecting that they in return will act in ways that are useful to him or her (like in Hume's mutual advantage), which does not require any real kindness. But neither is the person purely benevolent (like Shaftsbury's theory): the will to be useful is conditional on the confidence that that will is reciprocated. The friendly person wants to be useful to others, having confidence in their wanting to be useful to him or her. If we are to represent this mode of reasoning in modern terms, I suggest that the most useful framework to use is the rationality of we-rationality, as advocated by Hollis (1998).

If we think in these terms, we have to ask: *for whom* is the disposition of friendship rational – for people severally, for people collectively, or for both? Genovesi's catechism betrays some ambiguity on this matter, which is perhaps best resolved by taking his answer to be "for both". The content of the first eight propositions seems to be this: *We,* that is, human beings collectively, can achieve happiness only in societies; societies are possible only among people who are disposed to be useful to one another; within any putative society, everyone's having that disposition is possible only if everyone is disposed towards sincere friendship, and confident that the others are so disposed. It would be a natural continuation to say: So let us all cultivate the disposition of friendship. This reading would cohere with Genovesi's diagnosis of the failure of Naples to achieve economic development as the result of a collective deficiency of *buon costume.* However, the final propositions of the catechism warns everyone that if *they* fail to cultivate the virtues of friendship, there will be adverse consequences for *their* happiness. Significantly, these adverse consequences are in the *currency of sociality* rather than material self-interest: what the individual stands to lose are relationships with others – the main source of true happiness. Thus Genovesi is addressing his readers both individually and collectively. Individually, each of us can best achieve happiness by being ready to form relations of friendship with others who are similarly inclined. Collectively, we can best achieve happiness, and even economic development, by acting together in relations of friendship.

6   Happiness as reciprocity

Il più prezioso tesoro del Principe è la fiducia, la quale non dura se non è reciproca.

(Ferdinando Galiani)

A relational anthropology

After the analysis of the general framework of Genovesi's Civil Economy, in this chapter we consider directly the peculiarity of his vision of Civil Happiness. Genovesi's main reference point is Aristotle, as in his *Diceosina*, his book of ethics where his anthropology (theory of the human person) is fully presented. In all his works, we find an Aristotelian approach to happiness: "No man could work for anything other than his own happiness or he would be less than a man..." (*Autobiografia e Lettere*, p. 449). We also find: "God ... could not give men any attribute that was not ordered to their end, that is to their happiness" (*Lezioni*, I, chapter 1, §15). And, a few pages later: "Every person has a natural and inherent obligation to study and procure his/her happiness" (chapter 1, §39, p. 29). In the *Diceosina*, he writes: "There is no one so foolish or crazy ... not to seek the happiness of all his life, but of just a part" (p. 34). Therefore, goods, wealth, and economic development are useful to the measure in which they are ways to happiness, they are means to that end.[121]

As a "civic humanist" Genovesi says that the most important virtues are civil, because they construct *directly* "public trust". Although – as we saw previously – his *Lezioni* take into consideration the unintentional and providential role of private interests, we discovered that Genovesi's main line of argument is not about a spontaneous order of egoistic interests made by an invisible hand. Although Genovesi recognises the actual "invisible hand" mechanism, he claims that society, in order to flourish, also needs something more. What Smith entrusted to the invisible hand of the market, Genovesi entrusted mainly to the "visible network" of civil virtues which citizens and governments must create and maintain. In particular, Genovesi considers diffused trust (*"fede pubblica"*) to be the priority for the development of a nation.[122]

What's more, happiness flourishes from genuine interpersonal relationships, which are therefore not instrumental, but sincere relationships, because "man is naturally a sociable animal" and "society is an indelible property of our nature" (*Lezioni*, I, chapter 1, §§16, 18).

The following passage by Gaetano Filangieri beautifully connects civil life to happiness by means of a relational vision of the human person:

> Nature's Author would have been inconsequential in the most worrying of his productions, if he had not made man for society. Why, in fact, give him reason which only develops with communication and with the company of other human beings? Why add the exclusive gift of the word to the cry of sentiment, which is part of the language of all brutes?... Why make man susceptible to a multitude of passions, which would be of no use outside society, and could not serve a solitary being? Why inspire in him the ambition to please his fellows and command them, or at least their opinions? Why plant in their heart the seed of compassion, of charity, of friendship, and in a word, of all the passions which depend on the moral sense of a well-born soul, and give us the singular need to spread over others a part of our existence? Why not, finally, restrict all his appetites to the same sphere, in which all the other beings living on the surface of this globe are restricted, that is, in satisfying physical needs, which present themselves to man only at intervals and momentarily, and would then leave behind a void which would warn us of their inability to produce our happiness, and deliver the announcement that the soul, as the body, has its own needs, and that these needs cannot be satisfied without us falling prey to social affections?
>
> (Filangieri 2003 [1780]: 11)[123]

Happiness and positive interpersonal relationships are, in the Neapolitan tradition, two sides of the same coin. The same definition of virtue, that according to the classical tradition is the path towards true happiness, is *civil by nature*. In fact, from the *Diceosina* emerges a theory of virtue based on reciprocity.[124] It is impossible to consider this happiness as a synonym of *self-interest*, because it needs gratuitousness and is connected to a sincere relationship with others:

> There can be no human state less happy than that of being alone, which means being segregated from every commerce with our fellows. A beautiful, strong and true saying by Aristotle, is that a solitary man, content by himself, is either a divinity or a beast. What would he do without the life and bliss-giving breath of his fellows?
>
> (*Lezioni*, II, chapter 10, §11)

In his inaugural lecture in the chair of Civil Economy, in 1754, he stated that

> Some philosophers [i.e. Descartes] have said that our pleasures origi-nate from the awareness of some good belonging to us. It is very true; and this demonstrates that those pleasures derived from the awareness that great and upright reason, used for the happiness of others as well as our own, is the greatest good and greatest perfection of human nature.
>
> (*Scritti*, p. 78)

The idea became one of the pillars of the civil tradition in Neapolitan and Italian Enlightenment.

More than sociality: reciprocity

The meaning of civil virtue and public faith (*fede pubblica*) in the Neapoli-tan Civil Economy reveals itself fully when we look at the basic concepts of *sociality and reciprocity*. In Genovesi, these dimensions are explicitly rooted in a relational anthropology, the presence of which is also very clear in Doria and in Vico. According to Vico, for instance, society is a direct derivative of "man's civil nature".[125] His vision will be taken up and developed by many Neapolitan authors, from Palmieri to Filangieri, from Galanti to Pagano.

As we have already mentioned, Genovesi does not view relationships with other people basically as *means* for obtaining personal interests – even in the economic domain, although Genovesi does not deny that market is a nexus of instrumental contracts. Nevertheless, to him the market is *also* a place in which sociality can be exercised. The market is also based on the fundamental law of civil society, *mutual assistance*.

General sociality, in fact, is not enough for his theory: he needs reciprocity. Let us see why.

According to the Neapolitan economist, as in every other dimension of civil life, the market is founded on civil virtue and depends entirely on it. This idea was also present in the "Introduction" to *Della Vita Civile* (1710) of Paolo Mattia Doria:

> the true essence of civil life is the helpful exchanging of virtues and natural faculties, which men give to one another with the ultimate end of obtaining human happiness.

In this context, it is interesting to note that, in Naples, many economists of that time adapted Newton's theory of gravitation to their own philo-sophical systems. In his *Diceosina*, Genovesi argues that some passions are manifestations of self-love (*forza concentrativa*), although others reflect

"love of the species" (*forza espansiva or diffusiva*).[126] The whole of
Genovesi's theory of action is constructed upon the idea that any phenomenon, whether human, social and physical, can be explained as an "equilibrium" between these two opposite forces. To Genovesi, these two forces
are primitive. This conception provides the logical basis for the criticism
towards Mandeville's and Hobbes' egoistic conceptions of man that we
find throughout Genovesi's work. In his *Logica per gli giovanetti* (*Logic
for the Youth*) he wrote: "Hobbes founds all on *forza concentrativa*, and
the *forza diffusiva* springs only from a higher degree of the *concentrativa*,
that is fear" (chapter 5, §36).

The language and the concepts of Newtonian mechanics are also
present in Genovesi's political and economic theory. These brought him to
"see in political life a social machine made of centripetal and centrifugal
forces" (Venturi 1969: 566). In the *Lezioni* "forza concentrativa" and
"forza espansiva" (the expressions used in his *Diceosina*) are also called
"forza coattiva" (coercive force) and "forza direttiva" (directive force), a
semantic shift emphasising a recourse to the Newtonian idea of "force" for
explaining social matters in the *Lezioni*:

> It is true that as the attraction of bodies is maximal in their contacts
> and decreases proportionally to distances; in the same way the recip-
> rocal attraction and love among men is very great in the family, among
> companions, in the homeland, etc., and decreases with greater dis-
> tances.
>
> (*Diceosina*, pp. 42–43)[127]

In this passage there is the idea (that we also find in Hume and Smith)
that, in small societies, *sympathy* is dominant, whereas in larger ones *self-
interest* is the basic passion. It is interesting that, in Genovesi, this thesis is
justified by means of an explicit reference to the Newtonian theory of
mechanics. Newtonian themes appear also in a footnote to the *Lezioni* (I,
chapter 10, §26, footnote "z"):

> all solitary men are wild, cruel, unforgiving, since in solitude there is
> no room for the diffusive force of the human heart, and only the con-
> centrative force works, which makes men hypochondriac and brutal.

This passage is important because it links the Newtonian elements
present in Genovesi's thought with *reciprocity*, on which his theory of happiness depends. While Galiani used Newtonian Mechanics in order to
build the fundamental principle of his economic theory (self-interest),[128]
Genovesi used the same analogy – giving it a meaning closer to the original Newtonian one – as a cornerstone of his Civil Economy based on
"mutual attraction of bodies", on *reciprocal assistance*. Following the civic
humanist tradition, Genovesi argues that each person has a *natural right* to

the benefits of "reciprocal assistance" and a corresponding *duty* to assist other people (*Lezioni*, I, chapter 1, §18). Thus, a person's willingness to help those who stand in relations of *reciprocity* towards him or her is a virtue of the same kind as the virtues of justice and honesty. Genovesi understands economic relations as relations of reciprocal assistance: in an economic system, each agent is helping others to satisfy their wants. On this conception of Civil Economy, engagement in economic relations is an exercise of civil virtues.

Therefore, self-love and love of others are the two dimensions present in the human person: "those who pretend that one of these forces is born from the other are wrong. . . . These two forces in us are both primitive and tied together" (*Diceosina*, p. 42).[129]

Thus, the "expansive force" is not simply benevolence or that which today we would call "altruism", but has to do with interpersonal relationships, and its basic element is the inborn capacity for sympathy of the person. Both for Genovesi and the Scottish School, that capacity is a *natural* virtue, an inherent characteristic of our nature, which explains most human actions, in both big and small societies:[130]

> Yes, as in musical sympathy we are made to be touched by pleasure and interior satisfaction when we see another person ... and this happens to the most cruel and wretched as well. No one takes pleasure in pleasure if there is no one else to participate. . . . As when a chord of a guitar is touched, the octave resounds for the consonance of tension, but will not repeat the sound in unison if the tension is even slightly changed; in the same way, it seems, our natures are worked by the same rule and impressed in the same mould and so it is not possible that in an encounter, the air of one does not sympathetically move the other.
>
> (*Diceosina*, p. 42)

To Genovesi, then, the peculiarity of a fully flourishing human life is *reciprocity*. In particular, we wish to highlight the elements in his reflection that make us think he intuited the necessity for a new anthropological foundation of human relationality, civil society and the market.

In this context is his vision of marriage, which is very interesting, and surprisingly modern. According to him, in fact, the typical form of relationship within the marriage is *friendship*:

> love is an instinctive passion, that lasts very little among the wedded pair. But friendship is a reasonable affection, coming from consideration and choice. I don't pretend that the two persons are perpetually in love with one another; it is too hard, if not impossible. But they can, and ought to be friends. . . . The two are friends by nature and by choice, and among friends every good and every bad is put in

common. Nothing fosters friendship more than to share sincerely with the friend every pleasure and displeasure, and in this way the two hearts become one.

(*Diceosina*, pp. 282–283)

Such a vision of marriage is very surprising if we consider that, at that time, the kind of family Genovesi saw in Naples was patriarchal, and the basic relation between men and women was like master and servant – as Mill will say more than a century later.

This strict connection between reciprocity and friendship does not surprise if we consider the Aristotelian roots of Genovesi's vision of happiness: the typical characteristic of *philia* is, for Aristotle, reciprocity. In Chapter 9 we will see how close to this vision (and, in general, to Genovesi's theory of happiness) is Mill's idea of friendship in marriage.

The project to give philosophical foundations to sociality, which began in classical culture (we mentioned Aristotle), matured in the Middle Ages and then in Humanism, was only partially achieved. To Thomas Aquinas, for instance, interpersonal relationships are no more considered *accidens* (as in Aristotle) but are *substantial*, i.e. essential constituents of the person: there is no person without relationality. Yet this intuition never developed into a coherent anthropology for founding civil life: to Aquinas, only for the *divine* Persons of the Trinity are relationships *substantial*, not for the *human* persons. In Scholasticism, therefore, the human person was defined more by "individuality" than by the "relationship" with others. Civic humanists, as said, developed the phenomenic and the historical dimensions of sociality, but their philosophical reflections about human beings and political philosophy were not consistent with these social intuitions. From Civic Humanism did not come a new "civil" anthropology. Thus, when later Machiavelli and Hobbes started again to think deeply about the nature of humanity, they did not find any alternative "civil" anthropology to fight, but only generic references to Aristotle's sentences about the sociability of humans in the books of Bruni or Palmieri, not strong enough to withstand the individualistic and a-civil attack.

As a philosopher and scholar of social facts, converted from metaphysics to social sciences, Genovesi took the anthropological issue seriously. We should not exclude the possibility of him feeling there was a need for a theory that tried to combine the person and the relation-with-others. A generous interpretation of the brighter pages of Genovesi makes such a conclusion possible. Although possible, it is not at all an easy interpretation, because we cannot overlook the fact that Genovesi's anthropology never became a systematic theory in the modern sense. He failed to adequately develop and organise his brilliant intuitions. Nevertheless, it is my conviction that Genovesi deserves to be interpreted without ideological prejudices within the humanist and civil traditions. From such a perspective, Genovesi's attempt to write a relational anthropology, and his critique of the authors who identified "simple" sociality as the specific element of human nature, is still interesting and original.

According to Genovesi, I repeat, the originality of the human condition does *not* dwell in simple sociality. In line with classical thought,[131] he reminds us that not only humans but even animals are sociable. Human originality is to be found then in "mutual assistance", in *reciprocity*, which is both a natural inclination as well as a moral obligation to cultivate:

> Man is a naturally sociable animal: goes the common saying. But not every man will believe there is no other sociable animal on earth.... How is man more sociable than other animals?... [it is] in his recipro-cal right to be assisted and consequently in his reciprocal obligation to help us in our needs.
>
> (*Lezioni*, I, chapter 1, §17)

His relational vision of the person and society is most evident in his reflection on the wealth–happiness nexus, which we will look at closely in the following section.

Wealth and happiness

Genovesi and his school express strong convictions that the process of becoming civilised requires a fair distribution of wealth ("equality") for societies:

> The excessive wealth of a few citizens, together with the laziness of others, are suppositions for the majority's unhappiness and misery. This civil partiality is contrary to the common good. The only con-ditions in which a state can be said to be rich and happy is when every citizen has a decent job of a few hours in which he can comfortably cover his needs and those of his family.
>
> (Filangieri 2003 [1780]: 12)[132]

And Bianchini: "without too much amassing of goods, the idea of civility naturally brings with it the best distribution of comfort and ease" (1855: 12).[133]

Entering directly into the theme of happiness, he concludes in a fashion very similar to the present economists studying the paradoxes of happiness:

> Therefore, if civilization does not consist in mere wealth, it is equally true for mere industry; and the claim of many writers that *the happi-ness of the nations walks hand in hand with their ease*, is not always true. Even if there are a few cases in which well-being is the con-sequence of ease, happiness is not always its product.... We can

consider an individual rich, but one can live unhappily in the midst of wealth. Thus with numerical sums we can evaluate the nations' claims of wealth, but not their well-being.

(1855: pp. 13, 70)

This relationships between wealth and happiness emerges with extreme clarity in a study that Genovesi dedicated entirely to the "transformation problem" of wealth into happiness, i.e. the *Reasoning About the Use of Great Wealth in Regards to Human Happiness (Ragionamento intorno all'uso delle grandi ricchezze per riguardo all'umana felicità)*. It is not by chance that his *Ragionamento* has been put, by Genovesi, as an appendix at the end of his *Lezioni*, because it sums up and closes the main theme of his work. He wrote: "It is born from the things said up until now, and with all those things that have been added", for it often happens that "men ... not understanding the very end and true use of their goods ... where they thought they could be happy, they have become miserable" (*Lezioni*, II, *Ragionamento*, §1).[134] Therefore, Genovesi recalls that it "has been written often and in all times about the power and effect of wealth" in relationship with happiness (§2), but, on the other hand, there have been philosophers "who believed very happy those who have accumulated great wealth", claiming that "rich and commercial peoples don't distinguish between poor and unhappy men; *olbios* for the Greek means both rich and happy" (§4). Instead, "all savage, naked and simple peoples, not only laugh of the nations longing for riches, but they have a great compassion for them" (§4). Genovesi, however, calls experience the only judge on these two opposite parties about the relationship between wealth and happiness; and historical experience tells that "some rich people were very unhappy,... other, on the contrary, were very happy with their riches" (§6). For this reason a theory, and not just "facts" (§6), is needed to properly understand, beyond the common sense and the different historical facts, the relationship between wealth and happiness, given its complexity.

A first element of his theory is the importance of reason: "the great majority of men do not recur to the proper reason", because they are dominated only by passions. In this case, wealth works as a powerful tool that stimulates all kind of instincts, luxury in particular. Such passions push people to always desire new pleasures and stimuli. Civil life, furthermore, amplifies these desires, emulation and imitation being the most powerful forces operating in shaping needs and wants. Thus, the first conclusion that Genovesi reaches in his *Ragionamento* is that the cultivation of virtue is the tool for avoiding irrational passions and desires taking advantage and bringing people towards unhappiness: virtue is an education of the soul for putting passions under the control and power of reason – a conclusion in line with the classical Aristotelian–Tomistic theory of person and society (§§30, 31).

But the modern soul soon emerges too:

Here a question asked by Mr. Mandeville comes about: is it possible that in fertile and abundant country, under a happy climate, with arts and commerce, many people can, at the same time, become over-rich and keep all virtues of moderation, parsimony, diligence and prudence?

(§35)

He approaches this issue, not principally at the level of the individual or the single family (because each case is different from another), but in the context of civil life, of *Civil Happiness*, an analysis that he defines as "our principle intention".[135]

Genovesi's general argument points out that the corruption of virtues by excessive wealth can be a result of a bad "education" (§37). In fact, he claims, again in line with the great classical civil thought, "one has never read about a tranquil and happy republic without the flourishing of science, of a multitude of virtues and arts, which are the sole nourishment of our happiness" (§40). In such a context, he says that

not only can a State be happy with few riches of gold, silver, and gems, but also it can be happy without any at all of this; as long as ... virtue and industry have their reward,[136] ... that it knows how to live with its neighbouring populations, religiously conserving with them justice, the faith of contracts, friendship, and doesn't fall in love with getting rich at the expense of others.

(§41)

Then, he gives his economic explanation, based on "positional consumption", of why wealth doesn't necessarily bring happiness but, on the contrary, often brings with it unhappiness: "Glory has no place outside men's opinions, therefore every external thing, which men have commonly adapted as a sign of glory, can serve to distinguish and make them illustrious" (§44). These are mechanisms which bring people into the pursuit of increasing "relative happiness", not "absolute" happiness (§61). On the basis of this theory, he can support the thesis that there are plenty of examples throughout history showing "that abundant riches, rather than making a State greater and happier, have made it smaller and unhappy" (§73). But soon he recalls Mandeville's theory, a constant reference point in his writings:

Mr. Mandeville is against this doctrine. The cupidity of riches, he claims, is a force that stimulates and pushes people to work and to the search for the comforts that we all need, more if we live in a polite society. From that comes that if you will try to eradicate or suffocate it, you will make people immobile, and you will extinguish in them any spirit of industry.... It is a paradox, Mandeville claims, nevertheless true: the fatal enemy of work is not sluggishness but, actually, the scorn of any comfort and politeness.

(§80)

And he concludes: "Do we say here that economy and politics are against ethics or the rules of good custom (*buon costume*)? I answer then that cupidity, as every primitive passion, has not to be totally extirpated, because it is impossible, and even if it were possible, man would be dispossessed from all stimulating springs that move him" (§81). In fact, "cupidity for man is as the wind in the sea, the passions as the sails, reason is the steersman and the helmsman" (§81). Even here, in the analysis of the wealth–happiness nexus, we find Genovesi as *mediator* between classic and modern sensibility.

The happiness of others

In line with Aristotle and Thomas Aquinas, Genovesi sees the nature of happiness as being constitutionally relational. Thus, happiness is civil and connected to the freedom and choices of others.

In his *Lezioni* we find:

> Even among peoples that are corrupted by luxury and bad custom there is no one, a head of family or anyone else, who does not feel an inner pleasure in doing good things to other people, in making others happy.... It is a characteristic of man of not being able to enjoy a given good without sharing it with somebody else. Some say that it is self-love or pride (*superbia*) to show our happiness to others. I don't think so: it seems to me that there in us an inner need for us to communicate our happiness to one another.
>
> (*Lezioni*, I, chapter 16, §2, footnote)

A similar thesis can be found in a private letter dated 1763: "The law of loving the happiness of friends is not, according to me, a law that obliges only in certain times: it is an eternal law, it is in the nature of the world" (*Autobiografia e lettere*, p. 146). In these passages, some analogies with Smith's category of fellow-feeling can be found. But, in Genovesi's relational happiness, there is even more.

The following passage helps us to fully understand Genovesi's idea of happiness. It is a synthesis and natural ending for the flow of thought we have been mapping until now:

> tire yourselves for your interests; no man could do anything but for his own happiness; or he would be less a man: but don't desire the misery of others; and if you can and in as much as you can, try to make others happy. The more you work for interest, the more you must be

virtuous, unless you are a fool. It is a universal law that we cannot make ourselves happy without making others happy as well.

(*Autobiografia e Lettere*, p. 449)

With its Aristotelian and Thomistic flair, the paradox here lies in the statement that happiness comes from "making others happy". But is such an idea really paradoxical? If we think about it, at least three keys can unlock the paradox.

First, common and rational sense tell us that one cannot be happy if surrounded by those who are not: "if one wicked person only is enough for ruining a republic, as many examples show, how would it be possible to be happy where the majority were wicked?" (*Lezioni*, I, chapter 14, §14, pp. 203–204). On the same line, Paolo Mattia Doria wrote: "no-one can be happy if all his neighbours and the Republic are miserable and unhappy".[137] Although the positional theories of happiness claim that people gain happiness from a worsening of other people's happiness, nevertheless I am with Genovesi in thinking that it is perfectly reasonable to think that the unhappiness of others detracts from our own happiness.[138]

The second key to unlock the paradox calls into question the Civil Economy vision of the market. Even if the formal demonstration of market exchange as a positive sum game was lacking until marginalism, Genovesi was convinced that the market is mutually beneficial, particularly as a form of mutual assistance. As he wrote in *Lezioni*, the market is born when "the superfluous is exchanged for the necessary" (*Lezioni*, I, chapter 16, §5, p. 242). Thus, making oneself happy doesn't mean impoverishing others, but means making them rich as you enrich yourself and thus you become happier together. This is a basic idea of the market seen as civil because it is based on the same reciprocity that is the universal law of civil society.

The third key to unlock the paradox probably weighed heaviest in the Abbott's pocket. Among his other categories, Genovesi surely held the paradoxical gospel law of "giving to receive" and "losing to find" – that is, loving others to find one's own happiness. None of these keys locks the others out, but help each other in.[139]

Giuseppe Palmieri's position is also interesting. The title of his work, *Riflessioni sulla pubblica felicità relativamente al Regno di Napoli* (*Reflections on Public Happiness Relative to the Kingdom of Naples*) (1788), is directly connected to the *pubblica felicità* tradition: "Profits, the great springboard for human action, and the well-being to which we all aspire, will always make men run to where profits or well-being are better or where they come together more easily"; a few lines later, he adds the necessity for education in a way that "each is persuaded that to find one's own good, he must find it in procuring that of his fellows" (Palmieri 1788: 38–39). A few years later, in 1792, in *Della ricchezza nazionale* (*About National Wealth*), he affirmed the economic meaning of the "golden rule":

"'love your neighbour as you love yourself' is the best way for making humankind happy". He stated that, given nature stamped the imperative to be happy in us, it is even more true that one cannot obtain happiness without "making others happy" (1853 [1792]: 192).

All this confirms that "Genovesi's paradox" is not an isolated affirmation contained in a private letter, but a shared idea in a current of Modernity. In this tradition, happiness is fragile by nature precisely because it is constituently relational. A "good life" cannot be carried on without living with, and thanks to, others. It's about making "the others happy". Thus, we can never have full control over happiness. Plato and one important stream of western culture felt this to be a dangerous jump. But if the risk is not taken, genuine reciprocity cannot be produced and society will unravel. Such is also the most classical and, at the same time, contemporary dimension of Genovesi.

A short evaluation

After this long stay in Naples, few summarising words are needed. What, then, is Genovesi's and the Neapolitan idea of happiness in relation with sociality?

First of all, we have found many points in common between the Neapolitan School of Civil Economy and the eighteenth-century economic movement. At first sight, Genovesi looks closer to modern Political Economy than to mercantilists or physiocrats. He praised free commerce, considered markets as civil society and put the *city* as the central element of Civil Economy.

Like Montesquieu, Hume or Smith, Genovesi and Filangieri conceived of the market and even luxury as providential tools for the collapse of the *ancien régime*, based on inequality and unjust relationships. The unintended results mechanism is clearly present and works as an important tool for explaining social order. Nevertheless, the "cunning of reason" is not, in Naples, the principal mechanism for explaining civil society and markets: communal life needs more. In particular, in polemics from Mandeville and Hobbes, Civil Economy denies that self-interest is enough for building a good society, even if coupled with good legislation: civil virtue, intended as intentional love for the public good, is needed, in line with the Civic Humanist tradition. The merchant is not always a pro-social merchant.

For these reasons, friendship and public faith are also fundamental *economic resources* for development, as long as all civil virtues are. The market, in other words, is not a mechanism eliciting *cooperation without benevolence*: because it is an expression of civil society, it works properly only if based on civil virtues, that is, if it is conceived as a form of friendship.

Genovesi's most adequate definition is probably that of *mediator*:

although fascinated by the new modern ideas and philosophies, he tried to remain anchored to the millenarian tradition of good society based on civil virtues. Thus, in his work we find Locke together with Vico, Mandeville with Shaftesbury, Hobbes with Grotius, Hume with Montesquieu. In this sense Genovesi, and his school, can rightly be seen as an attempt to welcome modernity together with antiquity, luxury *and* virtue, wealth *and* happiness, civil society *and* commercial society: Public Happiness, Civil Economy. In Smith and the mainstream tradition of Political Economy, as we shall see in the next chapter, it was exactly these dimensions of Civil Economy that were lost: friendship and trust as economic resources, and the "publicness" of happiness that, after Bentham in particular, became an individual matter confused with pleasure.

Finally, the contemporary theories of social capital that associate economic development with civil virtues, and the explanations of the paradox of happiness based on the crowding-out of relational goods, are saying that Genovesi's and Civil Economy's intuitions, far from being just a premodern paradigm, can still have something relevant to say to contemporary social scientists.

The analysis of Genovesi's idea of the economy–sociality nexus is not over yet: after having discussed Smith's vision of the market and society we will make a more complete evaluation of the Neapolitan Civil Economy and Public Happiness.

7   Adam Smith

Economists ... are the trustees, not of civilisation, but of the possibility of civilisation.

(J.M. Keynes)

The market and civil society

This and the following chapters aim to show that Civil Economy was not just a Neapolitan or Italian matter, but, actually, many elements of that approach to economy and society were present also in Great Britain up until the first decades of the twentieth century. But – and maybe most important – key differences are present too.

Thus, in what follows I intend to show *in which sense* between the Italian and the British classical schools of Economics there are points in common with respect to the nexus happiness–wealth–sociality, and in which sense their approaches were instead significantly different. In fact, we shall see both real continuity and real differences between Italian Civil Economy and what I call the "civil English tradition".

Let us start, again, with Smith.

Smith, it is well-known, considers the market as a place for civil and human development, where people trade in horizontal relationships among equals. Furthermore, for Smith and the other masters of Scottish Enlightenment, such as Hutcheson or Ferguson, the market sets up the conditions for experiencing free and genuine human relationships in which true friendships – and other relational goods – can flourish. Markets, in fact, make it possible to go beyond the feudal logic of ally–enemy or master–slave. Commercial society sets up pre-conditions for equality, without which true friendships cannot exist.[140] To Smith, then, to depend on the "benevolence of our fellow-citizens" is not an expression of friendship or even fraternity, but of unjust and feudal relations. The commercial society, instead, allows us to choose our friendships freely and on a basis of equality – it is for these reasons that market society is strictly connected to the humanism of modernity based on "liberté, egalité", and, in the specific sense I just mentioned, also "fraternité". This is, in my opinion, the strong unity of Smith's intellectual project, from the *Theory of Moral Sentiments* (*TMS*) to the *Wealth of Nations* (*WN*).

At the basis of Smith's vision of the market and sociality is a relational anthropology which sets the stage for the whole market society to work. The first stages of this anthropology can be detected in the *incipit* of *TMS*:

> How selfish soever man may be supposed, there are evidently some principles in his nature, which interest him in the fortune of others, and render their happiness necessary to him.
>
> (*TMS*, I, 1, 1)

While the fortune of a person consists in being considered by others, misfortune lies in other people's indifference. According to Smith, even wealth and power are basically ways *to attract other people's attention*, means to be "recognised".[141] In fact, the basic idea present in the *Theory of Moral Sentiments* is that the desire to receive distinction and other people's admiration is the greatest driving force in individual actions. Like many classical authors, Galiani and Genovesi in particular,[142] Smith says wealth is a *means* for obtaining the distinction and admiration from others, upon which our happiness chiefly depends.[143]

Another basic relational component in Smith's system is *sympathy*, which plays a decisive role in his thought.[144] As highlighted by many scholars, it is evident that *sympathy* for Smith is something different than pure and simple altruism.[145] For these reasons, it is impossible to grasp the peculiarity of the Smithian system by focusing on the counter positions of egoism–altruism. As an anthropological "descriptive" category, Smithian "sympathy" is not a moral or normative evaluation of the person's actions. Smith describes the human person as *de facto* a *relational* reality. To Smith, therefore, sympathy is a much broader notion than altruism:

> Pity and compassion are words appropriated to signify our fellow-feeling with the sorrow of others. Sympathy, though its meaning was, perhaps, originally the same, may now, however, without much impropriety, be made use of to denote our fellow-feeling with any passion whatever.
>
> (*TMS*, I, 1, 1, 5)

A concept that, more than sympathy, can describe the content of the *TMS incipit* is "fellow-feeling". As Sugden notes:

> Smith proposes a very general psychological tendency for what he calls fellow-feeling and what would now be called *emotional contagion*. Fellow-feeling occurs when one person B has a lively consciousness of some affective state experienced by another person A,

and when B's consciousness has similar affective qualities to A's state, as perceived by B.

(Sugden 2005a: 97–98)

Fellow-feeling constitutes the key distinctive element of Smith's anthropology, that is based on the fundamental hypothesis that human beings derive pleasure from any form of fellow-feeling. Fellow-feeling is, in Smith's philosophy, experiencing sentiments similar to those experienced by another person, by virtue of one's consciousness of the other person's sentiments:

> But whatever may be the cause of sympathy, or however it may be excited, nothing pleases us more than to observe in other men a fellow-feeling with all the emotions of our own breast; nor are we ever so much shocked as by the appearance of the contrary.
>
> (*TMS*, I, 1, 2, 1)

Smith's theory of happiness is deeply connected with his theory of fellow-feeling, as Sugden (2005a) has shown. Smith, in fact, argues that fellow-feeling is a primitive natural sentiment. We experience it even in our most frivolous moments, as when we take pleasure in other people's laughing at our jokes, or are upset by their failure to laugh. Similarly, it is pleasurable to read a much-loved book to someone else for whom it is new, and who appreciates it: "we are amused by sympathy with [the listener's] amusement which thus enlivens our own" (*TMS*, I, 1, 2, 2). These short references to Smith's ideas on sympathy and fellow-feeling are enough for our aim, that is to show that his vision of happiness is anything but a theory based on the Aristotelian or Civic Humanism civil virtues. The emphasis on fellow-feeling as the main source of happiness, therefore, is not the element that puts Smith in continuity with the civil tradition.

Where are, therefore, the "civic roots" of Smith's thought?

Smith studied moral philosophy under Francis Hutcheson's guidance, whose theory of sociality and benevolence was very influential in the Scottish Enlightenment.[146] We also find the influence of Rousseau[147] and of the Platonist Shaftesbury. In particular, the Civic Humanist tradition arrived to Smith through the mediation of the natural law Dutch theorists, such as Grotius and Puffendorf.

Thanks to the fundamental contributions of Winch and Pocock, the literature on Smith over the past 20 years has gone beyond a narrow vision of him as the initiator of a new era in economic science, characterised by a spontaneous order guaranteed only by division of labour and self-interest. This new interpretation of Smith places his economic thought within the Scottish culture of the first half of the eighteenth century, which shared some cultural and civil characteristics with the Florence of the *Quattrocento*. Inspired in particular by Florence, Glasgow adopted all the civil values that made the Italian city civilisations and economies so great, even architecturally. As Pocock and others have shown, it is not by chance that Smith, for the most part, analysed the vocabulary of Civic Humanism. But, as we shall see soon, Smith's approach to the market is civil *in a different sense* than Genovesi's Civil Happiness.

Trust as reputation

If we take Genovesi's theory of trust as the reference point, we can immediately grasp that Smith and Genovesi are similar in their analysis of the relationship between trust, economic development and wealth/happiness. In particular, for both of them, the market *is* an important moment in civil life. It does not destroy, but, normally, edifies civil virtues. Civil and just institutions and free competition transform *self-interests* into common good (intended as growth and wealth). At the same time, for both authors, the market *is* civil society, but in different ways, as we shall see in the conclusion of this chapter.

For the time being, let us look closely at Smith's theory of trust in relation to the market. Smith's most direct discussion of the economic significance of informal trust is the following passage in the *Lectures on Jurisprudence*:

> Whenever commerce is introduced into any country probity and punctuality always accompany it. These virtues in a rude and barbarous society are almost unknown. Of the nations of Europe, the Dutch, the most commercial, are the most faithful to their word. The English are more so than the Scotch, but much inferior to the Dutch, and in some remote parts of this country they are far less so than in the more commercial parts of it. This is not at all to be imputed to national character, as some pretend. ... It is far more reducible to self-interest, that general principle which regulates the actions of every man, and which leads men to act in a certain manner from views of advantage, and is as deeply implanted in an Englishman as a Dutchman. A dealer is afraid of losing his character, and is scrupulous in performing every engagement. When a person makes perhaps 20 contracts in a day, he cannot gain so much by endeavouring to impose on his neighbours, as the very appearance of a cheat would make him lose. Where people seldom deal with one another, we find that they are somewhat disposed to cheat, because they can gain more by a smart trick than they can lose by the injury which it does their character.
>
> (1978 [1763]: 538–539)

This analysis reveals a sophisticated theory of trust; but there is no doubt that this is a theory of trust or (in modern terms) of social capital based on individual self-interest.[148] This is not to say that Smith does not recognise the motivating force of social approval, but that social approval itself derives from self-interest. Much of the *Theory of Moral Sentiments* is devoted to an analysis of the basic force of social approval and, even in the *Wealth of Nations*, Smith sometimes appeals to social approval to explain non-economic phenomena.[149]

Nevertheless, it is relevant that in his discussion of the *commercial* virtues, Smith does *not consider relationships other than trade*. In the above passage about the Scottish, the English and the Dutch, he seems to be arguing that, in a developed market economy, trading relationships alone are dense enough to reproduce the trust and reputation that are necessary for the market to work, and that it is sufficient that those trading relationships are based on rational self-interest.

Far from seeing civil virtues as *a precondition for markets* (as Genovesi does), Smith tends to see commerce as the first stage in the development of civic society, as the "creator" of civil virtues. This precedence is clear in Smith's economic history. In two chapters of the *Wealth of Nations*, he explains how, during the Middle Ages, the order and good government of the towns gradually spread to the surrounding country, undermining, as seen, previous relations of feudalism (pp. 397–427). However, it would be truer to the spirit of Smith's argument to say that the market *is* a network of relationships of equality and reciprocity: it is not so much a precondition for, as an essential constituent of, civic society.

This idea comes over very clearly in the famous passage at the beginning of the *Wealth of Nations* (chapter 2), in which Smith says that, to get our dinner, we do not address ourselves to the benevolence of the butcher, the brewer or the baker, but to their self-love. Immediately after this, Smith says: "Nobody but a beggar chuses to depend chiefly upon the benevolence of his fellow-citizens." The message is straightforward: market relations, being *between equals*, are more civil and human relations than the "vertical" relations of feudal society. It is more consistent with human dignity for us to satisfy our wants through the market than through pre-market relations of generosity, patronage and dependence. For Smith, then, *the market itself* is a dense network of relationships within which individuals, motivated primarily by self-love, cooperate as equals for mutual benefit.

Thus, Smith presents a theory of rational trust which is broadly similar to the modern theory of *reputation*. When there are dense networks of bilateral or multilateral associations, within which individuals cooperate as equals to secure mutual benefits, individuals are led by self-interest to build and maintain reputations for trustworthiness; and the trustworthiness so created is important for the functioning of markets. In principle, Smith's theoretical framework allows social approval to work as an additional factor in maintaining norms of trust, but he seems to think that commercial trust can be adequately explained in terms of self-interest alone.

Happiness as deception[150]

Smith shares the civil tradition's classical thesis about happiness that wealth is a means and not an end. But he does not emphasise the relational nature of the good life. His theory is more Stoic than Aristotelian or Thomistic. This was a consequence of various factors. Living in a Scottish protestant culture with a heavy dose of Calvinism, it was first a cultural reason. Smith, then, was influenced by Hume's scepticism about *sympathy*'s capacity to move people's actions in the "greater community". From Stoic philosophy, he drew the emphasis on individual virtues, prudence and self-command in particular, over civil virtues. The combination of these elements produced a social and economic theory that was not totally coherent with either his relational anthropology or his continuity with Civic Humanism.

The fact that Smith opens his *Theory of Moral Sentiments* with the thesis that happiness is connected with interpersonal relationships gives us the expectation of finding a well-developed theory on happiness. Instead, the word "happiness" rarely occurs in either his *Theory of Moral Sentiment* or his *Wealth of Nations*. The classical thesis of happiness is reaffirmed as the "ultimate end", not of intentional human action, but as an immanent fact of the natural order of things: "[t]he happiness of mankind, as well as other creatures, seems to have the original purpose intended by the Author of the nature, when he brought them into existence" (*TMS*, III, 5, 7). Rather than being the intentional aim of human action, human happiness is the "aim of the Creator", stamped on human nature. While we will see later that people are directly moved to action by other aims, Smith defines happiness within a Stoic perspective as "tranquillity and enjoyment" (*TMS*, III, 3, 30), "the ease of body and peace of mind" (*TMS*, VI, 1, 11).

He says the virtuous man can reach happiness, but with the Aristotelian distinction between happiness and pleasure missing, it is impossible to distinguish between the two concepts (*TMS*, VII, 2, 2, 5, VII, 2, 3). On the other hand, the distinction between wealth and happiness is clear – *goods are only a means and not an end.*

The more systematic analysis of happiness found in the *Theory of Moral Sentiments* is founded on deception. It is an interesting and original theory, but it is far from the classical tradition. It is in his treatment of the "effect of utility upon the sentiment of approbation", that he comes directly to grips with the question of the wealth–happiness nexus. "How many people" – Smith sadly asks – "ruin themselves by laying out money on trinkets of frivolous utility?" (*TMS*, IV, 1, 6). This observation exemplifies, in Smith's view, "the secret motive of the most serious and important pursuits". For, in fact, the "pleasures of wealth and greatness ... strike the imagination as something grand and beautiful and noble, of which the attainment is well worth all the toil and anxiety which we are so apt to bestow upon it". This is how "nature imposes upon us" and "it is well" – Smith characteristically adds – that nature does that. For it is

> this *deception* which rouses and keeps in continual motion the industry of mankind. It is this which first prompted them to cultivate the ground, to build houses, to found cities and commonwealths, and to invent and improve all the sciences and arts, which ennoble and embellish human life; which have entirely changed the whole face of the globe, have turned the rude forests of nature into agreeable and fertile plains.
>
> (*TMS*, IV, 1. 10, my italics)

Smith's illustration of the working of deceived human imagination is a piece of psychological analysis which finds its completion in the description of the *real* and actual condition of the rich, as people paradoxically sharing the same lot as the poor:

> It is to no purpose, that the proud and unfeeling landlord views his extensive fields, and without a thought for the wants of his brethren, in imagination consumes himself the whole harvest that grows upon them. The homely and vulgar proverb, that the eye is larger than the belly, never was more fully verified than with regard to him. The capacity of his stomach bears no proportion to the immensity of his desire, and will receive no more than that of the meanest peasant.
>
> (*TMS*, IV, 1, 10)

The fate of the rich, in fact, is *merely* that

> they only select from the heap what is most precious and agreeable. They consume little more than the poor, and in spite of their natural selfishness and rapacity, though they mean only their own conveniency, though the sole end which they propose from the labours of all the thousands whom they employ, be the gratification of their own vain and insatiable desires, they divide with the poor the produce of all their improvements. They are led by an invisible hand to make nearly the same distribution of the necessaries of life, which would have been made, had the earth been divided into equal portions among all its inhabitants, and thus without intending it, without knowing it, advance the interest of the society, and afford means to the multiplication of the species. When Providence divided the earth among a few lordly masters, it neither forgot nor abandoned those who seemed to have been left out in the partition. These last too enjoy their share of all that it produces. In what constitutes the real happiness of human life, they are in no respect inferior to those who would seem so much above them. In ease of body and peace of mind, all the

different ranks of life are nearly upon a level, and the beggar, who suns himself by the side of the highway, possesses that security which kings are fighting for.

(*TMS*, IV, 1, 10)

Smith's use of the *invisible hand* metaphor in the *TMS* parallels the logic of the *happiness paradox* in the current literature. In Smith's moral theory, the rich and the ambitious are moved by frivolous and temporary illusions. "Power and riches (IV, 1, 8) appear then to be, *what they are*,[151] enormous and operose machines contrived to produce a few trifling conveniences to the body ... which in spite of all our care are ready every moment to burst into pieces, and crush in their ruins their unfortunate possessor" (*TMS*, VI, 1, 9, my italics).

At the same time, in spite of the strong emphasis on negative individual disappointment in the self-deceit context, in fact, the "invisible hand" argument is invariably pointed at a positive social aspect. I have already mentioned Smith's and Hume's "secret revolution" theory connected with luxury: riches, ambition and rapacity are unintentional tools of social mobility and, at the end, of a fair "distribution of happiness" on earth.

Thus, the unintended consequences side of the argument does have a much wider scope in Smith, as he argues that the general rules of morality keep society together precisely because the individual, "[t]hough his heart ... is not warmed by any grateful affection" toward his fellows, "he will to act as if it was"; this is perhaps not ideal, but it is the arrangement which suits the "coarse clay of which the bulk of mankind are formed" (*TMS*, III, 5, 1). This, indeed, textually precedes, but logically completes and generalises Smith's own description of the *objective*, although unintended, function of the "proud and unfeeling landlord".

Which sociality in the market?

Smith, like Genovesi, was keenly aware of the ways in which human sentiments are responsive to interpersonal relationships. The Neapolitan, however, had a much stronger sense that these relationships are *valuable in their own right*, have an intrinsic value. We saw in the previous chapter that, for Genovesi, the chief advantage of society is the enjoyment of reciprocal relationships. For him, as we have seen, there is a uniquely human propensity for reciprocal assistance, which results from the interaction of rationality and sociality.

The contrast, not only with Smith's *Wealth of Nations* but also with Hume's *Treatise*, is now evident. Hume's explanation of mutual assistance as the product of rational self-interest would be foreign to Genovesi's approach – to whom human beings' peculiarity consists of "reciprocal assistance". Smith's idea that the uniquely human trait which governs Economics is the propensity to truck, barter and exchange would be equally foreign.

More deeply, the Scottish writers effectively remove economic relations from the realm of *genuine* sociality. Smith (and Hume) play down the role of moral sentiments in governing economic relations: they try to explain economic trust as the exercise of far-sighted self-interest. By drawing a distinction between private virtues, such as friendship, love and benevolence, and the public virtues of justice and the market, Smith opens the way for his version of the invisible hand argument: perhaps "Public Happiness" does not require civic virtue. We saw that Genovesi explicitly rejects this idea, which he attributes to Mandeville (*Lezioni*, II, chapter 10, §29).

At the same time, from their different eighteenth-century perspectives, Smith and Genovesi both see trust as a *modern* phenomenon. Smith thinks that trust is a product of commercial society; Genovesi's concern is that his society may lack the trust that is a precondition for commerce. Both theories provide reasons for thinking that trust is propagated within networks of associations of people who cooperate for mutual benefit.

The more radical and relevant difference between these two approaches to the market and society, however, is about the nature of the market in relation to civil society. For both theories there is no conflict between market and society, but, on the contrary, the market fosters good society, and a civil society favours the spread of the market. Smith, however, thinks that the kinds of relationality implied in market dealing is of a different *nature* with respect to the kind of relationality of the non-market domains of life, such as family life, friendship or civic commitment. To survive and reproduce, small societies or communities need sacrifice, love and affection; big or commercial societies, however, are kept together "by a different bond", by cooperation without benevolence: "Society" – Smith writes early in his philosophical work, in discussing merit, justice and beneficence (*TMS*, II, 3, 2) – "may subsist among different men, as among different merchants, from a sense of its utility, without any mutual love or affection". The mention of "merchants" here makes it clear that *society* parallels the *market* in this context (*TMS*, II, 3), where Smith is in fact discussing the establishment and the sustainability of society, as (thus he writes at the very outset) man "can subsist only in society".

This "neutral" form of cooperation is possible only in commercial society, and represents to Smith a step forward in history because it allows more wealth and Public Happiness. Markets also need ties, but the kind of ties it needs are "weak" ties (in Granovetter's words), whose nature is different from the strong ties of "non-market" domains. This property of markets is *contrasted with* friendship: "In civilised society he [man] stands at all times in need of the cooperation and assistance of great multitudes, while his whole life is scarce sufficient to gain the friendship of a few persons" (*WN*, p. 26).

Friendship *cannot be the normal basis of market relations*. Benevolence and sympathy are fundamental features of human beings, just because the human being is naturally social and needs cooperation to survive. But *the market* itself doesn't require them, and works even better without them (it is the praise of weak ties). By freeing us from vertical and unequal dependency, the market allows us to express *true* sociality – because it involves relations among equals – *before* and *after* the market.[152]

Human social dispositions are expressed in the market only in attenuated form: justice (required by the market) is sharply distinguished from friendship.

Smith's picture of the market is a "morally free zone": economic agents pursue self-interest and treat economic relations instrumentally. Providentially, the overall effect of this is to everyone's advantage, although not intentional for the single agents.

To Genovesi, as seen, market nature is "reciprocal assistance", exactly as civil society is. Of course, in Genovesi's line of thought, the strength of the relationality within the family is not exactly the same as in market; but, I claim, the *difference is in degree not in nature*. To Genovesi the market is civil society because market relations are *civil*, in the sense that they require the same civil virtues as in any genuine human relations. To Smith, however, the market is civil society because it is a tool that creates the precondition for a true friendship, but *outside the market*. At the same time, the market remains a place for instrumental, although civil, relations, for three reasons: (i) it is based on horizontal relations among equals, (ii) it is a precondition for true civil relations and (iii) only civil societies know markets. These are two possible readings and representations of markets, but only Smith's has become the usual understanding of the market–sociality nexus.

8   The Cambridge civil tradition

Political Economy does not treat of the whole of man's nature as modified
by the social state, nor of the whole conduct of man in society. It is concerned with him solely as a being who desires to possess wealth, and who is
capable of judging that end. . . . It makes entire abstraction of every other
human passion or motive.

(J.S. Mill)

Malthus on happiness and sociality

The main aim of this chapter is to show that the Cambridge tradition, as
far as the market–happiness–sociality nexus is concerned, follows Smith's
approach.

Right from its beginning, Malthus, "the first of the Cambridge economists" (Keynes 1933: 95–149), showed special attention to the wealth–
happiness nexus, an attention that represents an element of continuity in
the English classical tradition from Smith, to Malthus, to Marshall.

Unlike Italy or France, in Great Britain Public Happiness was not given
such a prominent position until the Utilitarian period, which arrived a few
decades later than on the Continent and with different accents.

Malthus, in particular, complained that the classical English School
gave too little attention to the Public Happiness theme (the toast of the
Continent). In a passage of the *Essay on Population*, where the main focus
is the nexus between the wealth of nations and the happiness of the poor,
he wrote:

The professed object of Dr. Adam Smith's inquiry is the nature and
causes of the wealth of nations. There is another inquiry, however,
perhaps still more interesting, which he occasionally mixes with it, I
mean an inquiry into the causes which affect the happiness of nations.

(Malthus 1966 [1798]: 303–304)

Here Malthus clearly distinguishes between happiness and wealth.
While, generally speaking, he does not deny that an increase in wealth

brings about an increase in the people's happiness, he does introduce two interesting elements:

a   Smith (and the classical English Political Economy) was, however, not sufficiently aware that the relationships between the two concepts were very complex and not to be taken lightly. Malthus criticised him for not having done enough investigation into *how* the wealth of nations is transformed into the happiness of the people – with special attention given to the redistribution problems associated with this transformation.
b   Probably influenced by what was happening on the Continent in those years, Malthus, at least in principle, legitimises the idea that the "happiness" of nations can constitute the object of another research, perhaps even more important than that of the "wealth" of nations.[153]

Therefore, Malthus' methodological position is emblematic of the process that was taking place in classical Political Economy in his time, namely the need that all important economists felt to delimit the new discipline's subject of study (wealth) in order to gain scientific status. Each economist chose a particular criterion for defining the boundaries of the discipline. However, thanks to the cultural environment of the time, characterised by a growing positivism, all cut out a new shape for Economics after the classical period when the economist was a social scientist dealing with all social dimensions of life.[154] Malthus was well aware that a restriction in the confines of Economics would cause a loss in the discipline's hermeneutic richness and social relevance. He knew it would mean that important dimensions of human activity, even economic activity, would be left out. This was methodology not substantially different from that of Smith, who, although he considered sociality an essential dimension of a fully human life, left it outside of economic interactions.

Something had to be sacrificed to the altar of the new science of objective and scientific measurements: one of the main victims was the interpersonal component of wealth.[155] We find this methodological attitude very clearly in the following passage of Malthus' *Principles*:

A man of fortune has the means of ... collecting at his table persons from whom he is likely to hear the most agreeable and instructive conversation.... It would not be denied, that these are some of the modes of employing wealth, which are always, and most justly, considered as much superior in respectability, to the purchase of fine clothes, spending on furniture, or costly jewels.... But it is a wide step in advance of these concessions, at once to place in the category of wealth, leisure, agreeable conversation.... The fact really is, that if we once desert matter in definition of wealth, there is no subsequent line of demarcation which has any tolerable degree of distinctness, or can be maintained with any tolerable consistency, till we have included such a mass of immaterial objects as utterly to confuse the meaning of the term, and render it impossible to speak with any approach towards precision, either of the wealth of different individuals, or different nations.

(1986 [1820]: 31–32)

Here the main reason which led post-Smithian economists to avoid dealing with interpersonal, qualitative aspects of economic transactions, is clearly stated. Malthus, maybe more so than Smith, was convinced not only that "enjoying conversations" with friends is an important and "superior" form of *using* wealth,[156] but even that the availability of "leisure and agreeable conversations" can rightly be considered as a *component* of the wealth of a person. However, he considered these components to be too ill-defined for inclusion in the economic domain, since economic analysis needs data and objective measurement, needs "matter". So, an economic science seeking to develop the first "scientific" reflections on economic relations chose to concentrate upon objective elements such as the theory of prices, or the laws of the redistribution of income or production. As a consequence, such a Political Economy did not find room for interpersonal relations seen as a source of well-being, as a component of that "wealth" of nations to which they devoted their intellectual efforts.[157] In particular, Malthus is inclined to restrict the definitions of wealth to that "which has an exchange value". Although he admits to the limits of such a position (1986 [1820]: 26 and *passim*), he pushes it to the point of affirming that a *gift cannot be wealth*, because, in his definition, "wealth cannot be given, but only exchanged" (1986 [1820]: 25).

This methodological avenue continues and gets richer with Marshall and his school.

Marshall, the "good economic science"

The Economics of the "man in flesh and blood" but not of "friendship"

Alfred Marshall wanted to study the real and concrete human being, so any human motive should, in principle, be taken into consideration by his Economics (1946 [1890]: 23ff.), although

> it will however probably be always true that the greater part of those actions, which are due to a feeling of duty and love of one's neighbour, cannot be classed, reduced to law and measured; and it is for this reason, and *not because they are not based on self-interest*, that the machinery of Economics cannot be brought to bear on them.
>
> (1946 [1890]: 24, my italics)

The criterion for cutting off the economic domain is, for Marshall, the possibility of measurement, where measurement means to him *money* measurement: economic goods are those that "can be measurable by a money price" (1946 [1890]: 33)[158] – a methodological stance in shaping the boundaries of economic *wealth* very close to that taken by Malthus.

The "right of citizenship" for altruism in Economics is not, however, an original element or even a rupture of his theory with respect to the economists who preceded him.[159] More generally, the idea that self-interest represents the dominant motive in economic matters was indeed considered by classical and neoclassical economists (from Mill to Jevons and Pareto) to be one of the most basic and universal economic laws – but this was more a common sense thesis than an essential requirement of the theory. So, the introduction of altruism did not affect the hardcore of the classical theoretical system. In fact, both Edgeworth and Marshall maintain full continuity with classical Political Economy.[160]

What is important, when considering our issues, is Marshall's approach to interpersonal relationships *within* Economics. He affirms that interpersonal relationships are not "goods" for the economic analysis.[161] In the *Principles* he wrote:

> The affection of friends, for instance, is an important element of well-being, but it is not reckoned as wealth, except by a poetic licence.
>
> (Marshall 1946 [1890]: 54)

And further on, defining individual wealth as the possession of "economic goods", he says: "it excludes his personal friendships, in so far as they have no direct business value" (1946 [1890]: 57).

The explanation of this choice lies in Marshall's more general theory of the relationship between economic and general welfare. In its famous opening, Marshall writes in the *Principles*:

> Political Economy or economics is a study of mankind in the ordinary business of life; it examines that part of individual and social action which is most closely connected with the attainment and with the use of the material requisites of wellbeing. Thus it is on the one side a study of wealth; and on the other, and more important side, a part of the study of man.
>
> (Marshall 1946 [1890]: 1)[162]

Marshall did not place these few lines at the beginning of his treatise by chance. In fact, they contain the essential elements upon which he built his entire vision of Economics:

i   Economics is not concerned with "well-being", let alone happiness, but with their "material requisites". The word "happiness" is no longer found. In England, after Bentham, it had become synonymous with Utilitarianism and hedonism, from which Marshall was trying to distinguish himself.[163] The expression *well-being* appears instead, which Pigou translated into *welfare* a few years later and made a central category of his theory.

ii As in the best of the English tradition, the material requisites of *well-being* are "wealth".

iii Wealth is only a part of the study of Economics, that "directly capable of a money measure". Thus, all human actions can become the object of Economics – not only egoistically motivated actions, but also altruistically motivated actions – as long as their value can be calculated in monetary prices.

iv Finally, the most important part of the study of Economics is the "study of man", and his actions.

With this affirmation Marshall threw himself into the tide of the marginalist revolution that was shifting the economic principle from the *object* (wealth, happiness) to the *subject*, that is, to the individual and the logic of choice.

Distancing himself from such authors as Jevons, Edgeworth, Pantaleoni and Pareto, Marshall affirms that Economics is not concerned with an abstract "economic man" but with man in "flesh and blood" (1946 [1890]: 27). In an effort to make Economics "more acceptable for the English *business community*" that was supporting his effort to introduce a professorship of Economics at Cambridge,[164] he included as many elements as possible about human actions within Economics. Mixing economic analysis with historical, sociological and geographical analysis, he tried to bring the abstract, economic model of the human being as close as possible to the real person. From this methodology to his vision of the wealth–happiness nexus the step is short:

> It is true that in religion, in the family affections and in friendship, even the poor may find scope for many of those faculties which are the source of the highest happiness. But the conditions which surround extreme poverty, especially in densely crowded places, tend to deaden the higher faculties. Those who have been called the Residuum of our large towns have little opportunity for friendship; they know nothing of the decencies and the quiet, and very little even of the unity of family life; and religion often fails to reach them.
>
> (1946 [1890]: 2)

This well-expressed passage clears up and develops the basic idea that was to accompany the entire humanist or civil tradition in England. Happiness mostly depends on factors external to Economics, like religion and the meaning of life, and above all on an *affective life and friendships*. Thus, in Marshall, we find the Aristotelian idea that happiness does not coincide with wealth, and that it is of a social nature. Nevertheless, even if extreme poverty doesn't automatically mean unhappiness, it does in fact determine those objective conditions which make it very difficult, if not impossible, to develop those dimensions of life, and those social relations, upon which happiness eventually depends. Therefore, even if the economist's job is concerned with material goods which have a monetary price, it still carries out an important social function of great ethical value, because it deals with the improvements of the *pre-conditions* for happiness.[165] However, true relationality – as affection, friendship or love, today "relational goods" – is not part of economic inquiries, they are matters "external" to Economics. In this sense too Cambridge tradition is close to Smithian classical Political Economy: the *market is a tool for true sociality, but market relations are only instrumental.*

Marshall's line of thought was followed by his heir in Cambridge Arthur Cecil Pigou, who moved the fulcrum of the issue at hand towards the other key word in Economics: *welfare.* In his *The Economics of Welfare* (1920: 16), he states that he intends to only deal with the economic aspects of general welfare (what he calls "economic welfare"), the part of total welfare that "can be expressed, directly or indirectly, by a money measure".[166] The affirmation is in full adherence to Marshall's methodology in that the economist is only concerned with the material prerequisites of well-being, but it is precisely this conviction which shows the importance he gave to happiness.[167]

The "transformation problem" of goods into happiness

In Marshall's theory of happiness, we must stop to look at another theme that is central to this research. Marshall and the Cambridge School's methodological choice to concentrate on the "means–wealth" which contributes to the "end–happiness" is justifiable if the underlying hypothesis holds; that is, that an increase in wealth brings more happiness, either directly or indirectly. The "Easterlin paradox" shows us today that this hypothesis is not obvious at all. On the contrary, in certain cases an increase in wealth produces systematic effects in other dimensions of life – religion, friendship and family affections – exactly those cited by Marshall. In other words, today we know that the "technology of happiness", the transformation of goods (*inputs*) into happiness (*outcome*) is more complex than Marshall thought.

These issues are at the heart of the contemporary debate on Economics and happiness – although the same methodological finesse is not always to be found.

However, in the last chapter of *Principles*, Marshall expresses an idea about these open questions, which his contemporary fellow economists, such as Pareto or Wicksteed, completely missed. I am referring to his analysis of the "standard of life".

The first idea we find in the last chapter (that develops an issue introduced in chapter 3 of the *Principles*) has an Aristotelian flavour and is very near to Scitovsky: "the true key-note of economic progress is the development of new activities rather than new wants" (1946 [1890]: 688), specifying that the question that "is of special urgency in our generation" is "the connection between changes in the manner of living and the rate of earning" (1946 [1890]: 688). In analysing this urgent question, he distinguishes between "the standard of life" and "the standard of comfort", specifying that the "standard of life is here taken to mean the standard of activity adjusted to wants. . . . The standard of comfort [is] a term that may suggest a mere increase of artificial wants, among which perhaps the grosser wants may predominate" (1946 [1890]: 689–690). Then he specifies that:

> [i]t is true that every broad improvement in the standard of comfort is likely to bring with it a better manner of living, and to open the way to new and higher activities; while people who have hitherto had neither the necessaries nor the decencies of life, can hardly fail to get some increase in vitality and energy from an increase of comfort, however gross and material the view which they may take of it. Thus a rise in the standard of comfort will probably involve some rise in the standard of life.
>
> (1946 [1890]: 690)

Unfortunately, this is not always the case. The rest of the chapter, in fact, is an analysis of the cases when rises in standard of comfort bring a *fall* in the standard of life. Marshall develops this analysis in particular in the labour market, and the burning question of the limitation of the hours of labour, and to the related issues of a minimum wage and redistribution of income.

A first application of this analysis is Marshall's recommendation for a general reduction of the hours of labour, which is likely to cause little net material loss and much moral good; a case where a reduction of income can lead to a higher standard of life. At the end of the chapter, Marshall explains why:

> Even if we took account only of the injury done to the young by living in a home in which the father and the mother lead joyless lives, it would be in the interest of society to afford some relief to them also. Able workers and good citizens are not likely to come from homes, from which the mother is absent during a great part of the day; nor from homes to which the father seldom returns till his children are asleep: and therefore society as a whole has a direct interest in the curtailment of extravagantly long hours of duty away from home.
>
> (Marshall 1946 [1890]: 721)

Analogies and differences

Marshall's analysis of the standard of life is the peak reached by the Smithian stream of British classical Political Economy. The methodological continuity is, in fact, real and profound. Wealth is not happiness; however, wealth can *instrumentally* foster both sociality and happiness, although the "technology of happiness" is a complex matter. The market is not the place for friendship, but without markets true friendship can hardly exist (because people are not equals and independent).

It cannot be denied, then, that there is also some continuity between the Italian "Public Happiness" tradition and that of the Anglo-Saxon "Wealth of Nations". Civil Economy and Political Economy both express the same "civil" idea to extend "home governance", *oikos-nomos*, from the private sphere to the public one, to the city, the *polis*, the *civitas*. Certainly, neither Smith nor Marshall fully shared Genovesi's theory on the happiness–sociality nexus, but if we dig deeper, we find that both schools see the objective of their disciplines as being the study of the ways to increase the "well-being" of the nations.

Nevertheless, the key difference between these two traditions is the following question: *which* sociality *within* the market? And therefore, *which* happiness *within* normal market interactions? The answers, as we have seen, are very different. In the final chapter we shall deal again with these central issues.

9 Happiness becomes pleasure

> Progress chiefly depends on the extent to which the *strongest* and not merely the *highest* forces of human nature can be utilised for the increase of social good.
>
> (A. Marshall)

The English happiness

In a parallel stream another tradition of thought was flowing in England, representing a strong rupture with respect to both Civil Economy and the Smithian British Political Economy. It is Bentham's Utilitarianism, one of the key episodes of the story we are telling.

The link between Smith's theory of happiness and the Utilitarian one still remains mysterious, and it is not easy to understand why English tradition shifted from the Smithian tradition to the hedonist and individualistic version of Utilitarianism that inspired neoclassical Economics at the end of nineteenth century.

What is sure is that, thanks to Bentham, the neoclassical paradigm converged fully with the anti-social western modern mainstream grounded in individualism and solitude. It was the advent of the *Robinson Crusoe* Economics, totally defined within the mind of the single individual.[168] Utilitarianism was the philosophy most responsible for the new formulation.[169] While there were exceptions like Menger and Walras (who were not hedonist), most of the leaders of the neoclassical subjectivist approach, in fact, based their economic theory on the hedonist philosophy, and were closer to an a-social anthropology like that of Machiavelli or Hobbes than to a relational anthropology like that of Smith or Genovesi. We will see that this was the case for hedonist founders of marginalism like Jevons and Pantaleoni, as well as for Wicksteed and Pareto, who were neither hedonists nor Utilitarians, but *just* individualists.

Thanks to Bentham and his school, happiness was an important theme in the English Utilitarian tradition. With expressions like *"the greatest happiness for the greatest number"* running high on the agenda, Utilitarianism at that time was certainly in touch with some social dimension.[170] In this case, however, it is imperative to distinguish between *social* theories and *relational* theories – in the sense specified in the Introduction. Utilitarian philosophy is sensitive to social themes regarding well-being, but it is not based on a relational anthropology: J.S. Mill, however, was in this respect an important exception. We will now concentrate on his work in more detail.

John Stuart Mill

A "relational" Utilitarian

John Stuart Mill is a philosopher–economist who should rightfully be considered a representative of the vision of Political Economy in continuity – although with important innovations – with the "Civil Happiness" tradition (and, for this reason, I put him before Bentham). Furthermore, I connect the exploration of his works to the two themes we are following, namely, his vision of happiness and its relationship with civic life.

Mill's conception of happiness is very articulated and rich, and is very much linked to his conception of liberty and political participation, developed mainly in his *On Liberty* (1859) and *Utilitarianism* (1863).[171] Although it has been the object of many studies,[172] some aspects of his theory of happiness are so central to the discussion we are developing that we need to analyse them further.

First, it must be said that, in spite of Mill being considered one of the founders of classical Utilitarianism, his position on the motivations for action and on the nature of happiness is substantially different from that of Bentham.

Second, a biographic datum. His encounter with Harriet Hardy marked a turning point in both his life and thinking. Mill defined his own relationship with the woman who years later became his wife "the friendship which has been the honour and chief blessing of my existence, as well as the source of a great part of all that I have attempted to do, or hope to effect hereafter, for human improvement" (1874, chapter 6 and 7). Mill treated the idea of the life of the couple and, in general, of the marriage as an "agape", that is, as a union made of reciprocity, which, at the same time, exalts both the individuality of each partner and their complementariness. In particular, Mill was convinced that the paradigm of the marriage relationship is *friendship*, a thesis – the key-idea of his *The Subjection of Women* – that places Mill among the first feminists ever; a vision that is surprisingly similar to that of Genovesi (mentioned in Chapter 6):

> When the two persons both care for great objects, and are a help and encouragement to each other in whatever regards these, the minor matters on which their tastes may differ are not all-important to them;

and there is a foundation for solid friendship, of an enduring character, more likely than anything else to make it, through the whole of
life, a greater pleasure to each to give pleasure to the other, than to
receive it.

(1975 [1869], chapter 4)

Mill, in criticising the man–woman relationship in marriage, was also
addressing a radical criticism towards any form of unequal or hierarchic
society, claiming that relationships of reciprocity were superior, more civil,
forms of human relations:

The true virtue of human beings is fitness to live together as equals;
claiming nothing for themselves but what they as freely concede to
everyone else; regarding command of any kind as an exceptional
necessity, and in all cases a temporary one; and preferring, whenever
possible, the society of those with whom leading and following can be
alternate and reciprocal.

(chapter 2, pp. 174–175)[173]

Therefore, his personal experience of reciprocity could have had an
important role in his social and even economic theory.[174] Surely his vision
of happiness was affected by his experience of reciprocity, as were his
theories of friendship and of liberty.

His theory of liberty and democracy, for instance, attributes great
importance to civil society. Although they may be noisy and not always
efficient, the intermediate bodies of civil society work as public forums for
dialogue and the decision-making process and so ensure democracy.

Mill exalted the individual without ever adapting his ideas to an atom-
istic vision. He liked to use the term *individuality* instead of individualism.
Also influenced by the cooperative and socialist–utopian movements, Mill,
over the years, matured the conviction that individuality is enriched only
through interpersonal relationships. Because the personality is inter-
subjective, it only flourishes in the interpersonal dimension (both the
public sphere and face-to-face relationships).[175]

Even the typical logic of the economic sphere, according to Mill, cannot
be separated from the civil dimension, because economic activity and the
market are part of civil life, are civil society. So the economy is a *public*
sphere, even though it is not *political* (but *civil*).

On the anthropological level, Mill refuses Bentham's view of the individual as being moved strictly by the desire to maximise pleasure or min-
imise pain. In "Remarks on Bentham's Philosophy", Mill clearly expresses
his position on this point by criticising the father of Utilitarianism for
embracing such a narrow vision of the motivation of human action. The
motives are too heterogeneous and complex to be reduced to the mere
pursuit of pleasure: "Motives are innumerable: there is nothing whatever

which may not become an object of desire or of dislike by association"
(Mill 1963 [1833]: vol. X: 13).

In particular, Bentham, according to Mill, gave too little importance to
sympathy, conscience, duty, justice and benevolence. In his *System of
Logic* (1862 [1843]) he confirmed his earlier position, expressed in his
"Remarks", and developed them thus:

> When the will is said to be determined by motives, a motive does not
> mean always, or solely, the anticipation of a pleasure or of a pain. . . .
> It is at least certain that we gradually, through the influence of associ-
> ation, come to desire the means without thinking of the end: the
> action itself becomes an object of desire, and is performed without ref-
> erence to any motive beyond itself.
>
> (Book 6, chapter 2, §4)

Mill, therefore, besides affirming the plurality of *motives* of actions –
which he distinguishes from the *motivation* which is what determines the
morality of an action – goes beyond the instrumental approach to rationality. Because Bentham's Utilitarianism is anchored to such an instrumental approach, consequentialism is a central feature of his philosophy.
Instead, for Mill, action is not necessarily a means to reach an end (pleasure) external to the action itself, but in certain cases may be an *end*
in itself. Such an approach to rationality, today also called "expressive"
(Hargreaves-Heap *et al.* 1992), is also close to Genovesi's account of
rationality and to Aristotle's as well.

Another point in which Mill's approach to rationality distances itself
from that of Bentham (and, later, from neoclassical Economics) is about the
so-called *psychological egoism*, that is the thesis that an individual's actions
are moved solely according to the maximisation of one's own pleasure and
objectives, without any reference to the others (as in Hobbes' political
theory). Although benevolence had a place in the thought of both Mill's
father (James) and Bentham, it was conceived only in the measure to which
helping others increased the subject's own pleasure. Thus, benevolence or
altruism were not considered as being *primitive* principles, but as leading
back to individual self-interest – not far from Hobbes' vision of altruism.

Mill very clearly criticised the psychological egoism thesis in his
"Remarks on Bentham's Philosophy". According to Mill, while Bentham
"distinguishes between two types of interests, the *self-regarding* and the
social" (Mill 1963 [1833]: 13–14), at the same time he maintains that even
the social is instrumental to individual interests; for Bentham, in other
words, only self-interest is primitive. Mill is critical towards this form of
reductionism, as is clear from the following passage of the "Remarks":

> That the pleasures or pains of another person can only be pleasurable
> or painful to us through the association of our own pleasures or pains

with them, is true in one sense (the only pleasures or pains of which we have direct experience being those felt by ourselves, it is from them that our very notions of pleasure or pain are derived), which is probably that intended by the author, but not true in another, against which he has not sufficiently guarded his mode of expression.

(Mill 1963 [1833]: 14–15)

Instead, Mill was convinced that "there are, there have been, many human beings, in whom the motives of patriotism or of benevolence have been permanent steady principles of action, superior to any ordinary, and in not a few instances, to any possible, temptations of personal interests" (1963 [1833]: 15).[176]

The paradox of happiness: the happiness of others

Mill's anthropology gives life to a different version of Utilitarianism's basic principle of happiness. Such version of happiness – not far from Aristotle's or Genovesi's – is especially affirmed in Mill's book, *Utilitarianism*, a book, as Nussbaum states, that

frustrates philosophers who look for a tidy resolution to the many tensions it introduces into the Utilitarian system. But it has proven compelling over the ages because it contains a subtle awareness of human complexity that few philosophical works can rival. Here as in his surprising writings on women, Mill stands out, an adult among the children, an empiricist *with* experience, a man who painfully attained the kind of self-knowledge that his great teacher lacked, and who turned that into philosophy.

(Nussbaum 2005: 182)

The following passage from *Utilitarianism* highlights Mill's intuitions on happiness.

I must again repeat, what the assailants of utilitarianism seldom have the justice to acknowledge, that the happiness ... is not the agent's own happiness, but that of all concerned. As between his own happiness and that of others, utilitarianism requires him to be as strictly impartial as a disinterested and benevolent spectator. In the golden rule of Jesus of Nazareth, we read the complete spirit of the ethics of utility. To do as you would be done by, and to love your neighbour as yourself, constitute the ideal perfection of utilitarian morality. As the means of making the nearest approach to this ideal, utility would enjoin, first, that laws and social arrangements should place the happiness ... of every individual, as nearly as possible in harmony with the interest of the whole ... so that not only he may be unable to conceive the possibility of happiness to himself, consistently with conduct opposed to the general good, but also that a direct impulse to promote the general good may be in every individual one of the habitual motives of action.

(1998 [1863]: chapter 2)

Mill re-evaluates the civil soul of happiness (the classical or Aristotelian one) and makes it central to his theory. Although it was already present in Bentham's early philosophy, it was overshadowed by the primacy of pleasure and self-interest. Mill's idea of happiness is especially different from Bentham's in the emphasis he puts on the *relational or civil nature of happiness*. His anthropological theory compelled him to stress that the human being has a natural drive towards "communion or unity with his/her fellows" (Berger 1984: 44), and therefore can only be happy in relationships with others.

The following passage from Mill's *Autobiography* should come as no surprise. It tells of a transformation in his philosophy of happiness:

I never, indeed, wavered in the conviction that happiness is the test of all rules of conduct, and the end of life. But I now thought that this end was only to be attained by not making it the direct end. Those only are happy (I thought) who have their minds fixed on some object other than their own happiness; on the happiness of others, on the improvement of mankind, even on some art or pursuit, followed not as a means, but as itself an ideal end. Aiming thus at something else, they find happiness by the way.... Ask yourself whether you are happy, and you cease to be so.

(1981 [1874]: chapter v)

This passage gives us, in a nutshell, some of the key themes of the classical and civil vision of happiness. Happiness is the final end, the *sommum bonum*, and has a paradoxical nature (the teleological paradox) because it can be obtained only if it is not instrumentally sought. It is found by making others happy, or in any case, forgetting about it. We have here the elements that we have found in Aristotle and in the Civil Economy tradition. Looked at from this perspective, it is correct to see Mill as the most relevant English representative of the classical tradition of "Civil Happiness". Happiness, to Mill, is *public* for the same reasons of the Civil Economy tradition: happiness is deeply related to civil and relational life; there is no happiness outside interpersonal relationships, in particular genuine interactions. In Mill's version, Utilitarianism's "greatest happiness" is actually a nineteenth-century continuation of the humanist tradition of *pubblica felicità*.[177]

Thanks to the relational depth of Mill's anthropology and political science, we find in his *Principles of Political Economy* the intuition that greater wealth can even bring less happiness. The search for happiness through greater wealth produces negative effects on other goods (which today are called environmental and relational goods). The following exposé of Mill's theory of "steady state", which has become well-known more recently thanks to environmental economists, is particularly inspiring to this regard:

> I confess I am not charmed with the ideal of life held out by those who think that the normal state of human beings is that of struggling to get on; that the trampling, crushing, elbowing, and treading on each other's heels, which form the existing type of social life, are the most desirable lot of human kind, or anything but the disagreeable symptoms of one of the phases of industrial progress.... I know not why it should be a matter of congratulation that persons who are already richer than any one needs to be, should have doubled their means of consuming things which give little or no pleasure except as representative of wealth;... It is only in the backward countries of the world that increased production is still an important object: in those most advanced, what is economically needed is a better distribution, of which one indispensable means is a stricter restraint on population.... Nor is there much satisfaction in contemplating the world with nothing left to the spontaneous activity of nature.... If the earth must lose that great portion of its pleasantness which it owes to things that the unlimited increase of wealth and population would extirpate from it, for the mere purpose of enabling it to support a larger, but not a better or a happier population, I sincerely hope, for the sake of posterity, that they will be content to be stationary, long before necessity compels them to it.
>
> (Mill 1920 [1848], vol. IV: chapter 6, §§, 6.5, 6.6, 6.8)

His vision of the economy also, in line with the Civil Economy tradition, gives room to genuine sociality *within normal market interactions*. Let us think, for example, of his vision of the cooperative movement:

> The peculiar characteristic of the civilized being is the capacity of cooperation; and this, like other faculties, tends to improve by practice, and becomes capable of assuming a constantly wider share of action.... Accordingly there is no more certain incident of the progressive change taking place in society, than the continual growth of the principle and practice of cooperation.
>
> (Mill 1920 [1848], book IV, chapter 1, §2, p. 698)

Mutuality, solidarity and fraternity (the basic principles of the classic cooperative movement), are, to Mill, considered to be part of the economic domain.

Bentham's hedonic happiness

In spite of its originality and promising fecundity, Mill's version of Utilitarianism didn't enter mainstream marginalist Economics. As we will see in the following pages, it was Bentham's Utilitarianism, and the way he reduced *happiness* to hedonist *utility*, which penetrated neoclassical Economics in Great Britain, especially in the works of Jevons, thus determining the direction Economics took in the twentieth century. So, with Mill, the brief season of Civil Happiness in English Political Economy ended. The sociologist Robert Michels, in 1918, began his book, *Economy and Happiness*, by correctly affirming that "modern economists have totally abandoned researches on happiness" (Michels 1918: x).[178] The kind of happiness that entered into neoclassical Economics was that of Bentham.

It is well-known that, according to Bentham, the individual is like a machine that maximises utility, a utility that is deeply rooted in the hedonist philosophy of pleasure.[179]

Nevertheless, when Economics *reduced* the classical understanding of happiness to pleasure, it shifted its concern from the *means* (wealth) to the *end* (utility–pleasure–happiness). Though the *end-happiness* may recall the Public Happiness tradition, the resemblance is utterly superficial. Once Economics broke away from the classical idea of happiness, happiness became pleasure and Public Happiness became the sum of individual pleasures. All connections with civil virtues and the "teleological paradox" of happiness were lost. Furthermore, whilst happiness was essentially a matter of relationships between people, hedonic utility, the new key concept, became defined as a relationship between *an individual and a thing* (according to Pareto and most of the neoclassical economists).

In Bentham's theory of *happiness*, happiness means simply *pleasure*. Bentham seems to ignore the long western philosophical tradition that had denied that happiness could be identified with pleasure (almost all philosophers apart from Epicureans and some sensists[180] of the eighteenth century such as Lametrie). Bentham appears in the tradition of happiness like a mushroom, jumping back to the Epicureans and ignoring (or seeming to ignore) the debate on happiness in Aristotle, in the Middle age (Thomas Aquinas), Spinoza, or in the eighteenth-century Public Happiness.

The reduction of happiness to pleasure is immediately clear in the opening of *An Introduction to the Principles of Morals and Legislation*, when Bentham affirms that "nature has placed mankind under the governance of two sovereign masters, pain and pleasure" (1789). Thus, Bentham's happiness has an individualistic nature and people are described as simply searchers of happiness-pleasure. This anthropological characteristic is "essential to the utilitarian programme" (Berger 1984: 10), in which social happiness is seen as an aggregation, or sum of individual pleasures. J.S. Mill clearly said that, in the Utilitarianism of Bentham (and his father James) "with happiness is intended pleasure" (Mill 1998 [1863]: chapter 10).

On the first page of *An Introduction*, Bentham said the "principle of utility" was foundational in his system, and thereafter the terms *happiness*, *pleasure* and *utility* are interchangeable as different ways of expressing the same basic concept of Utilitarianism: "By utility is meant that property in any object, whereby it tends to produce benefit, advantage, pleasure, good, or happiness" (chapter 1, §1.4).

Having Maupertius and Beccaria as the main sources for his thought on happiness, Bentham, above all, determined the individualist–hedonist methodology of the early neoclassical Economics. Thus, it was this side of the Latin tradition that ultimately influenced neoclassical Economics.[181]

(Anti-)classical hedonist Economics

Within neoclassical Economics, Bentham's identification of happiness with pleasure, took neoclassical economic science progressively further away from Civil Happiness and towards the search for individual utility. Jevons and Edgeworth in England, Pantaleoni in Italy, among others, channelled a simplified version of Bentham's Utilitarianism into mainstream Economics, also informed by psychophysics (not known to Bentham).

The hedonist philosophy played a central role in the works of Edgeworth, from *New and Old Methods of Ethics* (1877) to *Mathematical Physics* (1881). For Edgeworth, *happiness* means *pleasure*, and maximising happiness is translated into maximising pleasure (1881: 7, 16).[182]

When Jevons (1870) defined Economics as the "science of utility", he explicitly recognised his indebtedness to Bentham. Happiness entered the *mainstream* in total identification with pleasure, the new object of the new Economics. For Jevons pleasures are diverse only by "degree, not by kind" (Schabas 1990: 39). Economics deals with the "lowest" one. Jevons doesn't exclude that people can renounce pleasures coming from the economic domain for the sake of ethical or superior pleasures, but his ethical rule, like, Bentham's, is to maximise the sum of pleasures, both individually and socially. In the *Theory of Political Economy*, he states:

> The theory which follows is entirely based on a calculus of pleasure and pain and the object of economics is to maximise happiness by purchasing pleasure as it were, at the lowest cost of pain.
>
> (Jevons 1970 [1871]: 91)

Jevons, Edgeworth and Pantaleoni defined the object of Economics on the basis of the *economic principle*. To Jevons the economic principle is "maximize happiness", and to Edgeworth, "The first principle of economics is that every agent is actuated only by self-interest" (1881: 16). In the first hedonist–marginalist Economists, Economics was not a general theory of action, or a praxis; actually, it was defined on the basis of a hedonic content. This can be seen in Marshall, who chose money measurement as the criterion of demarcation – the hedonist economists chose the *motive* of actions for the delimitation of the field of Economics.

The leading Italian economist, Maffeo Pantaleoni, was the clearest on this point. The first two chapters of his *Principii di economia pura (Pure Economics)* (1898) are dedicated to the attempt to found Economics on a single *hedonic hypothesis* – his version of the "economic principle" – from which all economic laws can be derived as its corollaries. In spite of his great friendship with Pareto, he stuck to this anti-Paretian framework his entire life. He begins his book by stating that the hedonic hypothesis was the "keystone" of his entire theoretical building, "according to which men are actuated in the production, consumption, distribution and circulation of wealth, exclusively by the desire to obtain the maximum satisfaction of their wants that circumstances admit of" (1898: 9). A few pages later, quoting Edgeworth (1881), he states that the hedonistic postulate means to solve the problem of maximising pleasure and minimising pain. In this way, as with Jevons, he gave a hedonistic content to economic rationality, and thought to avoid a definition of economic rationality as a simple tautology.[183]

As far as sociality is concerned, the hedonist approach to Economics gives room to interpersonal relations, even non-instrumental ones. Edgeworth, and Pantaleoni, claimed that altruistic sentiments can also be sources of individual utility. They were not concerned with the "public" happiness; nevertheless, the individual was considered to form his tastes in all kinds of social interactions. Neoclassical Economics, being reliant on Psychology, was inclined to insert sociality into Economics by means of the concept of pleasure. This was a methodological attitude very close to the contemporary scholars of happiness, who intend to go "Back to Bentham" (Kahneman 1999).

Pantaleoni, Edgeworth and Jevons all attempted to refound Economics on a new economic principle – hedonic utility. For this reason it is really not correct to say that happiness is not central to neoclassical Economics: in fact, classical and Civil Happiness is out, but *Utilitarian happiness*, intended as pleasure or utility, has taken its place. Actually "lost in translation" were: the distinction between happiness and its material prerequisites; all connections with the non-instrumentality of happiness and its paradoxical logic; and its strict ties with civil virtues.

As an example of the strong methodological similarity between the first hedonist marginalist economists and most of the current studies on happiness, I will now look closer at one aspect of the theories of Edgeworth and Pantaleoni.

This generation of economists were very much interested in psychological laws, with the aim of basing the new economic science on solid ground, and introspection was considered as a scientific source of data for

Economics. Francis Ysidro Edgeworth, in explaining the law of diminishing sensitivity to stimuli – a very popular issue at that time – in his *Mathematical Psychics*, introduced the following consideration:

> But not only is the function connecting means and pleasure such that the increase of means does not produce a proportionate increase in pleasure; but this effect is heightened by the function itself so varying (on repetition of the conditions of pleasure) that the same means produce less pleasure.
>
> (1881: 62)

In other words, the function that specifies the amount of pleasure produced by different quantities of consumption in any given period – the utility function for consumption, as conventionally understood – *shifts according to the individual's consumption experiences in previous periods*. Edgeworth calls this the "Law of Accommodation". If we take a person's reference point to be some weighted average of his or her previous consumption, Edgeworth's hypothesis implies that a person's utility in any given period depends not only on the absolute quantity she consumes of each good in that period, but also on differences between those quantities and the corresponding quantities at the reference point. The psychological concept of "accommodation" used by Edgeworth is essentially the same as "adaptation", which present-day psychologists have used to explain reference-dependence.

Similarly, Maffeo Pantaleoni, in his analysis of wants, suggested that there is a tendency for a person's "hedonic scale" at any given time to depend on past consumption (1898: 53). In Pantaleoni, however, there is also an intuition that deserves attention for the present debate, namely the idea that the tendency for increases in income to generate new wants is stronger than the tendency for decreases in income to stifle existing wants: "The positive expansion of wants is, as a matter of fact, different from the negative expansion" (1898: 53). There would be, thus, an asymmetry in the relation income/wants–satisfaction, something similar to that emphasised by Kahneman in his *objective happiness* (1999).

This possible road of neoclassical Economics was not taken by the mainstream, mainly thanks to Pareto and, in a minor way, to Wicksteed – as we shall see in the next chapter.

10 The solipsistic foundation of contemporary Economics

> You talk of *cutting away a slice* from a concrete phenomenon, and examining this by itself; but I enquire how you can manage to cut away that slice?
>
> (B. Croce, letter to Pareto, 1900)

Pareto and Wicksteed: the definitive divorce between Economics and Civil Happiness

The economics of experimental facts

At this stage of the research, we have to register *two different methodological moves* in relation to Civil Happiness in Economics. The first, performed by hedonist marginalists, was the shift from the Aristotelian and Genovesi's Civil Happiness to *pleasure*. The second, as we shall see in this chapter, was the passage from happiness/pleasure to purely instrumental choices without any reference to the psychology of the subject. Most of the current scholars of happiness in Economics are going back to Bentham or Jevons, i.e. going back before the methodological move performed mainly by Pareto and Wicksteed. Let us see how.

Vilfredo Pareto and Philip Wicksteed are key figures for understanding the reasons why Civil Happiness was banished from the realm of neoclassical Economics.

More than any other economist, Pareto is, the main, responsible for the epistemological foundations for contemporary economic theory (see Bruni 2002). Over the decade overlapping the nineteenth and twentieth centuries, Pareto's economic works followed a number of objectives that are at the heart of today's economic theory. He criticised early neoclassical hedonist economists (Jevons or Edgeworth), and re-founded economic theory upon new epistemological bases. In particular he claimed that:

a   The whole of economic theory can do without the concepts of *pleasure* and *motives* – egotistical or altruistic – for an action. The theoretical economist can get all the data he/she needs from observing the choices of the market and its objective data of supply and demand. There's no need for hedonism or Utilitarianism.

b   From the analytical point of view, the theory of general equilibrium can be written starting from the *ordinal* "curves of indifference", because they are a "direct fact of experience". Thus he breaks away from the hedonistic concepts of marginal utility as well as total utility. He and his followers saw ordinal indifference curves as overcoming the theories of Marshall, Edgeworth and Pantaleoni, who were still dependent both on cardinal utility and marginal utility, and even that of Walras, dependent on the concept of marginal utility as well (the *rareté*).[184]

c   Psychological data are not necessary for Economics; choices are enough.

Breaking with *both* classical Political Economy and the Utilitarian and hedonist tradition which influenced most of the first generation of neoclassical economists, Pareto shows that economic theory only needs the "naked fact of choice", that it doesn't require hypotheses about the agents' motives – that was, instead, the key issue in the first generation of marginalist economists. Though he acknowledged in the *Manuale di Economia Politica* (chapter 2, §1) that Psychology had the potential to become an experimental science, he saw it as being too immature, of an inferior epistemic grade of confidence, and so offering fewer scientific guarantees than *empirical Economics*, based on "facts".[185] The first neoclassical economists, as J.S. Mill, used Psychology to found the laws of human behaviour because they considered it an experimental science:[186] deductions, on which social science is based for the construction of its own system of laws, rest upon the experimental data of psychological introspection. Pareto's economic theory broke away from this approach based on the psychological analysis of individual behaviour. It would seem that the "spiritualistic" climate of those years, which Pareto strongly reacted to in the name of empiricism, greatly influenced his attitude towards psychology.

In Pareto, the "experimental" or empirical dimension can mainly be found in objective verification, as in the hypothetical deductive method: for him, external experimental data is the primary element of science. This is the meaning of many of Pareto's assertions, including one mentioned in a letter to the philosopher, A. Naville: "Pure political economy has, therefore, great interest in taking the least possible from the domain of psychology" (in Busino 1964: xxiv); or, when he affirmed that one of the main achievements of the theory of choice was that "every psychological analysis is eliminated" (Pareto 1900a, preamble). However, it would be a mistake to deduce from these statements that, for Pareto, psychology is not a science. In the first section of chapter 2 of the *Manual*, he writes:

Clearly, psychology is fundamental to political economy and all the social sciences in general. Perhaps a day will come when the laws of social science can be deduced from the principles of psychology, just as some day perhaps the principles of the composition of matter will give us the laws of physics and chemistry by deduction; but we are still very far from that state of affairs, and we must take a different approach.

On this epistemological basis, he declared psychology off-limits for Economics, a methodological operation that stopped the process of dialogue between the two initiated by the first generation of marginal economists. In this sense, contemporary scholars (both economists and psychologists) working on happiness are "back to Bentham", or to Edgeworth, and therefore feel the need to retrieve psychological dimensions of choice lost after Pareto's positivistic shift.[187]

Getting back to our theme of well-being and happiness, Pareto worked to break away from economic theory of his time, which was still centred on the "metaphysical" and not on measurable utility. Thus he performed a few fundamental methodological operations in the development of twentieth-century Economics.

First of all, he introduced the famous neologism, *ophelimity*, as a substitute for utility, which he considered too vague and unscientific because it was still too "psychological". Introducing the concept in his first systematic work, the *Cours d'économie politique* (1896–1897) he advised Economics to rid itself of any consideration about people's well-being. From the Greek *ophelimos* (useful, advantageous), Pareto used *ophelimité* to signify "the convenient relationship, which makes it possible for something to satisfy a need or desire, whether it be legitimate or not" (1896–1897, §7), or as "a type of subjective utility" (§16); and specifies that "ophelimity's very characteristic of being subjective is fundamental. It must be kept in mind for all that follows" (§9).

Thus, Economics becomes "the science of ophelimity" (§16), which Pareto sees as being the relationship between a "man and a thing" (§7). It becomes also entirely individualistic, having nothing to do with social relationships, and therefore tells us nothing about well-being, and even less about happiness, private or public. Pareto thought that utility was still too much linked to the concept of well-being, a too-wide and ill-defined concept to be treated by Economics alone: "the term utility in its ordinary acceptance indicates the property of a thing to favour the development and prosperity of an individual, a race, or the entire human species" (§5). Again: "When we will speak of utility, we will assume material well-being as the distinctive criteria of scientific and moral progress" (§13). Thus, he repeated several times that although, alcohol has little "utility" when consumed in large quantities by an individual, it can also be "ophelimic" and therefore demanded, and that is all that counts for pure Economics. Economics became then the "science of ophelimity".[188] The introduction of ophelimity, nevertheless, served a methodological purpose, in that it represented the first step on a road that only Pareto's Sociology was to go down.

As a concept capable of refounding economic science, ophelimity didn't last long. Already in 1900, Pareto threw it out and demonstrated, instead, that the whole of economic theory could be founded on *choices*. Because the fact of choice is impersonal (since it abstracts from personalised dimensions of agents), "indifference curves" are more scientific than ophelimity and allow all economic theory to be drawn directly from facts.[189] With the "naked fact of choice" methodology, Pareto carried out the first part of his project which was to refound Economics and emancipate it from utility, pleasure and well-being, or happiness, a word which he rarely used and only as a synonym for well-being. The story is well-known and not worth taking any more time over, other than to make a few comments with regard to our specific discussion.

Economics as instrumentality

Restricting it even further than Marshall's "economic well-being", Pareto turned the field of Economics towards the study of *logical* actions, that is, choices based on *instrumental* rationality.[190] In fact, Pareto's criterion for distinguishing the economic field from the social one (non-economical) is given by the *logic* of the actions. He defines Economics as the study of logical actions that instrumentally and correctly tie the means to the end. Thus Economics became the exclusive kingdom of instrumental and logical behaviour.

In the *Manual* (1906), the distinction between logical and non-logical actions is well-established. In the *Trattato di Sociologia Generale*, Pareto repeatedly stated quite clearly that Economics deals with logical actions (1916, §§152, 262) whereas sociology deals with the "non-logical" ones, which are "by no means the same as 'illogical'" (§150), presented as a residual class. He subsequently defines logical actions as those

> that consist in means appropriate to ends and which logically link means with ends [...], not only from the standpoint of the subject performing them, but from the standpoint of other persons who have a more extensive knowledge – in other words, to actions that are logical both subjectively and objectively in the sense just explained.
>
> (§150)[191]

With this theory, Pareto rated well-being, happiness, and sociality as domains of Sociology, and thus banished them from the realm of Economics.

Furthermore, in the *Cours* (1896–1897, §386), and then in the *Manuale* (1906, Appendix §§45–46), and definitively in the *Trattato di Sociologia Generale* (1916), Pareto distinguished between two concepts, which he saw as being confused prior to his distinction: "The maximum of ophelimity *of* a community", and "the maximum of the ophelimity *for* a community" (1964 [1916], §2121 and ff.). Once the cardinal measurement of utility has been expelled from economic theory, the criterion of "sum ranking", which had guided the theory and *policy* of Utilitarian inspiration until then, could no longer be used to determine the "maximum of ophelimity *of* the community" – Pareto, this is a "metaphysical" concept because it implies *interpersonal comparisons* of ophelimity:

> If the utilities of single individuals were homogeneous quantities and could therefore be compared and reduced to a sum, our study would not, theoretically at least, be difficult. We would simply take the sum of utilities of the various individuals and so get the utility of the community they constitute – and would be taking us back to problems already examined. But the business is not so simple. The utilities of various individuals are heterogeneous quantities, and a sum of such quantities is a thing that has no meaning.
>
> (§§2126–2127)

According to Pareto it makes sense, instead, to speak in Political Economy of the "maximum of ophelimity *for* the community". In a community of individuals, all maximisers of individual ophelimity, the optima allocations will be multiple, but only a few of these (those that, in today's microeconomics, are located in the "Pareto curve") will be optima in the Paretian sense: "These are of two quite distinct types. Movements of a first type, P, are such that, beneficial to certain individuals, they are necessarily harmful to others. Movements of a second type, Q, are such that they are to the advantage, or to the detriment, of all individuals without exception" (§2128).

When the community stands at a "Q" point, that it can leave with resulting benefits to all individuals (thus obtaining that which we call today a "Paretian improvement"), "it is obvious that from the economic standpoint it is advisable not to stop at that point, but to move on from it as far as the movement away from it is advantageous to all" (§2129). When one of the Paretian optima P points is reached, the economist must give way to other spheres such as the political or the moral: "From the strictly economic standpoint, as soon as the community has reached a point P it has to stop" (§2129). The "P" points are the "maxima of ophelimity *for* the collective in Political Economy" (that today we call Pareto optima allocations), which may be determined "independently of any comparison between the ophelimities of different individuals" (§2130).

The "maximum utility *of* a community", impossible in Economics, is left to Sociology – notice that here Pareto uses the term "utility" and not ophelimity because society's choices are dictated on the basis of utility (that which is useful or beneficial) or on the basis of collective well-being or Public Happiness. In fact:

A government of course ... compares all the utilities it is aware of. Substantially, it does with a guess what pure economics does with scientific exactness: it makes certain heterogeneous quantities homogeneous by giving them certain coefficients.... In pure economics a community cannot be regarded as a person. In sociology it can be considered, if not as a person, at least as a unity.

(§§2131–2133)

Pareto's message is that the domain of Economics is very narrow, and therefore can say very little about the well-being or happiness of either the individual or the community, about private or Public Happiness. From this point of view, the most interesting things begin, later, in Sociology. In fact, in the second part of his life, Pareto abandoned the study of Economics and turned to Sociology. Economics as a social science was impoverished by his passage, at least from the perspective of happiness and sociality.

Wicksteed's *non-tuism*

Robinson Crusoe Economics

The work of Wicksteed is also unavoidable when tracing back the history of happiness in Economics, in particular its connections to sociality. More to the point, Wicksteed's conception of sociality had a major role in the definition of Economics as the ideal-type of anonymous and instrumental relationships. Such a methodological operation holds a great responsibility for the difficulty or incapacity of twentieth-century Economics of understanding happiness and its paradoxes.

Wicksteed occupies a high position in the ideal ranking of the greatest economists ever. His contribution to the theory of distribution (1894) is a classic in the history of economic analysis. Less emphasised and analysed by historians of economic thought is his methodology, although it has influenced the hard core of the contemporary Economics, mostly thanks to Lionel Robbins, one of his most enthusiastic followers.

Even less studied is the pillar of his economic methodology, that is the *non tuism*, a Latin expression (in English it would be pronounced "no-thouism", the Latin "*tu*" means in fact "thou"), a concept still deep-rooted in present Economics.[192]

Wicksteed was an unusual figure for an economist: a minister of the Unitarian Church, scholar of Medieval and Scholastic philosophy, theologian and translator of Dante and Thomas Aquinas.[193] His story is very peculiar: he aimed to infuse a moral outlook into neoclassical (Jevons' in particular) Economics. His theory of distribution is witness to his genuine social concern, but nobody contributed more than Wicksteed to creating an economic theory with no room for non-instrumental interpersonal relations.

With Wicksteed's *Common Sense of Political Economy*, the process of the eradication of interpersonal relations from economic analysis reached an advanced stage. Although he came from a different philosophical background (the Austrian tradition was very influential in his thought), Wicksteed reached conclusions similar to Pareto's in dealing with the interpersonal dimension in Economics.[194]

The *Common Sense of Political Economy* is the most mature and systematic exposition of Wicksteed's thought. In the *Introduction* he immediately asserts that the vast shift on economic science caused by neoclassical economists is the consequence of having based Economics on the "psychology of choice between alternatives" (Wicksteed 1933 [1910]: 2). It follows "that the general principles which regulate our conduct in business are identical with those that regulate our deliberations, our selection between alternatives, and our decisions, in all other branches of life" (1933 [1910]: 3). Then, Economics has nothing to say about wants and motives.

The *Common Sense* contains a methodology already present in the Italian Ferrara or Gossen (1981 [1854]: 54): Wicksteed starts his analysis from the behaviour of the isolated individual, Robinson Crusoe alone. Later (chapter 4), he introduces Friday: "Hitherto our examination of the administration of resources has been conducted purely from the personal or individual point of view.... We must now turn, making the momentous transition from personal to communal Economics" (Wicksteed 1933 [1910]: 127).

The most interesting part of the book can be found in chapter 5, entitled "Business and the economic nexus": here, with the praiseworthy intent of freeing economic science from egoism and hedonism, he takes away *personalised and genuine* human interactions from Economics. Indeed, in the *Introduction*, after defining Economics as the science of instrumental relations, he announces that: "the things and doings with which economic investigation is concerned will therefore be found to include ... the things a man can give to or for another independently of any personal and individualised sympathy with him or with his motives or reasons" (1933 [1910]: 4–5).

Economic relations as a game of chess

Wicksteed defines the "economic motive" as one of the worst confusions that prevented science from evolving (1933 [1910]: 163). The reasoning behind this is that many economists limited their studies to actions characterised by one particular motive, "the desire to possess wealth" (1933 [1910]: 163). The methodology of the "economic motive" (that of Pantaleoni and of most of the first marginalist economists) excludes altruism from the economic field, a serious limitation for Wicksteed, given his humanitarian and Christian ethics. Viewing Economics as *the science of human action*, he opens the economists' city walls to *all* motives (self- or other-regarding): "We are only concerned with the 'what' and the 'how', and not at all with the 'why'" (p. 165).

The economic relation is a positive-sum game: *alter* cooperates with *ego* because the relation is advantageous to both (p. 166). All positive-sum types of relations, where the other's interests are seconded as an indirect way of reaching one's own, "may be fitly called 'economic'" (p. 166). Then, having defined relations and economic conditions (pp. 168–169), Wicksteed emphasises that the methodological pillars, on which his Economics is built, are substantially different from those present "in the current treatment of Political Economy" (p. 169).

The first pillar is "that the economic relation is entered into at the prompting of the whole range of human purposes and impulses, and rests in a no exclusive or specific way on an egoistic or self-regarding basis" (p. 169). So, he can state: "It is often said or implied that the housewife, for example, is actuated by a different set of motives in her economic transactions in the market and her non-economic transactions at home; but this is obviously not so" (p. 170).

Similarly, Saint Paul would not be inspired by altruistic motives when at Aquila and Priscilla's home in Corinth, and then by egoism when he made tents – "the economic relation, then, or business nexus, is necessary alike for carrying on the life of the peasant and the prince, of the saint and the sinner" (p. 171). However, according to Wicksteed, he could not be altruistic towards *all people*, but only those "at large", that is, *external to that particular economic interaction*: "In his attitude towards himself and 'others' at large, a man may be either selfish or unselfish without affecting the economic nature of any given relation, such as that of Paul to his customers" (pp. 173–174).

A crucial passage is the following:

> As soon as he is moved by a direct and disinterested desire to further the purposes or consult the interests of those particular "others" for whom he is working at the moment ... *the transaction on his side ceases to be purely economic.*
>
> (p. 174, my italics)

In sum, for Wicksteed, Economics is compatible with any motive, including altruism. What it cannot tolerate is that the other becomes a "you" ("tu"). This is where his famous neologism comes from:

> It would be just as true, and just as false, to say that the business motive ignores egoistic as to say that it ignores altruistic impulses. The specific characteristic of an economic relation is not its "egoism" but its "non-tuism".
>
> (p. 180)

Economic relations are like a game: "It would be absurd to call a man selfish for protecting his king in a game of chess. ... If you want to know whether he is selfish or unselfish you must consider the whole organisation of his life" (p. 181). He repeats this idea in even clearer terms:

> Once more, then, if *ego* and *tu* are engaged in any transaction, whether egoism or altruism furnishes my inspiring motive, or whether my thoughts at the moment *are wholly impersonal*, the economic nature of the action on my side remains undisturbed. *It is only when tuism to some degree actuates my conduct that it ceases to be wholly economic. It is idle, therefore, to consider "egoism" as a characteristic mark of the economic life.*
>
> (p. 181, my italics)[195]

The last two phrases summarise Wicksteed's methodological project. The price paid for saving Economics from the criticism of being founded on egoism, with no room for altruism, was excluding *personalised face to face* relationships from Economics.

It is interesting to note that Wicksteed's theory of action is exactly the opposite to Pareto's, with respect to the domain of Economics. In fact, in reviewing Pareto's *Manual* (1906), Wicksteed criticised the book for having restricted the domain of Economics, which, for Pareto, makes up "a very small part of the actual phenomena of the business" (Wicksteed 1933 [1906]: 817). Pareto, according to Wicksteed, does not realise that his "curves of indifference" can cover a much greater area of human behaviour.

Economics: the realm of instrumental interactions

In Wicksteed's account, the only kind of interactions allowed within Economics definitively have an *instrumental* nature, so there is no place left for intrinsic or "expressive" motivations. This is very clear in Wicksteed's essay on "The scope and method of political economy", published in *The Economic Journal*. There, he wrote:

> [I]f a peasant adorns his ox-yoke with carving because he likes doing it and likes it when done, or if he carves a stool for his friend because he loves him and likes doing it for him and believes he will like it when done, the action is not economic; but if he gets a reputation for carving and other peasants want his work, he may become a professional carver and may carve a yoke or a stool because other people want them and he finds that supplying their wants is the easiest way for him to get food and clothes and leisure for his own art, and all things else that he desires. His artistic work now puts him into an economic relation with his fellows; but this example serves to remind us that there may be an indefinite area of coincidence between the economic and

non-economic aspects of a man's occupations and relations. That man is happy indeed who finds that in *expressing* some part of his nature he is providing for all his natural wants; or that in rendering services to friends in which he delights he is putting himself in command of all the services he himself needs for the accomplishment of his own purposes.
(Wicksteed 1933 [1914]: 773, my italics)

Wicksteed, like Pareto, requires that economic action is instrumental. Wicksteed, however, also thinks that most non-selfish behaviour is instrumental.

The most influential place where this methodology crystallised is Lionel Robbins' *The Nature and Significance of Economic Science* (1932), which – together with Pareto–Hicks–Samuelson's approach – has most influenced the epistemology of microeconomics in the twentieth century.

In the prologue to his *Essay*, Robbins explicitly recognises his indebtedness to the Austrians, Von Mises in particular, and to Wicksteed.

Economics became a matter of choices about scarce resources destined to alternative uses (Robbins 1932: 16). It is not by chance that Robbins goes back to the Robinson Crusoe metaphor, as in Wicksteed's work, but without Friday. The example of Robinson Crusoe's economy is adopted to demonstrate how even an isolated man has an economic problem (1932: 10). Thus, according to Robbins, starting from the isolated agent makes it possible to find the nature of the economic problem, since Crusoe also "has to choose. He has to economise ... This example is typical of the whole field of Economic Studies" (1932: p. 12).

Wicksteed's influence in this design is decisive, as Robbins himself recognises (Robbins 1932: ix; 1933: xxii, footnote 2). Robbins considers the chapter, "Business and economic nexus", where non-tuism is introduced, as the most important and original part of the *Common Sense*. Certainly, it is the part that influenced his method – and contemporary neoclassical Economics – the most.

Instrumental rationality and non-tuism are therefore two sides of the same coin: within the framework of instrumental rationality, *ego* establishes a relation with *alter* only *when* and *if* he needs her, and the counterpart is only seen as a means in order to achieve some goal which is *external* to the relation itself.

Wicksteed's good intention of freeing Economics from egoism and hedonism brought him to expel personalised interpersonal relations from economic enquires: the domain of economic analyses becomes that characterised from purely anonymous interactions, and is therefore instrumental. In his methodology there is surely room for any kind of relations, but only in a second moment, after the economic one: the economic relation is, in itself, anonymous and instrumental. Only in the redistribution of the surplus gained in the exchange can other personalised or *tuistic* considerations come into play.[196]

As a consequence, to Wicksteed, altruism is perfectly consistent with the absence of sympathy (intended à la Smith) within a given economic relation: the two concepts, today often confused, are, in Wicksteed's analysis, distinct. Altruism or egoism are, to him, the motivations underlying the anonymous and instrumental (non-tuistic) economic transactions.

A final consideration. There is a strong, deep and perhaps unexpected permanence of a *fil rouge* from Smith to Wicksteed passing the Cambridge tradition: *economic interactions are not the place for genuine relationships*. They are just means, although an important and civil means, for living a good life *outside* the market. Civil Happiness and economy remain two separate fields of life.

With Pareto and Wicksteed we would have brought together enough elements to understand that the turning of the century (from nineteenth to twentieth) has been the key moment of the epistemological break between neoclassic Economics and Civil Happiness.

Utilitarianism, Wicksteed and Pareto performed diverse operations, but all have converged to the same result: to expel from the economic horizon the face-to-face relationship, the "*tu*" that one faces in an economic transaction.

Wicksteed's and Pareto's move is still more fundamental than Utilitarianism with respect to the happiness–sociality–Economics nexus. In fact, the approach of the contemporary scholars working on happiness is Benthamite or Jevonsian, an approach where it is also allowed that people get happiness/pleasure from social interactions. In fact, the present Economics of happiness is a challenge to the Economics of Pareto and Wicksteed, *not to that of Jevons, Edgeworth or Pantaleoni*, to whom it is methodologically very close. And for this reason mainstream neoclassical Economics, still based on Pareto's and Wicksteed's methodology, has tremendous difficulties in understanding the interpersonal matter that is happiness. This strong continuity between Pareto's and Wicksteed's project and mainstream Economics can also be found in two of the strands of contemporary Economics that are often presented as "social" or "relational", that is, Game Theory and Becker's approach to human behaviour – as I try to suggest in the final section.

A note on the absence of the interpersonal dimension in the theory of rational choice

In this last section, I want to take a quick look at two lines of research which are both absolutely central to today's theoretical debate, and in full continuity with the historical and methodological analysis which we have followed until now. They are Gary Becker's economic approach to human behaviour and standard *Game Theory*.

Those who know Becker's School, will have found a strong assonance between his approach to human behaviour and Wicksteed's non-tuism. In the first page of his seminal paper, "A theory of marriage", a manifesto of his research project, Gary Becker wrote: "Indeed, economic theory may well be on its way to providing a unified framework for *all* behavior involving scarce resources, nonmarket as well as market, nonmonetary as well as monetary, small group as well as competitive" (1973: 814).

Much utilised in Economics today, Becker's methodology is based on the epistemological assumption that it is possible to analyse human behaviour by extending economic rationality's field of application over every intentional action in every domain, from politics to art, from religion to the family – the mere idea would have sent shivers up Pareto's spine.

Like Wicksteed, Becker had no problem including altruism in his analyses, which don't require self-interest as his studies on the family show. In fact, as Cartwright points out:

> contemporary economics provides models not just for the prices of the rights for off-shore oil drilling, where the market meets very nice conditions, but also for the effects of liberal abortion policies on teenage pregnancies, for whom we marry and when we divorce and for the rationale of political lobbies.
>
> (1999: 1)

Like Wicksteed, Becker analyses interpersonal relationships within a purely *instrumental framework* (1996). There is no place in either of his two theories for "relational goods" which need a certain dose of "non-instrumentality" to exist. Thus, it is not by chance that Ramon Febrero and Pedro Schwartz (1997) have put *in esergo* of *The Essence of Becker* Wicksteed's housewife example quoted above: there is, in fact, a clear similarity between Wicksteed and Becker.

The extension of the economic logic to a larger set of interactions – including those occurring within the family, where agents' utility functions are interrelated – has *ipso facto* overcome the necessity of assuming non-tuism. Today's economists do not have much difficulty in dealing with altruism.[197] Instead, they find intrinsic and relational elements hard to grasp, and repeatedly try to reduce them to forms of standard altruism. Thus, Becker is very close to Wicksteed when he analyses social interaction by a purely instrumental rationality: in both approaches there is no room for genuine interpersonal relationships within Economics.

The same applies to the strategic logic of conventional Game Theory: no room is left for non-instrumental behaviour. Playing the game is not in itself a source of utility; what matters are payoffs that are defined *before* the game starts and are not affected by sentiments, intentions, or fellow-feeling among players. *Alter* is not a "tu" with whom *ego* can have a personal relation, but is just a complex constraint of the latter's maximisation problem: the constraint is an "alive" maximiser facing another "alive" maximiser. As Hollis and Sugden observe, "game theory provides an elegant, universal logic of practical reason, offering much to anyone whose notion of rationality is instrumental and whose view of social world is individualistic" (1993: 32).[198] Describing Von Neumann-Morgenstern's methodology, Thomas Schelling notes how, in their world, a player "does not need to communicate with his opponent, he does not even need to know who the opponent is or whether there is one" (Schelling 1960: 105).

That interpersonal relations were not at the core of Game Theory's research programme was stated clearly by its founders, Von Neumann and Morgenstern. In the Introduction to *Theory of Games and Economic Behaviour*, commenting on the so-called Robinson Crusoe Economics, they wrote:

> The chief objection against using this very simplified model of an isolated individual for the theory of a social exchange economy is that it does not represent an individual exposed to the manifold social influences. Hence, it is said to analyse an individual who might behave quite differently if his choice were made in a social world where he would be exposed to factors of imitation, advertising, custom and so on.... Crusoe is given a number of data which are "dead"; they are the unalterable physical background of the situation.... Not a single datum with which he has to deal reflects another person's will or intention.
>
> (1964 [1944]: 10, 12)

After this statement one might expect that interpersonal elements would eventually enter economic analysis, that adding "alive" variables to the standard (or "dead") economic variables would have introduced emotions, identities and sentiments within Game Theory research programme. But it is enough to look a few lines later in the same Introduction, to realise that Von Neumann and Morgenstern were looking for something else:

> The study of the Crusoe economy and the use of the methods applicable to it, is of much more limited value to economic theory than has been assumed heretofore even by the most radical critics. The grounds for this limitation *lie not in the field of those social relationships which we have mentioned before* – although we do not question their significance – but rather they arise from the conceptual differences between the original (Crusoe's) maximum problem and the more complex problem.
>
> (1994 [1944]: my italics)

In the end, all "alive" variables bring with them is just greater complexity in calculating the maximum.[199] In doing so, Game Theory prevented itself from entering the territory of genuine human relationality. Pareto and Wicksteed, in the first half of the twentieth century, and Game Theory and Becker's methodology in the second half, have all contributed to determine the solipsistic foundation of contemporary economics, where genuine sociality is not necessary to *homo oeconomicus*'s happiness.

11 Conclusion

What can we learn from the Civil Happiness tradition?

It is quite easy to be persuaded that being happy is an achievement that is valuable, and that in evaluating the standard of living, happiness is an object of value (or a collection of objects of value, if happiness is seen in a plural form). The interesting question regarding this approach is not the legitimacy of taking happiness to be valuable, which is convincing enough, but its *exclusive* legitimacy. Consider a very deprived person who is poor, exploited, overworked and ill, but who has been made satisfied with his lot by social conditioning (through, say, religion, political propaganda, or cultural pressure). Can we possibly believe that he is doing well just because he is happy and satisfied? Can the living standard of a person be high if the life that he or she leads is full of deprivation? The standard of life cannot be so detached from the nature of the life the person leads.

(A. Sen)

In this research we have gone through more than 2,000 years of history of thought: what have we learned?

The main ambition of this book has been to show *why* contemporary economic theory no longer has the *methodological* tools for understanding the civil nature of happiness (and its paradoxes). I tried to underline some of the key reasons for explaining why twentieth-century Economics, after the work of Wicksteed and, significantly, of Pareto, this discipline has lost any connection with the terrain of Civil Happiness. Neo-positivistic philosophy, that in the first half of the twentieth century has dominated Neoclassical Economics, has determined the cultural environment where the a-civil Economics grows speedily, shaping the way of dealing with social interactions of both General Equilibrium Theory and the New Welfare Economics. The recent interest of economists for relational goods and for the interpersonal dimensions of happiness is, however, suggestive that the civil tradition in Economics is still alive.

The research has been shaped around the tension between, on the one hand, the attempt to provide evidence (both historical and theoretical) about the relational nature of happiness, and, on the one hand, to register a radical tendency by mainstream Political Economy to relegate genuine relationality *outside* the market.

Parallel to this basic tension, the research also contains an outline of another possible and honourable story – that of the civil tradition, which considers happiness as a matter of reciprocity and friendships; the market too, in this approach, intended as a form of reciprocity, can be a place for happiness, for Civil Happiness.

I see one "main lesson" from the past.

At the end of this long journey through Economics, happiness and sociality, we could have more elements for understanding why Easterlin's data about income and happiness has represented a paradox for contemporary Economics. In fact, to both Genovesi and Smith, as well as to Edgeworth or Pantaleoni, those data would probably not have looked paradoxical at all. But, during its historical development, economic theory has lost the methodological devices for understanding why more wealth can bring less happiness.

At this point, it is interesting to note that the "mainstream" explanations of the paradox of happiness – that of Easterlin, Layard, Frank, Frey and Stutzer, etc. – utilise a theoretical tool developed within the Cambridge tradition, a tradition that, as seen, was paying special attention to the distinction and connection between wealth–happiness, but, at the same time, considered genuine sociality something *external to the domain of economics.* In fact, most of the explanations of the Easterlin paradox today make use of the concept of *externality* – first developed by Marshall and Pigou – in particular *positional externality.* After the analysis of Marshall's methodology we can, perhaps, understand why the Cambridge approach to Economics is suitable for such an explanation of the paradox. At the same time, and again in continuity with Marshall, the kind of sociality implied by the concept of positional externality has nothing to do with personalised or genuine relationships of the Civil Happiness tradition: aspirations and positional treadmills can also be produced by fashion, television, "culture" in general. Family life, friendships and close relationships do not play any particular role: "Whether we like it or not, human beings are rivalrous, and it is time for mainstream economics to incorporate this key fact of human nature" (Layard 2005: 147).

In other words, the positional or aspirations theories of happiness are "social" – in the Crusoe's island example, positional competition cannot be at work – but the kind of sociality taken into account has no reference to the *relational nature* of happiness, and therefore to sociality considered as an essential direct ingredient for a good life. Like Marshall, those modern economists working on the paradox of happiness do not consider "relational goods", "the affection of friends" (in Marshall's words), economic goods – therefore, their theory of happiness can be called "positional" but *not* "relational".

In these theories, genuine sociality *is not a source of happiness.* What economics may need – I claim – is an analysis of the interaction between genuine (or non-instrumental) social interaction and subjective well-being.

Therefore, the lesson coming from "Civil Happiness" is also a general lesson addressed to Economics *tout court* (not only, then, to the field of the Economics of Happiness): genuine sociality matters in the economic domain probably more than current economic theory thinks. An economic theory more open to genuine sociality could better understand not only the "Easterlin paradox" but also those interactions (that are growing more and more in postmodern market societies) characterised by the presence of relational goods.

The best conclusion of this book is to register in current Economics, a new season of interest for the interpersonal dimension. Thanks also to the emergence of both experimental and behavioural Economics, words typical of the civil tradition are brought back to economic theories and models. Reciprocity, trust, intentions, fairness, esteem and similar concepts can be nowadays found even in the top Economics journals, showing that something new really is going on.

Also, the analysis of the specific connection between happiness and genuine sociality is developing. Kahneman *et al.* (2003), for instance, found in empirical research that in only one of 15 activities of daily living (i.e. praying) was affect balance (positive minus negative emotions) greater when people were alone rather than with others. People enjoy the other 14 activities, such as exercising, resting, commuting and working around the house, more when others were present than when they were alone.[200] In a similar line of enquiry, Meier and Stutzer (2004) find, using the German Socio-Economic Panel (GSOEP) for the period between 1985 and 1999, robust evidence that volunteers are more satisfied with their life than non-volunteers.

More in general, psychological studies offer plenty of data on the importance of relationality on happiness and life satisfaction. There has been increasing appreciation within psychology of the fundamental importance of supportive interpersonal relationships for well-being and happiness. Especially within the "eudaimonic" approach, many authors see a *universal* association between the quality of relationships and well-being: "Evidence supporting the link of relatedness to SWB is manifold. Studies suggest that, of all factors that influence happiness, relatedness is at or very near the top of the list ... Furthermore, loneliness is consistently negatively related to positive affect and life satisfaction" (Deci and Ryan 2001: 154).

Ryff *et al.* (2001) also reviewed evidence that positive relations predicted physiological functioning and health outcomes: "Central among the core criterial goods comprising optimal living is having quality ties to others. Across time and settings, people everywhere have subscribed to the view that close, meaningful ties to others is an essential feature of what it means to be fully human" (Ryff and Singer 2000: 30). In particular, Ryff and her colleagues show empirical and theoretical evidence on the strict nexus between interpersonal relationships–health–happiness: "Viewed from the standpoint of interpersonal flourishing and positive health, two key points emerge. First, studies of the beneficial and positive features of social relationships, be they secure attachments in childhood and adulthood, or loving and intimate relationships in adulthood, are rarely connected to health. Second, when health or biology has entered the picture, it is overwhelmingly on the side of negative social interaction and adverse health consequences, including an expansive array of physiological systems." (Ryff and Singer 2000: 34). Furthermore, reduction of genuine interpersonal relationships "predicted incident cardiovascular disease, decline in physical function, and decline in cognitive function" (ibid: 38).

In economic theory, the new concept of relational goods is slowly but steady emerging (Gui and Sugden 2005). Uhlaner defined them as goods that "can only be 'possessed' by mutual agreement that they exist after appropriate joint actions have been taken by a person and non-arbitrary others" (1989: 254). Relational goods are goods (in the Economics sense) which cannot be produced, consumed or acquired by a single individual, because they depend on interaction with others and are enjoyed only if shared with others. According to Uhlaner, "goods which arise in exchanges where anyone could anonymously supply one or both sides of the bargain are not relational" (1989: 255).

In research based on the data of *World Values Survey* (Bruni and Stanca 2005), we found robust evidence about the nexus between happiness and relational goods. For example, membership of a voluntary organisation – used as a proxy of relational goods – is associated to a statistically significant increase in life satisfaction. It is interesting to observe that the effect of volunteering for life satisfaction is quantitatively the same as that of moving up by *one decile* in the income scale. These results suggest that the relational component of participation to voluntary organisations, represented by the actual interaction with other people, has an independent positive effect on life satisfaction. Furthermore, time spent with the family has the largest effect on life satisfaction, and time spent with friends and with people from sport activities have positive and significant coefficients.

A last note, I am convinced that, in contemporary market societies, the idea of a sharp separation between market relations – seen as the domain of instrumental dealings – and non-market ones conceived as the realm of reciprocity and genuine sociality is not very useful for imagining a good society. Markets occupy today most of the social areas formerly covered by family, church or community. Quality of life, perhaps, could improve if we also begin to conceive of market relations as a form of friendship, or of reciprocity, and then design civil institutions that could make this possible. It is from this perspective that the tradition of Civil Happiness can still have something important to say. *Sit finis operis sed non querendi.*

Notes

Acknowledgements

1 "*Pubblica felicità* and *Economa civile* in the Italian Enlightenment", L. Bruni and P.L. Porta, *History of Political Economy*, 35, Supplement 1, 361–385, 2003; "The technology of happiness in the tradition of economic science", *Journal of History of Economic Thought*, 26, 1, 19–43, 2004; "Hic Sunt Leones: social relations as unexplored territory in the economic tradition", in B. Gui and R. Sugden (eds), *Economics and Social Interaction*, Cambridge: Cambridge University Press, 2005; "The 'happiness transformation problem' in the Cambridge tradition of Economics", *European Journal of the History of Economic Thought*, 11, 433–452, 2004; "Introduction", with L. Bruni and P.L. Porta (eds) *Economics and Happiness: Framings of Analysis*, Oxford: Oxford University Press, forthcoming.
2 "The paradoxes of happiness in economics" (March 2003); "Capabilities & Happiness" (June 2005).

Introduction

3 In this book I use expressions that are very similar: *civil, relational* (or "interpersonal relations" or "relationality"), *social* and *political*. Most of what social scientists have done in previous centuries has been an analysis of the distinctions between these basic concepts. This book has no ambition to write a new theory on this subject, but, maybe, to offer new content to the least-used of these words, namely "civil". It is useful to specify that, in what follows, I use "relational" in the sense specified by Gui and Sugden (2005), that is, "to refer to forms of human interaction in which the identity of the participants *as particular human beings* has affective or cognitive significance" (introduction). In this sense, *relational* is different from *civil*. In fact, on the one hand, there are forms of civil interactions that are not relational (i.e. contribution to a charity, commitment in NGOs); on the other, there are forms of relationships that are not civil (i.e. mafia relations). *Civil* (and *civic*) and *social* (or "sociality") refer here to the same concept, although *civil* (even more than *civic*) stresses the connection with *civil society* (and also because, in the twentieth century social has been associated, by many authors, sociologists in particular, to a plurality of concepts). As a consequence, I use civil in a sense distinguished from *political*. In the following chapters we will often discuss these expressions, with the aim of demonstrating the peculiarity of Civil Economy and Civil Happiness.

1 Happiness again

4 In general, however, these economists, and those who have followed them, were not aware of such an old tradition. Their reference points were far more recent: apart from Psychology's influence, Duesenberry's (1949) social theories of consumption, or the American Institutionalist tradition (from Veblen to Galbraith). In a parallel stream of research, the Dutch economist, Bernard Van Praag, in his doctoral thesis (1968), showed an unusual and heterodox interest in investigating wealth and well-being amidst the almost complete indifference of mainstream economists.

5 This study also offered important considerations concerning the "hopes" of people in different countries. For example, while Nigeria and the USA attributed the same value to health in relation to hope, for Nigeria, the economic factor was more important (90 versus 65) and, less obviously, Nigerians gave more weight to the family than the USA (76 versus 47).

6 In the following pages I will discuss the differences between the concepts of "happiness" and "life-satisfaction".

7 Cantril's data showed, for instance, that Cuba and Egypt were more satisfied than West Germany (1965: 258). He plotted satisfaction against the log of income and thus construed a lack of relationship.

8 A recent paper (Hagerty and Veenhoven 2003) challenges this thesis, claiming that growing GDP does go with greater happiness. Easterlin (2004) replied to this paper defending his classical thesis. In 1991 Veenhoven had already criticised Easterlin's thesis about international comparisons. He plotted the same data as Cantril, though using the same scale on both axes, and showed that the relationship follows a convex pattern of diminishing returns. A similar criticism has been put forward by Oswald (1997: 1817) and others, but the idea of a very low correlation between happiness and income growth is still the most accepted among economists working on happiness.

9 The same thesis can be found in Frank:

> When we plot average happiness versus average income for clusters of people in a given country at a given time..., rich people are in fact a lot happier than poor people. It's actually an astonishingly large difference. There's no one single change you can imagine that would make your life improve on the happiness scale as much as to move from the bottom 5 percent on the income scale to the top 5 percent.
>
> (2005: 67)

And Layard states: "Of course within countries the rich are always happier than the poor" (2005: 148).

10 Among psychologists the debate is more controversial still. Some, on the basis of data different from those of the *WVS*, challenge the correlations (also when other variables are under control) between income and happiness in general (*among* countries, *within* a country and *over time*): for a review, see Diener and Seligman (2003).

11 Obviously, the positive correlation between income and happiness among countries can derive from factors other than income: democracy, rights, health, etc. Research on the *World Values Survey* that I am currently working on (Bruni and Stanca 2005a, b) also shows a robust correlation (other variables under control) between income and happiness among countries.

12 It began with a brief article in the *American Journal of Sociology*. It was composed almost entirely of 41 graphs that demonstrated the course of a few social variables chosen as gauges of the quality of life in America during the great depression (Ogburn 1935).

13 In 1954, the United Nations nominated a commission for the task of improving the studies on living standards by defining more precisely the items which make up the *standard of living* concept as well as their indicators.

14 However, Sen's capabilities approach has been criticised for failing to provide convincing solutions for its diagnosis on the gaps in traditional theories of well-being. The HDI turned out to be crucial in development policies. According to Sen (2000), it represents the most important example of putting into operation his *capabilities approach*, which measures individual well-being on the basis of what a person is capable of doing with his goods.

15 For example, Robert Sugden writes: "Given the rich array of functionings that Sen takes to be relevant, given the extent of disagreement among reasonable people about the nature of a good life, and given the unresolved problem of how to value sets, it is natural to ask how far Sen's framework is operational" (Sudgen 1993: 1962).

16 In the "Preface to the second edition" of *Fragility of Goodness* (2001), Martha Nussbaum acknowledges a partial departure from Aristotle and a proximity to Stoic philosophy (for a sense of universal human dignity, a concept absent in Aristotle), Kant (liberty) and Rawls' (political liberalism).

17 Nussbaum's latest works propose a *normative* approach to well-being. Her theory is based on a list of fundamental capabilities, called *Central Human Functional Capabilities*, which equip human beings with the capability of *effectively* doing and being well. Though Sen shares the idea that the good life is not merely a subjective perception and that it should be measured by how people actually live, the methodological consequences of Nussbaum's response put him off:

> I certainly have no great objection to anyone going on that route. My difficulty to accepting that as the only route on which to travel arises partly from the concern that this view of human nature (with a unique list of functionings for a good human life) may be tremendously over-specified, and also from my inclination to argue about the nature and the importance of the type of objectivity involved in this approach. But mostly my intransigence arises, in fact, from the consideration that to use of the capability approach as such does not require taking that route, and the deliberate incompleteness of the capabilities approach permits other routes to be taken which also have some plausibility.
>
> (Sen 1993: 36)

18 What variables should be assessed in a national index? This will require serious discussion among scholars, as well as further research. Diener and Seligman (2003) have suggested that well-being includes positive emotions and moods (The Pleasant Life), engagement (The Good Life) and having meaning in life (The Meaningful Life).

19 "The subjective well-being index reflects the average between (1) the percentage of the public in each country that describes itself as 'very happy' or 'happy' minus the percentage that describes itself 'not very happy' or 'unhappy' and (2) the percentage placing itself in the 7–10 range, minus the percentage placing itself in 1–4 range, on the 10-points scale of life-satisfaction" (Inglehart 1996: 516).

20 Note the importance of marriage in this hierarchical model (Diener and Seligman 2003): in fact, marriage has been found to affect happiness in a significant and positive way (Diener 1984; Frey and Stutzer 2002).

21 On SWB, see also Diener and Lucas (1999), and Diener (1984).

22 Kahneman's approach to happiness is twofold: in some studies he explicitly

follows a hedonistic approach (Kahneman *et al.* (1997, 2003), but in other research (such as that with Nickerson *et al.* 2003), he reaches conclusion in line with the Aristotelian approach.

23 Ryff and others presented a multidimensional approach to the measurement of PWB that taps into six distinct aspects of human flourishing: autonomy, personal growth, self-acceptance, life purpose, mastery and positive relatedness. These six constructs define PWB (Ryff and Singer 1998). See also Keyes *et al.* (2002).

2 Explanations of the Easterlin paradox

24 Only very recently has his interest for this issue grown: see Sen 2005.

25 For a critical approach to this theory, see Lucas *et al.* (2002: 4).

26 It has to be acknowledged that Veenhoven's methodological position is different from the set-point theory. In his 1991 paper, he argued that happiness does not depend on social comparison or culturally variable wants, but rather reflects the gratification of innate human "needs"; and a few years later (1994) he rejected the set-point theory.

27 See www.eur.nl/fsw/research/happiness/prologue.htm.

28 On the basis of the distinction between objective and subjective happiness, Kahneman maintains the individual and social importance of improving the *objective* conditions of happiness, even if such improvements are not felt *subjectively*. To drive more comfortable cars or eat better food is an expression of a higher quality of life ("objective happiness", in Kahneman's terms) although, because of the hedonic and satisfaction treadmills, there can be no increase in subjective terms.

29 Similar experiments have also been reported in Layard (2005).

30 Although the paradoxes of happiness are more relevant in high-income societies, they don't have the monopoly on positional or consumer competition. Anthropologists tell us that positional competition exists in all types of societies. Even the act of giving is often another way of showing off one's high consumer level in order to reinforce one's status. In the *Theory of the Leisure Class* (1899), Veblen blamed the depersonalisation of social relations, typical of modern society, for the increase in conspicuous or positional consumption. While there are many ways to communicate one's social position in villages and small communities, consumption is the only way to say who we are in today's anonymous society. The tribe's witch-doctor earned respect for his family for generations, the mighty warrior as well, as did the person who taught one's children to read. Now the big cars and homes tell the neighbours, whom we don't know, just who we are. Goods have become almost the only means to communicate status in anonymous societies.

3 From the "civil" to the "uncivil" animal

31 In Greek philosophy there are many words for expressing the concept of what we now call happiness. In particular, the happy man is called *Makar*, *Eudaimon*, *Olbios*, or *Eutyches*. Nevertheless, in Plato, Aristotle, and also for Epicurean and Stoic philosophers, eudaimonia was by far the most used term. On this, see de Heer (1968).

32 The fact that we find these essential ideas in other cultural universes makes us think of them as an emanation from an archetype lying at the wellspring of human history. For example, Hinduism and its sacred text, *The Bhagavadgita*, is built around the idea that happiness arrives from virtue only if it is sought as an end and not as a means. The epic poem, *The Mahabharata*, also presents an idea of happiness as a by-product of non-instrumental and virtuous behaviour.

33 Elisabeth Anscombe (1958) was the first to translate eudaimonia into "human flourishing". There are some scholars who still maintain that "happiness", if qualified, translates the original meaning of eudaimonia more appropriately (Kenny 1999). In his *The Methods of Ethics*, Henri Sidgwick affirmed that "the English term Happiness is not free from a similar ambiguity". And adds, "It seems, indeed, to be commonly used in Bentham's way as convertible with pleasure" (1901 [1874]: 92). In a footnote (n. 2) he is even more explicit: "since by Stuart, as by most English writers, 'Happiness' is definitely conceived as consisting of 'pleasures' or 'Enjoyments'." The ambiguity has not diminished recently, as the philosopher Hill says: "By common opinion now, one can be happy for a few moments, then unhappy, then happy again, and so on; but the same does not hold for *flourishing as a human being*" (Hill 1999: 145).

34 Following the same line of thought, the "Aristotelian" Thomas Aquinas wrote that the *dilectatio* (pleasure) is the very *accidens* of the virtuous life. The relationship between happiness and pleasure is conceived by the Aristotelian theory in a substantially different way than by hedonism and Utilitarianism. In certain situations, in fact, happiness requires pain and sacrifice (see Veenhoven 2005).

35 Aristotle gives such essential importance to political life that he denies that children can be happy: "for this reason also a boy is not happy; for he is not yet capable of such acts, owing to his age; and boys who are called happy are being congratulated by reason of the hopes we have for them. For there is required, as we said, not only complete virtue but also a complete life" (I, 9, 1099b). Furthermore, only the free adult male can be happy.

36 Some modern Anglo-Saxon languages have kept the original meaning. In German, for instance, *glück* means both happiness and good fortune, and, in English, happiness comes from "to happen".

37 If happiness was not dependent on virtues but on good fortune (external events), then, Aristotle affirms, we could define a man as being happy only at the moment of his death, because, otherwise, events could turn against him at any second prior to that. Instead, if happiness is a life in conformity with virtue, then happiness can be dynamic yet permanent, because "we have assumed happiness to be something permanent and by no means easily changed" (NE, I, 10, 1100a).

38 This is the reason why a theory of happiness based on virtues is essentially an ethical theory.

39 Also, K. Polanyi (1957) has well illustrated that commerce and exchange depend on the needs of the *philia* or, better, on the maintenance of that reciprocal good will among its members, without which the community would cease to exist. We will find this theme at the heart of the Medieval and Humanistic reflections on civil life centred around the principle of reciprocity, in which the principle of the contract is also founded.

40 We can't help but recall *Raffaello's* masterpiece, "The School of Athens", as a splendid icon of these two souls of Greek philosophy. Plato, with *Timaeus* under his arm, pointing to the sky, expresses the contemplation of beauty in itself, while Aristotle, embracing the *Nicomachean Ethics*, indicates the *polis*, the civil life.

41 The expression "relational goods" is used by Nussbaum in a sense that is different from the use by economists today (see Gui and Sugden 2005).

42 Neera Kapur claims that the most genuine idea of friendship cannot be instrumental but is an end in itself, because, she argues, a consequentialist's motivational structure is incompatible with a disposition to one kind of friendship (1991: 483). That is the reason why a consequentialist ethics (like the Utilitarian) is not compatible with a theory of friendship, at least not in the classical

sense. The entire Ciceronian theory of friendship, later appropriated by Medieval monastic ethics (see *The Spiritual Friendship* by Aelred of Rielvaulx in the twelfth century), was based on the conviction that friendship cannot exist except among virtuous persons (*summa amiciitia proprie non est nisi inter bonos*). Thomas Aquinas called the virtue-friendship *amor amicitiae.*

43 It's not by chance, as Nussbaum remarks, that Aristotle gives particular attention to the catastrophes which can happen because of the *philia*, when he writes about catastrophes. He tries to deal with the problem by defining eudaimonia as a self-sufficient reality that is, however, dependent on other people.

44 In Aristotle's theory of eudaimonia, therefore, self-sufficiency, does not imply solitude.

45 Nevertheless, it would be too simplistic to say that Plato was not aware of the importance of civil life or of friendship (it would be enough to think of his theory of *Eros*). He saw man as a political animal, mainly because of his inability to fend for himself alone and his need to unite himself to fellow creatures (*Republic*, 369b–c). Plato gives great importance to the *polis*, to which he dedicates the *Republic* and the *Laws*. He recognises the importance of friendship and of love for reaching the truth (see *The Banquet* and *Letter VII*) as well as the importance of civil virtues, justice in particular. In any case, we can never fully understand Plato without recognising the fact that he put the individual and his *journey to reach the truth* at the centre of his metaphysical and ethical system. The relationship with the other is, above all, a means by which the individual, especially the philosopher, can reach perfection. At a certain point in his journey, one must detach himself from his fellows, take flight in solitude, and dedicate himself entirely to the search for truth alone with God alone.

46 Plato does not have a *relational* vision of the political life and the state in either the *Republic* or the *Laws.* While, in his *Politics*, Aristotle describes the origin of the state as the natural result of the single man associating himself into a family first, then with other families into a village, then with other villages into a state, Plato sees the State as an "enlargement" of the individual. He extended this vision to his theory of ethics. For example, justice has nothing to do with interpersonal relations, but is carried out when each individual, in one of the three classes, fulfils his office without interfering in that of the others. Just as the ultimate end of the individual is the good of the whole and not primarily the good of the single parts (which can be sacrificed if necessary for the good of the whole), the good of the State is the ultimate end of Plato's political vision. From here he gathers his idea of putting women and goods in common, which we read about in the *Republic*. It is an organicistic and holistic theory. It would be difficult to find a place for the relational and civic life in his *polis*. Today, we would say that Plato had a *political* vision and lacked a vision of the *civil* society.

47 See Bruni (2004c), Bruni and Zamagni (2004), Todeschini (2002).

48 The aim of the Cambridge School is ambitious: to show that the modern republicanism (the American cultural matrix in particular) was not only based on Locke's individualism, but was also deeply rooted in Civic Humanism and in Roman republicanism.

49 The Cambridge School's reading of Civic Humanism, in particular Skinner's, finds the roots of Humanism in the Middle Age and in Roman civil virtues. Whilst Baron and Garin associate the spring of Civic Humanism to the rediscovery of Aristotle's ethics in the *Quattrocento*, Skinner and his school consider Florentine Civic Humanism as an expression of an older tradition, mainly inspired by Aristotle but also by Cicero, Sallust and Seneca, that, before flourishing in Florence in the *Quattrocento*, gave life to the Italian municipalities (*comuni*) from the twelfth century onwards. It is, however, curious to note that

Hankins' book, an excellent work on Civic Humanism, ignores completely the work of Eugenio Garin.

50 Hankins (1995) challenges Baron's thesis of confining the *Quattrocento* Civic Humanism only to Tuscany, and he claims that all of northern Italy was the homeland of Civic Humanism. More in general, I think it would be wrong to confine Civic Humanism even to northern Italy alone. During the mid-1400s in central Italy, especially in the Marche and Umbria where the first *Montes Pietatis* were founded, Giacomo della Marca, Giovanni da Capestrano, disciple of Bernardino of Siena, and Bernardino da Feltre worked within the same civil direction. Giovanni Pontano was an important humanist in southern Italy, where he wrote on the civil virtues and was an important politician at the Aragon court in the mid-1400s (see Tateo 1972). There were also French and Spanish Schools, such as the School of Salamanca of the sixteenth and seventeenth centuries (see Chaufen 1999). In any case, Tuscany of the 1400s remains the ideal type for Civic Humanism.

51 Historic literature on Civic Humanism is abundant. Economic literature is nonetheless scarce, and almost all relevant literature can be still found in the volume *Wealth and Virtue*, edited by Istvan Hont and Michael Ignatief (1983). This English-language volume includes essays by Winch, Phillipson and Robertson dedicated to Smith and the Scottish Enlightenment.

52 A "first" and "second" humanism should not be taken in a strict chronological sense. B. Fazio, 1400–1457, who wrote *De viri felicitate*, is one example of the many authors who were already developing reflections during the civic period that were centred on the individual and his flight from the world.

53 Trinkaus (1965) completely missed the distinction in his study, dedicated to the idea of happiness in the Italian humanists. On the tail of the classical German tradition, he sees Humanism as a flight from the world, individualism, aestheticism, and a re-evaluation of the pleasures of modern life.

54 Coluccio Salutati, quoted in Garin (1994 [1947]: 36).

55 The title of the treatise itself, *De Avaritia* ("On avarice"), expresses a semantic shift of the category. In the height of the Medieval period, avarice was a vice, synonymous with an incorrect attitude towards wealth.

56 H. Arendt's civil philosophy has inspired the historical reading of Pococh's *Machiavellian moment*.

57 Leonardo Bruni, "Introduction" to the Italian translation of Aristotle's *Politics*, quoted in Garin (1994: 54).

58 Bernardino of Siena is perhaps the only humanist still remembered in books on the history of economic thought (see Schumpeter 1994 [1954]: 98), because of his being the first to have the intuition that the utility (*complacibilitas*) of a good should act as the measure of its value. The Scholastics thought that the "embodied labour" of a good indicated its "right price"; see Bernardino da Siena's *Prediche Volgari* (1989 [1427]).

59 Bruni translated Aristotle's *Politics* and *Nichomachean Ethics*, works which were little known even after the rediscovery of Aristotle's metaphysics by Scholastics (Aquinas in particular) and the Arabs (Averroe).

60 There was a strong, ideal tension in the civic humanists in general to take Christianity back to the purity of its origins, to re-evaluate its historical, communitarian and civic value. The classic works of Werner Sombart on the origins of capitalism brought this aspect out (1950 [1913], 1967 [1902]). He was among the first to retrace the roots of modern Economics to the Medieval period. He wrote that L.B. Alberti "canonised the doctrine of the 'holy economy' and of the 'holy household economy'" (Sombart 1967 [1902]: 258).

61 Imagining a perfect society during bad times is a phenomenon we find again in Modernity. Socialist utopian literature flourished in the climate of disappointment that followed the unfulfilled promises of the first industrial revolution.

62 Marshall, in his *Principles of Economics*, also emphasises this element in the European economic history. He quotes Westcott's *Social Aspects of Christianity:*

> The Reformation "was the affirmation ... of individuality.... Individuality is not the sum of life, but is an essential part of life in every region of our nature and our work, in our work for the part and for the whole. It is true, thought it is not the whole truth, that we must live and die alone, alone with God."
>
> (Marshall 1946 [1890]: 742–743, footnote 3)

63 For Kant, man's dominant inclination is his antisocial quality of wanting to turn everything towards his own interests, so that he expects resistance from all sides and, in turn, knows that he must tend to resist against the others (Kant 1784). A similar position is expressed by another lucid interpreter of his times: "We cannot love anything which is not related to ourselves ... only [self] interest produces friendship" (La Rochefoucauld 1993 [1678]: 44–45).

64 It seems that in Machiavelli's thought there is a latent contradiction between the civic perspective of the *Discorsi sopra la prima Deca di Tito Livio* and the *Prince*. In the former, commonly considered to be closest to Civic Humanism tradition, Machiavelli praises the "mixed constitution" that allowed Rome to maintain its republican roots (even, to some extent, during the Imperial involution). In the latter, Machiavelli makes clear his preference for a "strong" government, which he considers indispensable in a period of turmoil. Nevertheless, one can also find the same anthropological pessimism in his *Discorsi*: "Men never do good unless necessity drives them to it" (Book I, cap. 3).

65 Similar interpretations can be found in Mansfield (2000) and Rahe (2000).

66 Skinner (1999: 33 ff.) highlights the difference between fate and fortune, while philosophers of the Christian era, such as Boetio, had interpreted Fortune as *ancilla Dei*, thus harmonising her with Providence.

67 Machiavelli repeats that the goddess Fortune is attracted by the *vir*, the vir-tuos man: "*audaces fortuna juvat*" ("Fortune helps the audacious") went the ancient Latin song.

68 Therefore, I cannot but agree with the statement of P.A. Rahe who strongly contrasts Baron's and the Cambridge School's attempts to see Machiavelli in continuity with Civic Humanism.

69 We need, however, to be very cautious on this subject. Machiavelli's revolution was essentially anthropological (one may say based on social Psychology, or an early "behaviourism"), and constituted the basis for his political theory. There is in that a remarkable difference with Hobbes: the power conferred to the Leviathan by the people seeking protection, whereas in the case of Machiavelli it is the Prince who legitimates himself by offering protection to the subjects. The *Leviathan* is the product of a basic social need for security, and a result of a philosophical (pessimistic) vision of humanity; the *Prince*'s practical function is more about a "technique of power", more about the deliberate use of fear by the political actors to achieve and maintain power. I would thank Pasquale Ferrara for this note.

70 The thesis is taken again in the *Leviathan* (Part II, cap. XVII):

> It is true that certain living creatures, as bees and ants, live sociably one with another (which are therefore by Aristotle numbered amongst political creatures), and yet have no other direction than their particular judgements and appetites; nor speech, whereby one of them can signify to another what he thinks expedient for the common benefit: and therefore some man may

perhaps desire to know why mankind cannot do the same. To which I answer. First, that men are continually in competition for honour and dignity, which these creatures are not; and consequently amongst men there ariseth on that ground, envy, and hatred, and finally war; but amongst these not so. Secondly, that amongst these creatures the common good differeth not from the private; and being by nature inclined to their private, they procure thereby the common benefit. But man, whose joy consisteth in comparing himself with other men, can relish nothing but what is eminent.

We are actually in the opposite direction than that traced by Civic Humanism.

71 Text from eServer.org.
72 The Salamanca School (sixteenth century) inspired by scholasticism and Jesuits, strongly claimed the natural sociability of human beings: "it is in fact essential to man that he should never live alone" (Francisco di Vitoria); "a time when men wandered about in the manner of wild animals ... it is quite impossible that there could ever have been such a time" (Bellarmine) – quotations from Skinner (1978: vol. 2, 157).
73 More to the point, individuals gain security, whereas Hobbes' theory gains equality.
74 It is collected in the second volume of the *Fable of the Bees* (final edition).
75 See Bruni and Sugden (2000), section 2.

4 Public Happiness

76 See Farnie (1962).
77 See Hirschman (1977).
78 In 1826, the outstanding Italian philosopher Antonio Rosmini wrote: "The defect of economists is that they reduce to riches all the happiness of the state." The error, according to him, does not consist in working on wealth instead of happiness, because as he says, "the aim of any particular science has to have its limits" (2003 [1826]: 100). The error lies actually in transforming the means (wealth) to the end (happiness). In keeping with the Italian tradition, Rosmini sees happiness, Public Happiness in particular, as the *true* end (2003 [1826]: 102 ff.).
79 For more on Pietro Verri, see Bruni and Porta (2003).
80 Besides those already quoted, authors writing on "Public Happiness" in Italy between the seventeenth and eighteenth centuries included the Lombard Isidoro Bianchi (1779) and the Piedmontese Giambattista Vasco (1769), as well as many more minor authors.
81 According to Kant, action is moral if it conforms to universal moral rules. Thus, the categorical imperative can suggest behaviour that goes against personal happiness. Although Kant was directly fending off the view of happiness held by the incipient Utilitarian and sensist philosophies, he was also critical of the Aristotelian eudaimonian ethics because it only considered personal happiness as the motivation for taking action. According to Kant, in other words, Aristotle's error (and that of all eudaimonistic ethics) is that it did not distinguish between one's own happiness and ethical universal considerations: to Kant, as is well known, morality has to do with the "justice" (that is an interpersonal matter) and not primarily with the "goodness".
82 Hegel's *Philosophy of Law* represents an important passage in the interpretation of civil society in modernity. In a reductive interpretation of Smith and the Scottish Enlightenment, he made the *civil society* coincide with *commercial society* and distinguished the civil or commercial society from the State. The

civil becomes synonymous with the economic, intended as the place for individual interests and instrumental relationships. In the civil society, relationships between individuals are purely instrumental, characterised by self-interest because everyone is an end in himself and everything else is nothing (1979 [1821], §182). The founding principle of the civil/economic becomes "the egotistic end" (§183), and civil society becomes the arena of the private interests of everyone against everybody (§289). Hobbes' natural state of *bellum omnium contra omnes* wedded the civil society. For Hegel, this is the reason why the civil society is neither the family (reciprocity being the founding principle), nor the State (which is an external necessity with respect to both the family and the civil society) (§261). Hegel's interpretation of the civil – throughout the Marxian vehicle, and the reactions against it – is very important in order to understand the eclipses of civil society in modern political thought, as distinguished from both private and political sphere.

83 It should be noted that Jefferson's expression, "pursuit of happiness", that by the Historical Cambridge School is seen as an expression of a humanistic root in the American constitution, has actually very little to do with the tradition of Public Happiness. It is more similar to French hedonism than to the "good social living" of the Neapolitans. It may be curious to note that Jefferson, like Wicksteed afterwards, was a member of the Unitarian Church, which did not believe in the "social" Trinity.

84 The "Organicism" is the political vision of the whole antiquity. The most important pre-Christian reference point of the organic vision of society is the *apologus* of the Roman Menenius Agrippa who tells the allegory of the belly by which the patricians are the entry point through which all nourishment for plebes and for the body of Rome enters (Livy ii, 32, see also W. Shakespeare's *Coriolanus*, Act I). The Christian reference is Saint Paul's vision of the Church as the "body of Christ". The entire medieval *Christianitas* was conceived as a body with concordance of interests among the different classes and persons.

85 An economist among the first to question the organic vision of society, and in contrast with Smith's vision, is Thomas Malthus. In his *Essay on the Principle of population* he wrote: "the wealth of a society may increase (according to his definition of 'wealth') without having any tendency to increase the comforts of the labouring part of it" (Malthus (1966) [1798]: 304).

86 See Winch (1978).

87 It would be incorrect to state that in Smith's *WN* there is no reference to the conflict between the different classes, i.e. between undertakers and employees, or between landlords and the State, but these conflicts are regarded as the "pathology" of the system, and not as the normal situation.

88 First Manuscript, "Wages of labour", chapter 1. A number of Marxists are probably still convinced today that this is a good answer to Smith's overoptimistic bent.

89 In fact, Genovesi sometimes also uses the expression "private" and "common" happiness, where *common* is used as synonymous for *public*.

90 The Pius XII papal encyclical letter, "Mystici Corporis" ("Mystic Body", 1943), that defined the Church as an organic society, refers to "the inferior members" and "higher members" of the same body, the Church (§57).

91 Quoted in Frigo (1988: 108).

5 Genovesi and the Neapolitan School of Civil Economy

92 Bartolomeo Intieri was himself a disciple of Galileo and Torricelli and a representative of the Florentine tradition of Civic Humanism. Intieri had

studied Mathematics and Physics, and far more than anything else, he became prominent as an inventor of machines for agriculture. Following the vision of Civic Humanism, he stuck to the idea that sciences must be of practical and civil utility, rather than objects of mere intellectual speculation: "I do not appreciate those who spend their whole time in reading Geometry and Arithmetic without caring to see the fruit of their labours" (quoted in Venturi 1962: 553). Therefore, in Naples he spent his whole energy and talent in inventing new machines, for example for the cultivation and storage of grains. He believed science should lead to technical improvement, which in turn is conducive to social improvement through reforms and the promotion of Public Happiness. To Intieri, mechanics and technology *were both tools for Public Happiness*. The seat, where this intellectual and practical evolution took place, was the "Accademia delle scienze", founded in Naples in the 1732 by Celestino Galiani (another key figure in Neapolitan culture) and Bartolomeo Intieri. The *Accademia* was, at the same time, the place of the diffusion of Galilean, Lockean and Newtonian ideas. It also became the workshop where technical experiments were conceived and realised for the improvement of the arts and the economy of the Kingdom of Naples. The idea of linking together in a chain of continuity Civil Economy and mechanics was mainly due, in Naples, to the Florentine Intieri – and the Chair that was established by him in 1754 in Naples is, also, an icon of Intieri's cultural approach. It is interesting to report that the man he chose to be the first incumbent of the new Chair, Antonio Genovesi, was known as a philosopher and he was certainly *not* the best reputed economist in Naples: at the time, Naples hosted Broggia, and, above all, Ferdinando Galiani, the author of *Della Moneta*. The choice of Genovesi was, however, in line with Intieri's cultural vision and political philosophy.

93 In this book I freely interchange the expressions "school" and "tradition", well aware that not all agree with such usage.

94 Antonio Genovesi was born on 1 November 1713 in Castiglione (today called "Castiglione del Genovesi"), a small town near Salerno, into a noble family in decline. He entered the ecclesiastic life at an early age and, in 1737, was ordained into the priesthood. In 1738 he moved to Naples where he studied philosophy and attended lessons by Vico, whose thinking remained a constant source of inspiration. Founding his own private school in 1739, he taught philosophy and theology. In those years, he became acquainted with Celestino Galiani (the uncle of Ferdinando, the economist) who helped him obtain a university professorship in metaphysics, in 1741 and, later in 1745, in Ethics. Already by 1743, he had published the first part of his *Elementa Metaphysicae*. In the meantime, he became friends with another important author of "Public Happiness", Ludovico Antonio Muratori, and become part of Bartolomeo Intieri's intellectual circle in Massa Equana, a cultural and scientific environment where Genovesi's methodology grew and was nurtured, up to the transformation, as he said, from metaphysics to Economics, from "metafisico to mercadante". In 1753 he wrote a manifesto for a reform programme for his Kingdom: *Discorso sopra il vero fine delle lettere e delle scienze* (*Discourse Over the True End of Letters and Sciences*, republished in *Scritti*, from which I quote), and in 1757 a *Ragionamento sulla fede pubblica* would later become an important chapter (Vol. II, chapter 10) of the *Lezioni*. Between 1765 and 1770 Genovesi published his most important works: *Lezioni di commercio o sia di economia civile* (*Lectures in Civil Economy*, the first edition 1765 (Volume I) and 1767 (Volume II): in the present text indicated as *Lezioni*), *Logica per gli giovanetti* (*Logic for the Youth*, 1766), *Diceosina o sia della filosofia del giusto e dell'onesto* (*Diceosina, that is the Philosophy of the Just and Honest*, 1766:

indicated as *Diceosina*) and *Scienze metafisiche* (*Metaphysical Sciences*, 1767). All of these works have yet to be translated into English. The *Lezioni* were published in different editions from 1765 to 1770, on the basis of a still-unpublished manuscript of his lectures in Naples, *Elementi di commercio* (1757–1758). The first Neapolitan edition was reprinted in Milan (1768) and later in Bassano (Venice) in 1769, with few variations. Genovesi himself republished a second edition of the *Lezioni* in Naples (first volume 1768, second volume 1770), with variations with respect to both the first Neapolitan edition and the Milanese–Bassano edition. In 2005 the important critical edition of the *Lezioni* has been published thanks to M.G. Perna, which reproduces the second Neapolitan edition, with indications of the variations with respect to the first Neapolitan edition and to the Milanese one. This critical edition also embodies the manuscript of the *Elementi di Commercio*. All quotation of Genovesi's *Lezioni* are from this critical edition.

95 His economic and philosophical works made a remarkable impact in Spain, Portugal and Argentina.

96 The labelling of Genovesi as a "mercantilist" was basically due to his defence of domestic commerce and a certain diffidence towards international trade.

97 Also in his *Logica* (1766) he used the expression "Economia Civile" (Chapter 5, XLIX).

98 Edoardo Baviera, *True Christian political and economic method for princes, knights, citizens, and for every person in any condition*, written in the seventeenth century (quoted in Frigo 1988: 89).

99 There are various reasons for the decrease in the value of civil life in Latin Europe and the return to the land. The shifting of the economic and commercial axis from outside the Mediterranean basin, following the discovery of the Americas, is one. The reaction of the Catholic Counter-Reformation to the Protestant theological and political theories was certainly another factor. In particular, as a reaction against the Lutheran ecclesiology that conceived the Church as a *congregatio fidelium*, the restatement of the Catholic Church as a "visible" and "unequal" society founded upon the hierarchical principle was strong (see Skinner 1978: vol. 2, chapter 5). This "hierarchisation" of the Catholic Church has characterised the Latin Europe up to the Vatican Council II (1965), when the definition of Church as an "unequal and hierarchical society" gave way to "people of God"– a conception of the Church based on the priority of the "communion principle". In other words, after Civic Humanism had affirmed the equality of citizens and the importance of freedom, including economic liberty, social and political theories typical of unequal societies returned with great strength in the 1600s and 1700s.

100 The vision of the leading Italian economist of the nineteenth century, Francesco Ferrara, was decisive, even if he was not the only one to decree the end of the Italian civil tradition. It was he who indicated France and England as the nations of economic science and considered the Italian classical writers as easily-to-be-forgotten, minor players. After Ferrara, the leaders of the Italian School, Pareto, Pantaleoni, Barone, De Viti de Marco, and their followers, Ricci, Amoroso, De Pietri Tonelli, etc., threw themselves into the international debate and showed no interest in standing up for an Italian classical tradition. In the 1900s, a few economists like Luigi Einaudi, Rabbeno, Cusumano and Luzzatti felt closer to that civil tradition. Today, scholars are speaking again about Civil Economy and so returning to the authors of the Italian classical tradition (see Bruni and Zamagni 2004). See also Fernandez Lopez (2004).

101 Genovesi's teaching influenced the economists who took his Chair after him well into the 1800s, and his thinking inspired practically all of the economists

in southern Italy (Di Battista 1990: 46). Although they never reached the philosophical and methodological weight of Genovesi, Giacinto Dragonetti's work, *Sulle virtù e sui premi* (*On Virtues and Prizes*, 1787 [1766]), and Ludovico Bianchini's *Della scienza del bene vivere sociale* (*On the Science of Good Social Living*, 1855), continued Genovesi's approach to unite "civil life" and "Public Happiness".

102 Genovesi uses the expression "felicità civile" in his *Lezioni* (I, chapter 2, §11, p. 38).

103 Filangieri, in his *Scienza della Legislazione (Science of Legislation)*, tried to go beyond this theory of Montesquieu, by affirming that every form of government requires virtue and love for the public good (Book 1, chapter 12).

104 This is an indication that it is not so easy to call Genovesi a mercantilist.

105 See Ruggiero (2000).

106 Genovesi was probably also influenced by John Cary: see Reinert (2005).

107 An explanation of this can be Genovesi's reading of Hume's *History of England*, in 1765 (see *Scritti*, p. 188) – although Genovesi was familiar with Hume's philosophical works much earlier.

108 The last three lines – from "Luxury comes..." – of the above quotation are not present in the first edition, but added in the second revised Neapolitan edition of 1768 (volume I) and 1770 (volume II).

109 This is an idea that shares some similarities with the mechanism of the "circulation of elites", elaborated as a formal sociological theory at the end of the nineteenth century by Pareto, Mosca and Michels: see, for instance, Pareto (1964 [1916], §§2026 and ff.).

110 All words in bold are added by Genovesi in the second Neapolitan edition of the *Lezioni* (1768). It is interesting to note that all additions are expressions of a more positive attitude towards the virtuous effects of luxury that Genovesi developed over the years.

111 A few years later, Genovesi was clear in acknowledging that *private interests don't always or naturally become public virtue*: "The profit of the merchant has not to be confused with that of the State. The merchant can get rich, and the State ruins" (Genovesi, *Lezioni*, I, chapter 17, §9, footnote "b") – an idea that also appears many times in Smith's *Wealth of Nations*.

112 "*Id curarunt in nostra Italia maximus Galilaeus et alii praeclarissimi physici, qui antequam methodus geometrica in physicam importaretur, innumera et maxima naturae phaenomena hac ratione explicarunt*" (G.B. Vico, *De Antiquissima Italorum Sapientia*, 1710, quoted in Amerio 1947: 58).

113 The same concept was expressed by another civil philosopher in Naples, a contemporary of Vico, Paolo Mattia Doria, in the very first sentences of his *Della Vita Civile* (1710): "In order to make up for this rather impossible goal in men to possess all the virtues and properties, while each possesses only a few, [Providence] congers up the invention of the civil society" (*Introduction*).

114 On the role of providence in social order, see the classical work of J. Viner (1972).

115 Vico is certainly the most "civil" of modern philosophers: see Botturi (1991).

116 The direct influence of Vico upon Genovesi and other economists is not easy to spot. There were philosophical differences between them (i.e. the role of reason in actions). Nevertheless, Vico was a universal reference point in Naples in eighteenth-century philosophy.

117 This section draws on Bruni and Sugden (2000, §4).

118 *Buon costume*, literally "good custom", has no simple translation into English. The closest equivalent is probably "common decency". It signifies customary standards of acceptable or decent behaviour; it is that basic level of virtue which everyone is entitled to expect of everyone else.

119 In this previous version, he calls the catechism "of the common reason".
120 The emphasis on dispositions is made still clearer when, in revising a few years later the catechism for the *Lezioni*, Genovesi inserts a new proposition between those formerly numbered 8 and 9, which declares that "It is not possible for men to be mutually persuaded of the virtue of their fellows if they are not really virtuous. In fact the simulation of virtue is sooner or later found out" (*Lezioni*, II, chapter 10, §10, p. 140). This revision seems to be Genovesi's response to the classical problem that Hume presents in the person of the "sensible knave"; like Hume, Genovesi responds to the problem by arguing that our interests (happiness) are better served by settled dispositions towards trustworthiness than by instrumental reasoning at the level of actions.

6 Happiness as reciprocity

121 On this point, we note the strong assonance with Smith, who – as we will see – saw happiness as being an immanent end which God had placed in human nature, rather than an intentional aim of human action.
122 Genovesi drew many of his ideas on public faith from Paolo Mattia Doria's *Vita Civile.*
123 Mario Francesco Pagano, another great figure in Naples, explicitly moved in the same direction as Genovesi:

> More than any other animal, man is made for society, and his natural state is sociable.... Thus, that horrid beast, naked and alone, covered only with hair, running through the woods armed with a long club and belting out horrible roars, by indicating his stupid and senseless face, the profound dullness of soul, does not deserve the name of man. The savage is only a sketch of a man.

And with clear reference to Aristotle's famous phrase that only beast or a god can live without society, he concludes, "When solitary man is sufficient onto himself, when he can supply his own needs, either knowledge is of no use ... or is himself or a god" (Pagano, in Actis-Perinetti 1960: 43–44).
124 It has to be noted that Genovesi's idea of virtues is complex. In general, in his economic writings, "virtues" always means "civil virtues" (not individual ones such as courage, or temperance). In his comment to Montesquieu's *Eprit del lois*, for instance, he wrote: "that word virtue is ambiguous.... I call virtue the soul disposed to not invading and not violating the others' rights" (1777, I, p. 122, footnote 3). And again: "The virtue, that is to be content with our rights without invading those of others" (1777, I, p. 123, footnote 4). Or: "The good citizen who is happy with his rights does not invade those of the others" (1777, I, p. 129). It is an idea of virtue, therefore, very close to the concept of justice, then an interpersonal and civil matter.
125 Vico's anthropology is based on the idea that "homo est natura socialis" (*De Uno*, quoted in Botturi 1991: 350), and his egotistical passions (both powerful and operative) do not change his sociable nature and his need to relate with others: on this point as well as a comparison with Hobbes, see Botturi (1991: 343 and ff.).
126 As is well-known, the concept of contrasting *forces*, although present in Galileo and in other scientists at the time, only with Newton would become the key element of mechanics (Newton's third law claims that for every force there is an equal and opposing one).
127 A very similar thesis can be found in Hutcheson, and it is not esoteric to suppose an influence of the Scottish philosopher on Genovesi – given the

latter's acquaintance with Scottish moral philosophy. In fact, in Hutcheson's early *Inquiry into Our Ideas of Beauty and Virtue*, of 1725, we read: "The universal benevolence toward all men, we may compare to that principle of gravitation, which perhaps extends to all bodies in the universe; but increase as the distance is diminished, and is stronger when bodies come to touch each other" (quoted in Silver 1990: 1489).

128 Ferdinando Galiani had explicit recourse to Newtonian gravitational theory: as, in Newton's mechanics, planets remain in their orbits because of the action of gravitational law, the same is true in economic transactions, where "love of money, namely the desire of living happy, is in the man exactly what gravity is to physics (1803 [1751]: 91). In Galiani's methodological approach, there is the conviction that love for money is as exact and scientific as the law of gravity. In particular, love of money is the equivalent to the desire of being *happy*. Galiani did not specify which kind of happiness he had in mind, but it is very probable that he meant the hedonist happiness, as the Utilitarian and hedonist economists will do later. The "Public Happiness" of Genovesi and the Neapolitan School was not a central element in Galiani who cannot rightly be considered a representative of Naples' Civil Economy. Finally, as the law of gravity is the cornerstone of the new mechanics, and all the other laws can be derived from it, the same holds that laws of economic theory can be deduced from the economic principle – as one century later the Italian marginalist economist Maffeo Pantaleoni wrote (1889), basing his theory on Galiani and Genovesi among others. In fact, in *Della Moneta* we find the definition of the economic principle (quoted above), which will become the first rule of Italian neoclassical pure Economics.

129 Another great figure of Neapolitan and European Enlightenment, Mario Francesco Pagano, was inspired by the same interpretation of Newtonian theory. He also applied it by analogy to the dynamics of human Psychology and sociality in his "Saggi Politici" (*Political Essays)*: "Mothers and sources for all the others, the two original and central forces are attraction and repulsion; the first is called centripetal because it tends towards the centre, the other has the contrary effect and is called centrifugal. Now, beings are generated by the concentrative force…" (Pagano, in Actis-Perinetti 1960: 39).

130 Nevertheless Genovesi doesn't embrace the anthropological thesis, like the Platonist Shaftesbury, that man is fully altruistic by nature. Reciprocity is an anthropological dimension more basic than altruism. In *Lezioni* he writes:

> I've yet to see a fully disinterested man. He would have to be less than a man; because he would have to be without any of the principle instincts common to human nature: 1. The instinct that makes him preserve his existence. 2. The instinct that makes him seek comfort. 3. The instinct to distinguish himself. Now such a man would be an animal like the mammoth that is so sought after by the Muscovites, or like the Egyptian Sphinx, or the Arab Phoenix.
>
> (*Lezioni*, II, chapter 13, §25, pp. 206–207, footnote)

131 For more on human and animal sociality in the history of thought, see Laurent (2003).

132 Filangieri adds a phrase that would be useful in a modern study on Economics and the quality of life: "An assiduous work, a life difficult to preserve, is never a happy life. This is the miserable condition of Sisifo. No instant was for him, because he had to give them all to his work" (2003 [1780]: 12).

133 With such a vision of good living, Bianchini criticised J.B. Say, who saw in "the greatest production and consumption" the "protruding and highest side

of civilisation". In fact, "we cannot consider ourselves to be all the more civilised by reaching ever higher levels of production and consumption ... because the material side is the less important side, and [such a consideration] leaves behind all those things that together form the most elevated part, namely, the most noble of the nation's moral and civil life" (1855: 12).

134 In the various editions of the *Lezioni*, the last chapter of the second volume, "Ragionamento intorno all'uso..." is not numbered: for this reason I call this chapter simply "Ragionamento".

135 This statement serves to confirm that "Public Happiness" is a dominant theme in Genovesi's entire work, even if he never made "Public Happiness" the object of a specific book, as his "friend Muratori" did (*Lezioni*, II, *Ragionamento*, §34).

136 The theme of the "reward of virtues" is central in the Neapolitan culture. Giacinto Dragonetti dedicated a treatise to "On Virtues and Prizes" (1766), a treatise to which – according to Benedetto Croce – "Genovesi gave more than a hand" (Genovesi, *Scritti*: 205, footnote 5).

137 P.M. Doria, *Della vita civile*, quoted in Giarrizzo (1985: 324).

138 The textbooks of basic economic courses give the "malaise" which people feel when seeing the poor along their roads as one of the explanations of altruism (contribution to public good). But, at a more macro level, what the world (the western in particular) is experiencing today with terrorism says a lot in this regard.

139 In Dante's *Purgatorio*, we find a theory on love and happiness similar to Genovesi's. Virgil explains to Dante that, in love, the usual economic laws ("by companionship each share is lessened") do not apply; it happens, instead, exactly the opposite: "For there, as much the more as one says Our, So much the more of good each one possesses, And more of charity in that cloister burns." This is one of the most beautiful ideas of what today we call "relational goods" – I am indebted to my colleague and friend Luigi Giusso (1998) for this discovery. But Dante, astonished by the functioning of such an unusual law, asks his guide Virgil: "How can it be, that boon distributed, The more possessors can more wealthy make Therein, than if by few it be possessed?" (*Purgatorio*, XV, 61–63). Virgil suggests he considers the characteristic of Christian love which "So much it gives itself as it finds ardour. So that as far as charity extends, O'er it increases the eternal valour" (*Purgatorio*, XV, 70–72). The difference between private/material goods and love is that love's value grows the more it is used, as with all virtues. Mutually giving and sharing love, it multiplies as in a trick of mirrors: "And the more people hitherward aspire, More are there to love well, and more they love there, And, as a mirror, one reflects the other" (*Purgatorio*, XV, 73–75). Genovesi often quotes Dante in his own works.

7　Adam Smith: sociality outside of the market

140 See Silver (1990: 1481).

141 Todorov (1998) maintains that Smith inherited the importance of the "gaze of others" from Rousseau, whom he knew from the mid-1750s.

142 For example, Galiani writes in *Della Moneta*: "among all the passions which appear in the human soul, none is more vehement and strong in moving man than the desire to distinguish himself and be superior among others" (1803 [1751]: 9).

143 In this thesis we find the same basic idea that is still inspiring the current theories on positional consumption, from Veblen to Frank.

144 On the difference between Hume and Smith's concept of *Sympathy*, see Fontaine (1997); see Hollis (1998) for a different interpretation.

145 Fontaine (1997) brought out how Smith's *sympathy* is *other-oriented*, and distinguished it from the modern empathy, that is an ethically neutral concept that indicates putting oneself in another's shoes without altruistic or egotistic considerations.

146 Francis Hutcheson, in *Remarks upon the Fable of the Bees* (1750), writes in the first page:

> There is no mortal without some love towards others, and desire of the happiness of some other persons as well as his own. Men naturally perceive something amiable in observing the characters, affections and tempers of others, and are struck with a harmony in manners, some species of morality, as well as with a harmony of notes. They are fond of the approbation of each other, and desirous of whatever either directly procures approbation and esteem, or, by a confused association of ideas, is made an evidence of any valuable ability or kind disposition. Wealth and power are in like manner desired, as soon as we observe their usefulness to procure any kind of pleasures.

147 As a young professor in Glasgow in 1757, Smith reviewed the *Discourse on the Origin of Inequality Among Men* for the *Edinburgh Review*.

148 For a critical analysis, see Bruni and Sugden (2000), on which the following pages are based.

149 At one point, for example, Smith discusses the social effects of the proliferation of small religious sects. In this discussion, he assumes that the main motive for moral behaviour is our desire for the approval of others. Thus, moral behaviour is sustained by the value of reputation, which in turn depends on there being a network of associations, so that contraventions of morality become generally known. By providing networks of association in anonymous cities, religious sects promote "regular and orderly" morals among the common people (*Wealth of Nations*, pp. 795–796). The logic of this analysis is very similar to that of the modern theory of social capital, but with the additional feature that networks of association provide channels for the transmission not only of information, but also of approval and disapproval.

150 This section and the following are based on Bruni and Porta (2005a).

151 He adds: "we rarely view it in this abstract and philosophical light" (IV, 1, 9).

152 We have to avoid getting confused by some sentences, also present in Smith's works, that seem to admit that friendships also operate in economic environments and not just in the private or family spheres, such as the following: "Colleagues in office, partners in trade, call one another brothers; and frequently feel towards one another as if they really were so" (*TMS*, VI, 1, 15). Here Smith is describing the action of sympathy as a general anthropological mechanism operating in all kinds of ordinary environments. Furthermore, it is most probable that in that passage Smith is referring to relationships between partners, not to people who are *trading with one another*. Notwithstanding, in the following years, his vision of the market as a separate domain of life based on a special logic became more and more the dominating methodology of his social system, as it emerges fully in the *WN*.

8 The Cambridge civil tradition

153 In any case it is necessary to note that Malthus did not follow the "Public Happiness" tradition in his own economic theory. The object of his research was wealth, its distribution in particular, not happiness, even if the theme evidenced here is always present in his writings (see in particular the first chapter of his *Principles of Political Economy*).

154 For Ricardo the criterion of demarcation was constituted by the "laws for distributing wealth". For Mill and most classical economist followers of Smith, it was "wealth", and for the French Bastiat it was "exchange", and so on.

155 In this regard, there would be much to say about the power of attraction that the paradigm of physics held over economists in the second half of the nineteenth century, such as Jevons, who saw it as *the* paradigm of every science. Only recognising quantitative and measurable variables, the physics paradigm determined the methodological framework for the marginalist revolution at the end of the nineteenth century.

156 Something similar to what Hirschman (1996) calls "commensality".

157 We saw in Chapter 1 how the comparison between the different nations' well-being are today based on indicators embodying the aspects that Malthus threw out.

158 The same thesis is present in Pigou (1920, chapter 1). For Marshall and his school the domain of Economics is determined by the *strength* of man's motives – "not the motives themselves" – strength that "can be approximately measured by the sum of money" (Marshall 1946 [1890], p. 15).

159 The first name that comes to mind is Edgeworth (1881: 53): see Collard (1978).

160 What represented, instead, a real step forward with respect to English classical writers, was Marshall's analysis of wants. Many leading neoclassical economists of the first generation, such as Menger (1871, chapter 1, §1), Jevons (1870, chapter 3), or Pantaleoni (1898, chapter 3), in emphasising subjective and psychological elements in the economic life, in focusing then on *people* rather than *things*, brought back to the attention of economists the theme of *wants*, which at that time was resting, forgotten, in the works of some thinkers of the classical tradition (from Scholastic philosophers to Genovesi). For these economists, the psychology of wants was an essential part of Economics. In this way wants became (if only for a short while) the *bridge* between the interpersonal dimension and the analytical content of Economics. In fact, in order to deal with wants, economists must shift their attention from the isolated individual agent (Robinson Crusoe-like) to the agent embedded in a social environment, given the fact that most of our wants are generated by interactions with others. "To know which sentiments of soul, which faculties of mind … push man to deliberately modify the forms of the world in which he lives" (Pantaleoni 1925: I, 11): this was a common subject in the first "continental" marginalist synthesis. The early neoclassical economists hoped to develop an analysis of demand which could explain how human wants are formed and vary, calling for psychological and interpersonal explanations. Marshall was well aware of these recent trends in Austria and Germany, and in particular of the great emphasis "continental" economists put on wants and their social formation. In fact, these authors occupied an important place in his *Principles*, where *demand* and *consumption* are central. Marshall's theory of wants is also centred on the thesis that economic activity is performed in society, so the creation and modification of wants are *interpersonal matters*. "Desire for distinction", "emulation", "desire for excellence" (Marshall, 1946 [1890]: 87 ff.) were considered by Marshall among the most powerful determinants of wants, and therefore of consumer demand. At the same time, he included among the tasks of Economics *just* an "elementary analysis" of the theory of wants: "though it may have its beginning within the proper domain of economics, it cannot find its conclusions there, but must extend far beyond" (1946 [1890]: 90–91). In a footnote (p. 91), he adds that a profound analysis of wants, as was conducted by continental economists, "is a task not without interest" (he refers explicitly to Menger). Nevertheless "the rigid boundary which English

writers have ascribed to their science has excluded such discussions": for him, the call for continuity with English tradition was therefore stronger.

161 Menger too was very explicit in his *Manual*: despite his general statement that "goods" are all things capable of satisfying humans wants (1871, §1), the father of the Austrian School then denies that "happiness, well-being, love, friendship" are "goods", and calls them instead "free manifestations of personality" (1871, footnote 1). The explanation of this methodological choice is related to the "materiality" of goods: to him economic goods are "things", commodities (1871). The same conclusion, although starting from different epistemology and methodology, was reached by Marshall.

162 The same concept is restated at the beginning of chapter 2 (p. 14).

163 Marshall's well-known disagreements with hedonism and Utilitarianism distanced him from his colleague at Cambridge, the Utilitarian philosopher H. Sidgwick (see Groenewegen 2003).

164 See Groenewegen (1994, cap. XV; 2003).

165 Even his choice to use the word "good" (in the singular) instead of "commodity" in his *Principles* indicates the "goodness" he attributed to the economic sphere, as well as to its role in human flourishing. As we have seen, the Latin application of the word "bonum" or "good" to economical affairs goes back to Scholasticism and even before (the juridical ancient schools).

166 Pigou used the term "welfare" instead of "well-being", yet the meaning, in fact, remained the same until Sen made a distinction between the two terms years later.

167 This methodological attitude was also developed by Keynes, in particular in his social philosophy writings, such as *Economic Perspectives of our Grandchildren* (Keynes 1930), where he distinguished between "basic" and "relative" needs: to Keynes, economic or material growth can satisfy the basic needs, but the relative ones have only a tiny and indirect connection with income.

9 Happiness becomes pleasure

168 For more on these themes, see Bruni (2000).

169 In the next chapter I will briefly consider Bentham's ideas on happiness and pleasure.

170 It must be noted that Utilitarianism was never a single doctrine. According to Sidgwick, the expression Utilitarianism "is applied to several distinct theories, having no necessary connection with one another, and not even referring to the same subject-mother" (1901 [1874]: 411).

171 Mill thinks that freedom is *part* of well-being – a position, today, very close to that of Dasgupta (2001). It is a stand also similar to Sen, although Sen insists on treating well-being and freedom as *distinct* concerns. On this tension between Mill and Sen, see Qizilbash (2005) and Sugden (2005b).

172 In particular, see Berger (1984) and Urbinati (2002).

173 On Mill's idea of friendship in marriage, see Morales (1996).

174 Mill's substantial modification of the liberal framework of his *Principles of Political Economy* to include, in the second edition of 1849, an important chapter on the conditions of the working class, cooperation, the right to work and women's work can be directly traced to the influence of Harriet.

175 This is the basis for Mill's theory on the right to work, which is motivated by the fact that work must be well distributed because we all need to work to satisfy our primary needs, so that we can then aspire to more, that is, to the cultivation of our humanity.

176 In the previous chapters we saw a similar position in Genovesi and his school. It is interesting to find a similar thesis in the Scottish philosopher Adam

Ferguson, a contemporary of Smith. In his *An Essay on the History of Civil Society*, he criticises those (Hobbes among them) who won't admit any human behaviour not motivated by self-interest:

> This term *interest*, which commonly implies little more than our regard to property, is sometimes put for utility in general, and this for happiness; insomuch that, under these ambiguities, it is not surprising we are still unable to determine, whether interest is the only motive of human action, and the standard by which to distinguish our good from our ill. So much is said in this place, not from any desire to have a share in any controversy of this sort, but merely to confine the meaning of the term *interest* to its most common acceptation, and to intimate our intention of employing it in expressing those objects of care which refer to our external condition, and the preservation of our animal nature. When taken in this sense, it will not surely be thought to comprehend at once all the motives of human conduct. If men be not allowed to have disinterested benevolence, they will not be denied to have disinterested passions of another kind. Hatred, indignation, and rage, frequently urge them to act in opposition to their known interest, and even to hazard their lives, without any hopes of compensation in any future returns of preferment or profit.
>
> (1767: section II, 22–23)

177 Mill's intuition about the paradoxical nature of happiness, or of the "teleological paradox", is taken up and further developed in the thought of another proponent of classical Utilitarianism, Henry Sidgwick. In *The Methods of Ethics* (1901 [1874]), Sidgwick defines the mechanism which Mills and others highlighted as being a "fundamental paradox": the "greatest happiness" cannot be reached by who "seeks it as a direct end" (p. 130), because happiness requires "the practice of virtue, without any particular consideration of what appears to him to be his interest" (p. 174).

178 The absence of the entry "happiness" in the *New Palgrave Dictionary of Political Economy* attests to this.

179 According to Martha Nussbaum, "For him [Bentham] pleasure is a single homogeneous sensation, containing no qualitative differences. The only variations in pleasure are quantitative. They can vary in intensity, duration, certainty or uncertainty, propinquity or remoteness, and, finally, in causal properties" (2005: 173).

180 *Sensism* is the doctrine that reduces all knowledge to sensation: for sensists there is no need to have recourse to the intellect or to any faculty other than "sense". The reference text of sensism is Condillac's *Traité des sensations* (1754), though for example, Hobbes and Gassendi were also sensists. Sensism therefore is more radical than empiricism. Empiricism, in fact, needs something different from pure sensations. Locke, for instance, was an empiricist but not a sensist, because to him the principle of all knowledge comes from *perception*, which presupposes "*intelligence*" (as in the title of his *Essay*); and the latter cannot be included under "sensation". To the sensists, instead, sensations are primitive.

181 Among Bentham's *Fragments* we find: "I remember well that it was from Beccaria's little book *Dei delitti e delle pene* that I drew the first hint of the principle of utility" (quoted in Beccaria 1994 [1764]: 563). Cesare Beccaria is by far the best known and influential personality of eighteenth-century Milan. As is well known, in his twenties, Beccaria, though a younger member of the group of "Il Caffé", already enjoyed a superior international reputation, indeed the highest of the group. This followed the appearance of his

pamphlet, *Dei delitti e delle pene* (*Of Crimes and Punishment*), in 1764. Empress Maria Theresa took the bold step of creating a Professorship of *Scienze Camerali* for him in Milan at the *Scuole Palatine* in 1769. I have no space here to delve into his *Elementi di economia pubblica*, reflecting Beccaria's own teaching. It is significant in the present context that in chapters 41 and 42 of his pamphlet on crimes and punishment ("Of the means of preventing crimes" and "Of sciences"), some commentators incline to read a short history of civil society in a Fergusonian fashion, although Beccaria liked to also stress his distance from Genovesi's school, and did not want to adopt Genovesi's *Lezioni* in his chair in Milan: (see the critical note of M.L. Perna to Genovesi's *Lezioni*'s critical edition). His conception was Utilitarian. It was Beccaria who effectively contributed to the launch of the famous *dictum* that laws are to be considered – as he writes in the introduction (*A chi legge*) of his 1764 pamphlet, thus making use of a formula of Scottish origin – from the standpoint of "the greatest happiness of the greatest number". For more information about Beccaria and the Milanese School, see Bruni and Porta (2003).

182 Edgeworth presents a much more complex theory of utility, happiness and interpersonal relationships than that which emerges from this single phrase. To a lesser degree, the same can be said for Jevons. For more on such themes, see Bruni (2004a), Bruni and Sugden (2005), Bruni and Zamagni (2004), Zamagni (2005).

183 Pantaleoni was convinced that the economic principle requires a hedonic content. In contrast to other hedonists like Jevons or the Italian De Viti de Marco, he claimed that hedonism is quite different than that simple "law of the least means". The formal "law of the least means" was considered by many of his contemporaries, who were still tied to the classical paradigm, to be the economic principle. According to Pantaleoni, a "formal" economic principle, such as the minimum means law, is too general and does not help in explaining economic behaviour, or for distinguishing it from a non-economic one. On this, see Bruni (2002).

10 The solipsistic foundation of contemporary Economics

184 Hicks, Samuelson, and then the principal economists who worked on the theory of choice, pushed the "experimental turn" of Pareto's theory of choice to its extreme consequences. The theory of "revealed preferences", and the neo-positivist programme associated with it, reached their highest popularity among the economists in the 1960s, and even today Samuelson's "formal" approach is often used in the theory of decisions, in microeconomics, in Game Theory and connected disciplines. Therefore, it is not outrageous to say that the framework of microeconomics have been a continuation and development of the Paretian revolution that took place at the end of the nineteenth century: see Bruni (2002).

185 What in the twentieth century has been called "the demarcation problem" (how to distinguish science from what is not), one of the key issues of the history of modern thought (from Kant to the philosophers of the Vienna Circle), was also of fundamental importance to Pareto. Differentiating his Economics and sociology from literature ("novels") and science from metaphysics, was of fundamental importance to him. Pareto, all too simply, found the solution in the distinction between the objective (i.e. science) and the subjective (i.e. non-science). Because of this, in economic science, he made a radical choice by basing it on "objective" facts and rejecting all of the subjective and psychological aspects of preferences.

186 "Ethology, the deductive science, is a system of corollaries from psychology, the experimental science" (Mill 1862 [1843]: II, p. 453).

187 On this, see Bruni and Sugden (2005).

188 On the meaning and the contradictions of Pareto's usage of ophelimity, see Bruni (2002, chapters 1, 4).

189 Edgeworth introduced the indifference curves in 1881, but in his *Mathematical Psychics* the foundation for the curves was still the hedonistic utility, which he considered a measurable, cardinal quantity (as do present-day psychologist– economists like Kahneman). According to Pareto the existence and (cardinal) measurability of utility was instead a great epistemological weakness of Economics. He thought he could overcome it by working from choices as primitive data and, from them, construct functions which represent "preference indexes", which he did in his more mature works like the *Manuale* (1906) and the French *Manuel* (1909). In previous works (Bruni 2002) I have tried to show *if* and *in which sense* Pareto accomplished his purpose of eliminating hedonism from pure Economics.

190 In Pareto's theory we find an instrumental idea of rationality, which is, however, different from the approach that is at the basis of rational choice today, because of the role that *objectivity* plays in it. In fact, Pareto points out that from the subjective standpoint almost all actions are "logical": "in the eyes of the Greek mariners sacrifices to Poseidon and rowing with oars were equally logical means of navigation" (1964 [1916]: §150). Logic requires objectivity, an objectivity primarily furnished, for Pareto, by those "who have a more extensive knowledge" (§150), that is, the scientist, the external observer, an exogenous criterion with respect to the agent.

191 A tautological flaw immediately strikes us, that is, defining a "logical" action as the one that "logically" binds the means to the end.

192 Steedman (1995) has analysed Wicksteed's non-tuism, but his aim was to show the overcoming, thanks to this new concept, of the tendency for *self-interest* to be considered as basic hypothesis of Economics. Steedman, however, escaped the aspects of non-tuism most relevant in the research at hand. This section is dedicated entirely to Wicksteed's non-tuism.

193 The recent literature has shown (Steedman 1994) that his economic theory was very much affected by his religious and ethical vision.

194 First of all, Pareto's influence in Wicksteed's mature Economics has to be acknowledged – in Bruni (2002, chapter 5), I have discussed the differences between the two authors. When he reviewed Pareto's *Manual* in the *Economic Journal*, Wicksteed was really impressed by the book: "it is a work which is likely to modify and stimulate economic thought to an extent quite disproportionate to the numbers of its readers. It will probably be understood by few, but every one who understands it will be influenced by it." Given the technical difficulties of the book, he "looks forward to a long period of continued and intensified study, and probably to the exposition and comments of other students, before attempting to estimate its full significance" (1933 [1910]: 815). He actually had such a period of study: four years, for writing his *Common Sense of Political Economy*, a work that "bears witness everywhere to the extent to which Wicksteed himself had been affected" by Pareto's *Manual* (Robbins 1933: xviii). In fact if we compare the *Common Sense* with his older *Alphabet of Political Economy* "superficially, the two theories are the same.... But a closer inspection will reveal important points of difference" (Robbins 1933: xviii) in which it is too easy to single out Pareto's influence: (a) the *Alphabet* starts from marginal utility, the *Common Sense* from the "relative scale of preferences"; (b) in the *Alphabet*, utility is objective and measurable, in the *Common Sense* the idea of measurability gives way to that of "order of preferences". In sum, "there is no feature of the presentation which does not bear evidence of reformulation and

improvement. In all this, the influence of Pareto is very strongly discernible" (Robbins 1933: xix).
195 Note some parallel with Marshall: in rejecting hedonism, allowing higher motives, but accepting the main instrumental structure of Economics, putting this "higher" motive outside Economics. Wicksteed brings them in, but just as preferences.
196 It is interesting to note how much Welfare Economics, in particular the methodological separation between the "first" and "second" theorem, has been influenced by such a methodology (thanks to Robbins' mediation).
197 In discussing dilemmas of rational choice theory, Martin Hollis points out that the main methodological assumption in contemporary Game Theory, its *sine qua non* condition, is not non-tuism but "philosophical egoism", which he defines as follows: "Provided that the adjusted pay-offs are as stated, it makes no difference whether Adam and Eve are selfish sods or ardent altruists. The sorry outcome depends solely on assuming that Adam is directly moved only by what Adam wants overall, and Eve directly moved only by what Eve wants overall" (Hollis 1998: 17). Therefore, I do not agree with Binmore, who claims that "like arithmetic, Game Theory is not a manifesto for hedonism or egoism or any other *ism*" (1994: 103): Game Theory, in fact, can need philosophical ego*ism*.
198 It should be added that some very recent contributions present attempts at inserting non-instrumental elements within rationality: "sympathy" (Sally 2000), "trust" (Pelligra 2003), or "fellow-feelings" (Sugden 2005a).
199 After the 1950s, the original attitude of Game Theory towards interpersonal relations has been reinforced by the spread of Nash methodology (Mirowski 1999: 304–305). Nash has pushed forward the solipsistic nature of the theory: "Our theory [. . .] assume[s that] each participants act independently, without collaboration or communication with any of the others" (Nash 1996: 22).

11 Conclusion

200 This experiment, carried out by using the DRM (Day Reconstruction Method), is interesting also because it avoids the central problem of causality.

Bibliography

Actis-Perinetti, L. (1960) *Gli illuministi italiani*, Turin: Loescher.

Ahuvia, A. and Friedman, C. (1998) "Income, consumption, and subjective well-being: toward a composite macromarketing model", *Journal of Macromarketing*, 18, 153–168.

Amerio, F. (1947) *Introduzione allo studio di G.B. Vico*, Turin: Società editrice Internazionale.

Anscombe, G.E.M. (1958) "Modern moral philosophy", in *The Collected Philosophical Papers of G.E.M. Anscombe, Vol. 3, Ethics, Religion and Politics, 1981*, Oxford: Basil Blackwell, pp. 26–42.

Antoci, A., Sacco, P. and Vanin, P. (2005) "On the possible conflict between economic growth and social development", in Gui, B. and Sugden, R. (eds) *Economics and Social Interaction*, Cambridge: Cambridge University Press.

Argyle, M. (2001) *The Psychology of Happiness*, New York: Taylor & Francis.

Aristotle (1980) *Nicomachean Ethics*, Oxford: Oxford University Press.

Aristotle (n.d.) *Politics*, The Internet Classics Archive. Online, available at: classics.mit.edu/index.html.

Baron, H. (1955) *The Crisis of the Early Italian Renaissance*, Princeton: Princeton University Press.

Baron, H. (1988) *In Search of Florentine Civic Humanism: Essays on the Transitions from the Medieval to Modern Thought*, Princeton: Princeton University Press.

Baroni, C. (2003) "The road to virtue: Adam Smith and the economy of happiness". Paper presented at the conference, "The Paradoxes of Happiness in Economics", Milan–Bicocca, March.

Bartolini, S. (2004) "Perché la gente è così infelice? Una spiegazione basata sul rapporto tra tempo libero e felicità", in Bruni, L. and Porta, P.L. (eds) *L'economia e i paradossi della felicità*, Milan: Guerini.

Batkin, L.M. (1992) *L'idea di individualità nel Rinascimento italiano*, Bari: Laterza.

Baumeister, R.F. and Leary, M.R. (1995) "The need to belong: desire for interpersonal attachments as a fundamental human motivation", *Psychological Bulletin*, 117, 497–529.

Bazzichi, O. (2003) *Alle radici del capitalismo: medioevo e scienza economica*, Turin: Effatà Editrice.

Becattini, G. (2002) *Miti e paradossi del mondo contemporaneo*, Rome: Donzelli.

Beccaria, C. (1994 [1764]) *Dei delitti e delle pene*, Turin: Einaudi.

Beccaria, C. (1770) *Ricerche intorno alla natura dello stile, in Edizione Nazionale delle Opere di Cesare Beccaria* (1984–) Luigi Firpo (ed.) Milan: Mediobanca, various volumes, 1984 onwards (ongoing).

Beccaria, C. (1804) *Elementi di economia pubblica*, in *Edizione Nazionale delle Opere di Cesare Beccaria* (1984–) Luigi Firpo (ed.) Milan: Mediobanca, various volumes, 1984 onwards (ongoing).

Becchetti, L. and Santoro, E. (2005) "The wealth–unhappiness paradox: a relational goods' Baumol disease explanation", in Bruni, L. and Porta, P.L. (eds) *Handbook of Happiness in Economics*, Cheltenham: Elgar.

Becker, G. (1973) "A theory of marriage: part I", *The Journal of Political Economy*, 81, 813–846.

Becker, G. (1996) *Accounting for Tastes*, Cambridge, MA: Harvard University Press.

Bellamy, R. (1987) "'Da metafico a mercatante': Antonio Genovesi and the development of a new language of commerce in eighteenth-century Naples", in Pagden, A. (ed.) *The Language of Political Theory in Early Modern Europe*, Cambridge: Cambridge University Press.

Bentham, J. (1789) *An Introduction to the Principles of Morals and Legislation*, Burns, J.H. and Hart, H.L.A. (eds), London: Athlone Press.

Berger, F.R. (1984) *Happiness, Justice, and Freedom: the Moral and Political Philosophy of John Stuart Mill*, Berkeley: University of California Press.

Bernardino da Siena (1989 [1427]) *Prediche volgari sul Campo di Siena*, Delcorno, C. (ed.), Milan: Rusconi.

Bianchi, I. (1779) *Meditationi su vari punti di felicità pubblica e privata*, Lodi: Pallavicini.

Bianchini, L. (1855) *Della scienza del bene vivere sociale* (*On the Science of Good Social Living*). Naples: Dalla Stamperìa Reale.

Binmore, K. (1994) *"Playing Fair", Game Theory and Social Contract*, Cambridge, MA: MIT Press.

Binmore, K. (2001) "Review" of Broome (1999), *Utilitas*, XIII, 127–129.

Blanchflower, D.G. and Oswald, J. (2000) "Well-being over time in Britain and the USA", NBER Working Paper No. 7487. Cambridge, MA: National Bureau of Economic Research.

Bobbio, N. (1993) *Thomas Hobbes and the Natural Law Tradition*, Chicago: Chicago University Press.

Borcherding, T.E. and Filson, D. (2002) "Group consumption, free-riding, and informal reciprocity agreements", *Journal of Economic Behavior and Organization*, 47, 237–257.

Botturi, F. (1991) *La sapienza della storia. Giambattista Vico e la filosofia pratica*, Milan: Vita e Pensiero.

Bracciolini, P. (1994 [1429]) *De Avarizia*, transcribed with notes by Giuseppe Germano, Livorno: Belforte.

Bradburg, N.M. (1969) *The Structure of the Psychological Well-Being*, Chicago: Aldine.

Brennan, G. and Petitt, P. (2004) *The Economics of Esteem: an Essay on Civil and Political Society*, Oxford: Oxford University Press.

Brewer, A. (1998) "Luxury and economic development: David Hume and Adam Smith", *Scottish Journal of Political Economy*, 45, 1, 78–98.

Brickman, P. and Campbell, D.T. (1971) "Hedonic relativism and planning the good society", in Apley, M.H. (ed.) *Adaptation-level Theory: a Symposium*, New York: Academic Press, pp. 287–302.

Brickman, P., Coates, D. and Janoff-Bulman, R. (1978) "Lottery winners and accident victims: is happiness relative?" *Journal of Personality and Social Psychology*, 37, 917–927.

Brink, D.O. (1999) "Eudaimonism, love and friendship, and political community", *Social Philosophy and Policy*, 16, 252–289.

Broome, J. (1999) *Ethics Out of Economics*, Cambridge: Cambridge University Press.

Bruni, F. (1987) "La nozione di lavoro in Adam Smith", *Rivista di filosofia neo-scolastica*, LXXIX, 67–95.

Bruni, L. (2000) "Ego facing Alter: how economists have depicted human interactions", *Journal of Public and Cooperative Economics*, 71, 295–313.

Bruni, L. (2002) *Vilfredo Pareto and the Birth of Modern Microeconomics*, Cheltenham: Elgar.

Bruni, L. (2004a) *L'economia la felicità e gli altri*, Rome: Città Nuova.

Bruni, L. (2004b) "The technology of happiness in the tradition of economic science", *Journal of History of Economic Thought*, 26, 1, 19–43.

Bruni, L. (2004c) "The 'happiness transformation problem' in the Cambridge tradition of Economics", *European Journal of the History of Economic Thought*, 11, 433–452.

Bruni, L. (2005) "Hic Sunt Leones: social relations as unexplored territory in the economic tradition", in Gui, B. and Sugden, R. (eds) *Economics and Social Interaction*, Cambridge: Cambridge University Press.

Bruni, L. and Porta, P.L. (2003) *"Pubblica felicità* and *Economia civile* in the Italian Enlightenment", *History of Political Economy*, supplement 1, 35, 361–385.

Bruni, L. and Porta, P.L. (eds) (2004) *L'economia e i paradossi della felicità*, Milan: Guerini.

Bruni, L. and Porta, P.L. (eds) (2005a) *Economics and Happiness: Framings of Analysis*, Oxford: Oxford University Press, forthcoming.

Bruni, L. and Porta, P.L. (eds) (2005b) *Handbook of Happiness in Economics*, Cheltenham: Elgar.

Bruni, L. and Stanca, L. (2005) *Watching Alone: Relational Goods, Happiness and Television*, mimeo, Milan–Bicocca.

Bruni, L. and Sugden, R. (2000) "Moral canals: trust and social capital in the work of Hume, Smith and Genovesi", *Economics and Philosophy*, 16, 21–45.

Bruni, L. and Sugden, R. (2005) "The road not taken: how Psychology was removed from Economics, and how it might be brought be back", *Economic Journal*, forthcoming.

Bruni, L. and Zamagni, S. (2004) *Economia civile: efficienza equità pubblica felicità*, Bologna: Il Mulino.

Bruni, Leonardo (1558) *Aristotelis Stagiritae Politicorum siue de republica libri octo Leonardo Aretino interprete cum D. Thomae Aquinatis explanatione...*, Venice: VenetiisVenetiis impressum, Lucantonio eredi.

Burchkardt, J. (1869) *La civiltà del rinascimento in Italia*, Florence: Sansoni.

Busino, G. (1964) "Note bibliographique sur le Cours", in Pareto, V. (1975) *Corrispondance: 1890–1923*, a cura di G. Busino, Oeuvres Complètes, 19, Géneve: Droz, pp. 1165–1172.

Butt, B. (1978) *On Economic Man*, Canberra: Australian National University Press.

Campbell, A., Converse, P.E. and Rodgers, W.L. (1976) *The Quality of American Life: Perceptions, Evolutions, and Satisfactions*, New York: Russell Sage Foundation.

Cantril, H. (1965) *The Pattern of Human Concerns*, New Brunswick: Rutgers University Press.

Carabelli, A. (2003) "Keynes on happiness": Paper presented at the Conference, "The Paradoxes of Happiness in Economics", Milan–Bicocca, 21–23 March 2003.

Cardini, F. (1986) "Figure della vita quotidiana quattrocentesca", in Barbieri, R. (ed.) *Uomini & tempo medievale*, Milan: Jaca Books.

Carlyle, T. (1898 [1850]) *Letter-Day Pamphlets*, London: Chapman and Hall.

Carstensen, L.L. (1995) "Evidence for a life-span theory of socioemotional selectivity", *Current Directions in Psychological Science*, 4, 151–156.

Cartwright, N. (1999) *The Dappled World: a Study of the Boundaries of Science*, Cambridge: Cambridge University Press.

Cattaneo, C. (2001 [1859]) *Del pensiero come principio di economia pubblica*, Milan: Libri Scheiwiller.

Chafuen, A.A. (1999) *Cristiani per la Libertà – Le Radici Cattoliche dell'Economia di Mercato*, Macerata: Liberilibri.

Clark, A.E. and Oswald, A.J. (2002) "Unhappiness and unemployment", in Easterlin, R. (ed.) *Happiness in Economics*, Cheltenham: International Library of Critical Writings in Economics, Elgar, pp. 166–177.

Collard, D. (1978) *Altruism and Economy: a Study in Non-selfish Economics*, Oxford: Martin Robertson.

Cooter, R.D. (1984) "Prices and satisfactions", *Columbia Law Review*, 84, 1523–1560.

Copleston, F. (1962) *A History of Philosophy*, New York: Image Books Edition.

Corneo, G. (2002) "Work and television", Center for Economic Studies & Ifo Institute for Economic Research CESifo, Working Paper No. 829.

Croce, B. (1900) "Sul principio economico. Lettera al professore Vilfredo Pareto", *Giornale degli Economisti*, 21, 15–26.

Dahl, R. (1989) *Democracy and its Critics*, New Haven: Yale University Press.

Darwall, S. (1999) "Valuing activity", *Social Philosophy and Policy*, 16, 1.

Dasgupta, P. (2001) *Human Well-Being and the Natural Environment*, Cambridge: Cambridge University Press.

Davis, J. (2003) *The Theory of the Individual in Economics: Identity and Value*, London: Routledge.

Deci, R.M. and Ryan, E.L. (2001) "On happiness and human potentials: a review of research on hedonic and eudaimonic well-being", *Annual Review of Psychology*, 52, 141–166.

De Heer, C. (1968) *Makar, Eudaimon, Olbios, Eutuches: a Study of the Semantic Field Denoting Happiness in Ancient Greek to the End of the 5th Century B.C.*, Amsterdam: Adolf M. Hakkert.

De Luca, G.B. (1680) *Il Principe Cristiano pratico (The Practical Christian Prince)*, Rome: Stamperia Camera Apostolica.

Di Battista, F. (1990) *Dalla tradizione genovesiana agli economisti liberali: saggi di storia del pensiero economico meridionale*, Bari: Cacucci.

Diener, E. (1984) "Subjective well-being", *Psychological Bulletin*, 95, 3, 542–575.

Diener, E. and Biswas-Dieder, R. (2002) "Will money increase subjective well-being?", *Social Indicators Research*, 57, 119–169.

Diener, E. and Lucas, R.E. (1999) "Personality and subjective well-being", in Kahneman, D., Diener, E. and Schwartz, N. (eds) *Well-Being: Foundations of Hedonic Psychology*, New York: Russell Sage Foundation, pp. 213–229.

Diener, E. and Oiski, S. (2004) "The nonobvious social psychology of happiness", *Annual Review of Psychology*, 54, 277–295.

Diener, E. and Seligman, M.E.P. (2002) "Very happy people", *Psychological Science*, 13, 81–84.

Diener, E. and Seligman, M.E.P. (2003) "Beyond money: toward an economy of well-being", *Psychological Science in the Public Interest*, 5, 1–31.

Diener, E., Gohm, C.L., Suh, E.M. and Oishi, S. (2000) "Similarity of the relations between marital status and subjective well-being across cultures", *Journal of Cross Cultural Psychology* 31, 4, 419–436.

Diener, E., Scollon, C.N. and Lucas, R.E. (2003) "The evolving concept of subjective well-being: the multifaceted nature of happiness", *Advances in Cell Aging and Gerontology*, 15, 187–219.

Doni, A.F. (1552) *Mondo savio e pazzo*, Venice: Ripubblicata in Widmar (1964).

Doria, P.M. (1710) *Della vita civile*, Naples.

Dragonetti, G. (1787 [1766]) *Delle virtù e dei premi*, Palermo: Reale Stamperia.

Duesenberry, J. (1949) *Income, Saving and the Theory of Consumer Behavior*, Cambridge: Harvard University Press.

Easterlin, R. (1974) "Does economic growth improve human lot? Some empirical evidence", in Davis, P.A. and Reder, M.W. (eds) *Nation and Households in Economic Growth: Essays in Honor of Moses Abromowitz*, New York and London: Academic Press.

Easterlin, R. (1995) "Will raising the incomes of all increase the *happiness* of all?", *Journal of Economic Behaviour and Organisation*, 27, 35–48.

Easterlin, R. (2001) "Income and *happiness*: towards a unified theory", *The Economic Journal*, 111, 465–484.

Easterlin, R. (ed.) (2002) *Happiness in Economics*, Cheltenham: International Library of Critical Writings in Economics, Elgar.

Easterlin, R. (2004) *Feeding the Illusion of Growth and Happiness: a Reply to Hagerty and Veenhoven*, mimeo.

Easterlin, R. (2005) "Towards a better theory of happiness", in Bruni, L. and Porta, P.L. (eds) *Economics and Happiness: Framings of Analysis*, Oxford: Oxford University Press.

Edgeworth, F.Y. (1877) *New and Old Methods of Ethics*, London: James Parker.

Edgeworth, F.Y. (1881) *Mathematical Psychics*, London. Reprinted New York: Kelly.

Ellison, C.G. (1991) "Religious involvement and subjective well-being", *Journal of Health and Social Behaviour*, 32, 80–90.

Elster, J. (1983) *Sour Grapes*, Cambridge: Cambridge University Press.

Esposito, R. (1998) *Communitas*, Turin: Einaudi.

Fanfani, A. (1968) *Storia economica*, Turin: Utet.

Farnie, D.A. (1962) "The commercial empire of the Atlantic, 1607–1783", *The Economic History Review*, XV, 2, 205–218.

Febrero, R. and Schwartz, P. (1997) *La Esencia de Becker*, Barcelona: Editorial Ariel.

Ferguson, A. (1767) *An Essay on the History of Civil Society*, Edinburgh: Millar & Caddel. Reprinted from the original by "Fondazione Feltrinelli", Milan, 2001.

Ferguson, A. (1792) *Principles of Moral and Political Science: Being Chiefly a*

Retrospect of Lectures Delivered in the College of Edinburgh, London: Strahan, A. and T. Cadell.

Fernandez Lopez, M. (2004) "Neapolitan independence and the economics of Antonio Genovesi". Paper presented at the AISPE Conference, Palermo, October.

Ferrara, F. (1934–1935) *Lezioni di economia politica, 2 vols*, Bologna: Nicola Zanichelli.

Filangeri, G. (2003 [1780]) *La scienza della legislazione*, Naples: Grimaldi & C. Editori.

Fishkin, J. (1997) *The Voice of the People*, Yale: Yale University Press.

Fontaine, P. (1997) "Identification and economic behaviour: sympathy and empathy in historical perspective", *Economics and Philosophy*, 13, 264–268.

Frank, R. (1985) *Choosing the Right Pond*, New York: Oxford University Press.

Frank, R. (1997) "The frame of reference as a public good", *Economic Journal*, 107, 1832–1847.

Frank, R. (1999) *Luxury Fever*, New York: Free Press.

Frank, R. (2005) "Does absolute income matter?", in Bruni, L. and Porta, P.L. (eds) *Economics and Happiness: Framings of Analysis*, Oxford: Oxford University Press.

Frey, B.S. (1997) *Not Just For the Money: an Economic Theory of Personal Motivation*, Cheltenham: Elgar.

Frey, B.S. (2002) *Inspiring Economics*, Cheltenham: Elgar.

Frey, B.S. and Oberholzer-Gee, F. (1997) "The cost of price incentives: an empirical analysis of motivation crowding-out", *American Economic Review*, 87, 746–755.

Frey, B.S. and Stutzer, A. (1999) "Maximising happiness?", Working Paper No. 22, Institute for Empirical Research in Economics, University of Zurich.

Frey, B.S. and Stutzer, A. (2001) "Happiness, economy and institutions", *The Economic Journal*, 111, 918–938.

Frey, B.S. and Stutzer, A. (2002) *Happiness in Economics*, Princeton: Princeton University Press.

Frey, B.S. and Stutzer, A. (2005) "Testing theories of happiness", in Bruni, L. and Porta, P.L. (eds) *Economics and Happiness: Framings of Analysis*, Oxford: Oxford University Press.

Frigo, D. (1988) "La 'civile proporzione': ceti, principe e composizione degli interessi nella letteratura politica d'antico regime", in Mozzarelli, C. (ed.) *Economia e corporazione*, Milan: Giuffré, pp. 81–108.

Galiani, F. (1803 [1750]) *Della Moneta*, Collezione Custodi di scrittori classici di economia politica, Parte Moderna, Tomo III, Milan: De Stefanis.

Garin, E. (1988) *La cultura del rinascimento*, Milan: Il Saggiatore.

Garin, E. (1994 [1947]) *L'umanesimo italiano*, Bari: Laterza.

Genovesi, A. (1753) "Discorso sopra il vero fine delle lettere e delle scienze", in *Scritti Economici*, edited by M. Perna, Naples: Istituto Italiano per gli studi filosofici.

Genovesi, A. (1757–1758) "Elementi di Commercio", in *Lezioni, di commercio o sia di economia civile*, Critical Edition, edited by M.L. Perna, Naples: Istituto Italiano per gli studi filosofici.

Genovesi, A. (1766) *Logica per gli giovanetti*, Naples: Stamperia Simoniana.

Genovesi, A. (1777) *Spirito delle leggi del signore di Montesquieu con le note dell'abate Antonio Genovesi*, volume I, Naples: Domenico Terres.

Genovesi, A. (1963) *Autobiografia e lettere*, Milan: Feltrinelli.

Genovesi, A. (1973 [1766]) *Della diceosina o sia della filosofia del giusto e dell'onesto*, Milan: Marzorati.

Genovesi, A. (1979) *Scritti*, Milan: Feltrinelli.

Genovesi, A. (1984) *Scritti economici*, edited by M.L. Perna, Naples: Istituto Italiano per gli studi filosofici.

Genovesi, A. (2005 [1765–1767]) *Lezioni di commercio o sia di economia civile*, Critical Edition, edited by M.L. Perna, Naples: Istituto Italiano per gli studi filosofici.

Giarrizzo, G. (1985) "Un 'Regno governato in provincia': Napoli tra Austria e Spagna (1690–1740)", in *Paolo Mattia Doria fra rinnovamento e tradizione*, Galatina: Congedo Editore.

Giusso, L. (1998) *Economia Metodo Morale*, Catania: Il Cinabro.

Gossen, H. (1981 [1854]) *The Laws of Human Relations, with an Introduction by N. Georgescu-Roegen*, Cambridge, Mass: MIT Press.

Groenewegen, P. (1994) *A Soaring Eagle: Alfred Marshall 1842–1924*, Aldershot: Edward Elgar.

Groenewegen, P. (2003) "Alfred Marshall on homo oeconomicus: evolution versus utilitarianism", in Laurent, J. (ed.) *Evolutionary Economics and Human Nature*, Cheltenham: Elgar, pp. 114–133.

Gualerni, G. (2002) *L'altra economia e l'interpretazione di Adam Smith*, Milan: Vita e Pensiero.

Gui, B. (1987) "Eléments pour une définition d'«économie communautaire»", *Notes et Documents*, 19–20, 32–42.

Gui, B. (1994) "Interpersonal relations: a disregarded theme in the debate on ethics and economics", in Lewis, A. and Warneryd, K.E. (eds) *Ethics and Economic Affairs*, London: Routledge, pp. 251–263.

Gui, B. (2002) "Più che scambi incontri. La teoria economica alle prese con i fenomeni relazionali", in Sacco, P. and Zamagni, S. (eds) *Complessità relazionale e comportamento economico: marteriali per un nuovo paradigma di razionalità*, Bologna: Il Mulino, pp. 15–66.

Gui, B. and Sugden, R. (2005) *Economics and Social Interaction*, Cambridge: Cambridge University Press.

Hagerty, M.R. and Veenhoven, R. (2003) "Wealth and happiness revisited – growing national income *does* go with greater happiness", *Social Indicators Research*, 64, 1–27.

Hankins, J. (1995) "The 'Baron's thesis' after forty years and some recent studies of Leonardo Bruni", *Journal of the History of the Ideas*, 56, 309–338.

Hankins, J. (ed.) (2000) *Renaissance Civic Humanism*, Cambridge: Cambridge University Press.

Hargreaves-Heap, Shaun *et al.* (1992) *The Theory of Choice – A Critical Guide*, Oxford: Blackwell.

Hausman, D.M. and McPherson, M.S. (1996) *Economic Analysis and Moral Philosophy*, Cambridge: Cambridge University Press.

Hegel, G.W.F. (1967 [1821]) *Philosophy of Right*, trans T.M. Knox, London: Oxford University Press.

Herrnstein, R.J. and Murray, C. (1994) *The Bell Curve: Intelligence and Class Structure in American Life*, New York: Free Press.

Hill, T.E. Jr. (1999) "Happiness and human flourishing in Kant's ethics", in Paul,

E.F., Miller, F.D. and Paul, J. (eds) *Human Flourishing*, Cambridge: Cambridge University Press, pp. 143–175.

Hirsch, F. (1977) *Social Limits to Growth*, London: Routledge.

Hirschman, A.O. (1977) *The Passions and the Interests: Political Arguments for Capitalism Before its Triumph*, New Jersey: Princeton University Press.

Hirschman, A.O. (1982) "Rival interpretations of market society: civilizing, destructive, or feeble?", *Journal of Economic Literature*, 20, 1463–1484.

Hirschman, A.O. (1984) "Against parsimony: three easy ways of complicating some categories of economic discourse", *American Economic Review*, 74, Papers and Proceedings 2, 89–96.

Hirschman, A.O. (1996) "Melding the public and private spheres: taking commensality seriously", *Critical review*, 10, 4, 533–550.

Hobbes, T. (1954 [1651]) *Leviathan*, London: Dent & Son.

Hobbes, T. (1998 [1642]) *On the Citizen*, Cambridge: Cambridge University Press.

Höllander, H. (2001) "On the validity of utility statements: standard theory versus Duesenberry's", *Journal of Economic Behaviour and Organization*, 45, 227–249.

Hollis, M. (1998) *Trust Within Reason*, Cambridge: Cambridge University Press.

Hollis, M. and Sugden, R. (1993) "Rationality in action", *Mind*, January, 1–34.

Hont, I. and Ignatief, M. (1983) *Wealth and Virtue: the Shaping of Political Economy in the Scottish Enlightenment*, Cambridge: Cambridge University Press.

Hume, David (1975 [1777]) *Enquiries Concerning Human Understanding and Concerning the Principles of Morals*, Oxford: Oxford University Press.

Hume, David (1978 [1740]) *A Treatise of Human Nature*, Oxford: Oxford University Press.

Hume, D. (1983 [1778]) *The History of England*, six vols, London: T. Cadell. Reprinted by Liberty Fund: Indianapolis.

Hutcheson, F. (1750) *Remarks Upon the Fable of the Bees*. Online, available at: www.ecn.bris.ac.uk/het/hutcheson/remarks.htm.

Huizinga, J. (1987 [1919]) *L'autunno del medioevo*, Milan: Rizzoli.

Inglehart, R. (1996) "The diminishing utility of economic growth", *Critical Review*, 10, 508–531.

Jevons, S. (1970 [1871]) *Theory of Political Economy*, London: Macmillan.

Kahneman, D. (1999) "Objective happiness", in Kahneman, D., Diener, E. and Schwartz, N. (eds) *Well-Being: Foundations of Hedonic Psychology*, New York: Russell Sage Foundation.

Kahneman, D. (2000) "Experienced utility and objective happiness: a moment-based approach", in Kahneman, D. and Tversky, A. (eds) *Choice, Values and Frames*, New York: Cambridge University Press and the Russell Sage Foundation, pp. 673–692.

Kahneman, D. (2003) "Experienced utility and objective happiness: a moment-based approach", in Brocas, I. (ed.) *The Psychology of Economic Decisions – Volume One: Rationality and Well-Being*, Oxford: Oxford University Press.

Kahneman, D., Diener, E. and Schwartz, N. (eds) (1999) *Well-Being: Foundations of Hedonic Psychology*, New York: Russell Sage Foundation.

Kahneman, D., Krueger, A.B., Schkade, D.A., Schwarz, N. and Stone, A.A. (2003) *A Survey Method for Characterizing Daily Life Experience: the Day Reconstruction Method (DRM)*, mimeo, Princeton.

Kahneman, D., Wakker, P.P. and Sarin, R. (1997) "Back to Bentham? Explorations of experienced utility", *Quarterly Journal of Economics*, 112, 375–405.

Kant, I. (1959 [1784]) "Idea for a Universal History from a Cosmopolitan Point of View" in Gardiner, P. (ed) *Theories of History*, 22–34, New York: Collier.

Kant, I. (1992 [1798]) *Conflict of Faculties*, Lincoln: University of Nebraska Press.

Kapur, N. (1993) *Friendship: a Philosophical Reader*, Cornell: Cornell University Press.

Kapur, Neera Badwhar (1991) "Why it is wrong to be always guided by the best: consequentialism and friendship", *Ethics*, 101, 483–504.

Kaviraj, S. and Khilnani, S. (eds) (2001) *Civil Society: History and Possibilities*, Cambridge: Cambridge University Press.

Keely, L.C. (2000) *Why Isn't Growth Making Us Happier?*, mimeo, Oxford.

Kenny, C. (1999) "Does growth cause *happiness*, or does *happiness* cause growth?" *Kyklos*, 52, 1, 3–26.

Keyes, C.L.M., Shmotkin, D. and Ryff, C.D. (2002) "Optimizing well-being: the empirical encounter of two traditions", *Journal of Personality and Social Psychology*, 82, 6, 1007–1022.

Keynes, J.M. (1930) *Essays in Persuasion*, London: Macmillan.

Keynes, J.M. (1933) *Essays in Biography*, New York: Harcourt, Brace and Company.

Lane, R. (2000) *The Loss of Happiness in the Market Democracies*, Yale: Yale University Press.

Laurent, J. (ed.) (2003) *Evolutionary Economics and Human Nature*, Cheltenham: Elgar.

Layard, R. (1980) "Human satisfactions and public policy", *The Economic Journal*, 90, 737–750.

Layard, R. (2005) "Rethinking public economics: the implications of rivalry and habit", in Bruni, L. and Porta, P.L. (eds) *Economics and Happiness: Framings of Analysis*, Oxford: Oxford University Press, forthcoming.

Lebergott, S. (1993) *Pursuing Happiness*, Princeton: Princeton University Press.

Leibniz, G.W. (1972) *Political Writings (Cambridge Texts in the History of Political Thought)*, edited by P. Riley, Cambridge: Cambridge University Press.

Loria, A. (1904) *Verso la giustizia sociale*, Milan: Società editrice milanese.

Lubac de, H. (1977) *Pico della Mirandola: L'alba incompiuta del Rinascimento*, Milan: Jaka Books.

Lucas, R.E., Clark, A.E., Georgellis, Y. and Diener, E. (2002) *Unemployment Alters the Set-Point for Life Satisfaction*, Working Paper 2002/17, Delta, Paris.

Lykken, D. and Tellegen, A. (1996) "Happiness is a stochastic phenomenon", *Psychological Science*, 7, 186–189.

Machiavelli, N. (1513) *The Prince*. Online, available at: machiavelli.thefreelibrary.com/Prince.

MacIntyre, A. (1984) *After Virtue*, second edition, Notre Dame: University of Notre Dame Press.

Malthus, T.R. (1966 [1798]) *An Essay on the Principle of Population*, London: Macmillan.

Malthus, T.R. (1986 [1820]) *Principles of Political Economy*, "The Works of Thomas Robert Malthus", volume five, edited by E.A. Wrigley and David Souden, London: W. Pickering.

Mandeville, B. (1923 [1714]) *The Fable of the Bees: or, Private Vices, Publick Benefits*, edited by F.B. Kaye, 2 vols, Oxford: Clarendon Press.

Mansfield, H.C. (2000) "Bruni and Machiavelli on Civil Humanism", in Hankins, J. (ed.) *Renaissance Civic Humanism*, Cambridge: Cambridge University Press, pp. 223–246.

Marmot, M. (2004) *The Status Syndrome: How Social Standing Affects Our Health and Longevity*, New York: Times Books.

Marshall, A. (1946 [1890]) *Principles of Economics*, London: Macmillan.

Marx, K. (1906 [1867]) *Capital: a Critical Analysis of Capitalist Production*, edited by F. Engels, London: Swan Sonnenschein & Co.

Marx, K. (1994 [1857–1858]) *Grundrisse: Foundations of the Critique of Political Economy*, in Hausman, D.M. (ed.) *The Philosophy of Economics*, Cambridge: Cambridge University Press, pp. 119–142.

Matravers, M. (2005) "Happiness and political philosophy: the case of Nancy Mitford versus Evelyn Waugh", in Bruni, L. and Porta, P.L. (eds) *Economics and Happiness: Framings of Analysis*, Oxford: Oxford University Press, forthcoming.

Meier, S. and Stutzer, A. (2004) "Is volunteering rewarding in itself?", IZA Discussion Papers 1045, Institute for the Study of Labor (IZA).

Menger, C. (1871) *Grundsätze der Volkswirtschaftslehre*, Vienna: Braumüller.

Michels, R. (1918) *Economia e felicità*, Milan: Società Editrice Libraria.

Mill, James (1869) *Analysis of the Phenomena of the Human Mind*, London: Longmans, Green, Reader & Dyer.

Mill, J.S. (1862 [1843]) *System of Logic, Ratiocinative and Inductive*, London: Parker, Son, and Bourn.

Mill, J.S. (1920 [1848]) *Principles of Political Economy*, edited by W.J. Ashley, London: Longman Green & C.

Mill, J.S. (1963) [1833]) "Remarks on Bentham's philosophy", in Robson, J.M. (ed.) *Essays on Ethics, Religion and Society*, Collected Works, Vol. X, Toronto and London: University of Toronto Press; Routledge & Kegan Paul.

Mill, J.S. (1975 [1869]) *The Subjection of Women*, Oxford: Oxford University Press.

Mill, J.S. (1981 [1874]) *Autobiography and Literary Essays*, Collected Works, Vol. I, edited by John M. Robson and Jack Stillinger, Toronto and London: University of Toronto Press, Routledge & Kegan.

Mill, J.S. (1991 [1859]) *On Liberty and Other Essays*, edited by John Gray, Oxford: Oxford University Press.

Mill, J.S. (1998 [1863]) *Utilitarianism*, Collected Works, Vol. X, edited by John M. Robson and Jack Stillinger, Toronto and London: University of Toronto Press, Routledge & Kegan.

Millar, D.H. (1991) "An alternate approach to social philosophy and political economy, foresight institute" Online, available at: www.foresight.org/essays/econlove.html#Note1.

Mirowski, P. (1999) "Review" of *A Beautiful Mind*, by S. Nasar, *Economics and Philosophy*, 15, 302–307.

Morales, M. (1996) *Perfect Equality: John Stuart Mill on Well-Constituted Communities*, Lanham, MD: Rowman & Littlefield Publishers.

Muratori, L.A. (1749) *Della Pubblica Felicità*, Lucca.

Muratori, L.A. (1751) *Della carità cristiana*, Venice.

158   Bibliography

Muratori, L.A. (1824) [1743] *Cristianesimo felice*, Turin: Tipografia Bianco.

Myers, David G. (1999) "Close relationship and quality of life", in Kahneman, D., Diener, E. and Schwartz, N. (eds) *Well-Being: Foundations of Hedonic Psychology*, New York: Russell Sage Foundation, pp. 374–391.

Naiplaul, V.S. (2000) *Letters Between a Father and Son*, London: Abacus.

Nash, J. (1996) *Essays on Game Theory*, Cheltenham: Edward Elgar.

Neumark, D. and Postlewaite, A. (1998) "Relative income concerns and the rise in married women's employment", *Journal of Public Economics*, 157–183.

Nezlek, J.B. (2000) "The motivational and cognitive dynamics of day-to-day social life", in Forgas, J.P., Williams, K. and Wheeler, L. (eds) *The Social Mind: Cognitive and Motivational Aspects of Interpersonal Behaviour*, New York: Cambridge University Press, pp. 92–111.

Ng, Y.K. (1978) "Economic growth and social welfare: the need for a complete study of happiness", *Kyklos*, 31, 4, 575–587.

Ng, Y.K. (1997) "A case for *happiness*, cardinalism, and interpersonal comparability", *Economic Journal*, 107, 1848–1858.

Nickerson, C., Schwarz, N., Diener, E. and Kahneman, D. (2003) "Zeroing the dark side of the American dream: a closer look at the negative consequences of the goal for financial success", *Psychological Science*, 14, 531–536.

Nuccio, O. (1987) *Il pensiero economico italiano: le fonti (1050–1450). L'etica laica e la formazione dello spirito economico*, Sassari: Gallizzi.

Nuccio, O. (1995) *La civiltà italiana nella formazione della scienza economica*, Milan: Etas Libri.

Nussbaum, M.C. (1986) *The Fragility of Goodness: Luck and Ethics in Greek Tragedy and Philosophy*, second edition 2001, Cambridge: Cambridge University Press.

Nussbaum, M. (2005) "Mill between Aristotle and Bentham", in Bruni, L. and Porta, P.L. (eds) *Economics and Happiness: Framings of Analysis*, Oxford: Oxford University Press, forthcoming.

Nussbaum, M. and Sen, A. (1993) *The Quality of Life*, Oxford: Oxford University Press.

Offer, A. (2003) "Economic welfare measurements and human well-being", in David, Paul A. and Thomas, Mark (eds) *The Economic Future in Historical Perspective*, Oxford: Oxford University Press.

Ogburn, W.F. (1935) "Indexes of social trends and their fluctuations", *American Journal of Sociology*, 40, 822–828.

O'Neil, B. (2000) *Approaches to Modelling Emotions in Game Theory*, "Proceedings of the Conference on Cognition, Emotion and Rational Choice", UCLA, April.

Osberg, L. and Sharpe, A. (2002) "An index of economic well-being for Selected OECD Countries", *Review of Income and Wealth*, 48, 3, 291–316.

Oswald, A.J. (1997) "*Happiness* and economic performance", *Economic Journal*, 107, 1815–1831.

Pagano, F.M. (1962 [1789]) *Ragionamento sulla libertà del commercio del pesce in Napoli diretto al regio tribunale dell'ammiragliato e consolato di mare da Francesco Mario Pagano, avvocato dei poverini esso tribunale e regio professor di dritto nell'università napoletana*, Naples, reprinted in Venturi, pp. 842–853.

Palmieri, G. (1788) *Riflessioni sulla pubblica felicità relativamente al Regno di Napoli*, Milan: Pirotta e Maspero.

Palmieri, G. (1853 [1792]) *Della ricchezza della nazione*, Livorno: V. Mauzi.
Palmieri, G. (1997) *Dalla Pubblica felicità alla Ricchezza nazionale: Scritti di economia politica*, edited by M. Proto, Manduria: Piero Lacaita Editore.
Palmieri, M. (1981 [1440]) *Della vita civile*, Firenze: Olscki.
Pantaleoni, M. (1925) *Erotemi di economia*, 2 vols, Bari: Laterza.
Pantaleoni, M. (1970 [1889]) *Principi di economia pura*, Padova: Cedam.
Paoletti, F. (1804 [1772]) *I veri mezzi di render felici le società*, in Scittori classici di Economia Politica, Milan: De Stefani.
Pareto, V. (1896–1897) *Cours d'économie politique*, Lausanne: Rouge.
Pareto, V. (1900a) "Sunto di alcuni capitoli di un nuovo trattato di economia politica del prof. Pareto", *Giornale degli Economisti*, X, March, 216–235; June, 511–549.
Pareto, V. (1900b) "Sul fenomeno economico: lettera a Benedetto Croce", *Giornale degli Economisti*, 21, 139–162.
Pareto, V. (1906) *Manuale di economia politica, con una introduzione alla scienza sociale*, Milan: Società editrice libraria.
Pareto, V. (1909) *Manuel d'économie politique*, Geneva: Giard & Brière.
Pareto, V. (1960) *Lettere a Maffeo Pantaleoni*, 3 vols, Rome: Banca Nazionale del Lavoro.
Pareto, V. (1964 [1916]) *Trattato di sociologia generale*, Firenze: Barbera. English edition, Mind and Society.
Pareto, V. (1975) *Corrispondance: 1890–1923*, edited by G. Busino, Oeuvres Complètes, 19, Geneva: Droz.
Patrizi, F. (1964 [1553]) *La città felice*, in Widmar, B. (ed.) *Scrittori politici del '500 e '600*, Milan: Rizzoli.
Pelligra, V. (2003) "The not-so-fragile fragility of goodness: the responsive quality of fiduciary relationships". Paper presented at the Conference "The Paradoxes of Happiness in Economics", Università Bicocca, Milan, 21–23 March.
Phelps, C. (2001) "A clue to the paradox of *happiness*", *Journal of Economic Behavior and Organization*, 45, 293–300.
Pigou, A.C. (1920) *The Economics of Welfare*, London: Macmillan & Co.
Plato (1997) *Collected Works*, Indianapolis: Hackett Publishing Co.
Pocock, J.G.A. (1975) *The Machiavellian Moment: Florentine Political Thought and the Atlantic Republican Tradition*, Princeton: Princeton University Press.
Polanyi, K. (1957) "Aristotle discovers the economy", in Polanyi, K., Arensberg, C.M. and Pearson, H.W. (eds) *Trade and Market in the Early Empires: Economies in History and Theory*, New York, London: The Free Press, Collier-Macmillan, pp. 64–94.
Porta, P.L. and Scazzieri, R. (2002) "Pietro Verri's Political Economy", *History of Political Economy*, 34, 83–110.
Putnam, R. (2000) *Bowling Alone*, New York: Simon and Schuster.
Qizilbash, M. (2005) "Capability, happiness and adaptation in Mill and Sen". Paper presented at the conference "Capabilities & Happiness", Milan–Bicocca, 16–18 June.
Quadri, G. (1947) *Nicolò Machiavelli e la costruzione politica della coscienza morale*, Firenze: La Nuova Italia.
Rahe, P.A. (2000) "Situating Machiavelli", in Hankins, J. (ed.) *Renaissance Civic Humanism*, Cambridge: Cambridge University Press, pp. 270–308.
Reinert, S.A. (2005) "Republican mercantilism out of the context: on the Italian

reception of John Cary's essay on the State of England". Paper presented at the Conference for the 250 anniversary of the "Cattedra of Commercio e Meccanica, Istituto per gli studi filosofici", Naples, 6 May.

Rochefocauld, Francois de la (1993) *Massime*, Milan: Newton Compton.

Robbins, L. (1932) *The Nature and Significance of Economic Science*, London: Macmillan.

Robbins, L. (1933) "Introduction" to Wicksteed, P.H., *Common Sense of Political Economy*, London: Macmillan.

Robertson, D.H. (1956) "What does the economist economize?", in *Economic Commentaries*, London: Staples Press Limited.

Romagnosi, G.D. (1835) *Collezione degli articoli di economia politica e statistica civile del professore G.D. Romagnosi*, Firenze: Stamperia Piatti.

Rosmini, A. (2001) *Grande dizionario antologico del pensiero di Antonio Rosmini*, Vol. 4, Rome: Città Nuova-Edizioni rosminiane.

Rosmini, A. (2003 [1826]) *Politica prima*, Vol. 35 of "Opere edite ed inedite di Antonio Rosmini", Rome: Istituto Studi Filosofici, Centro Internazionale di Studi Rosminiani, Città Nuova.

Rothschild, E. (2003) *Economic Sentiment: Adam Smith, Condorcet and the Enlightenment*, Harvard: Harvard University Press.

Ruggiero, G. (2000) *Gaetano Filangieri: Un uomo, una famiglia, un amore nella Napoli del Settecento*, Naples: Alfredo Guida.

Ruhm, C. (2000) "Are recessions good for your health?", *Quarterly Journal of Economics*, 115, 617–650.

Ryff, C.D. (1995) "Psychological well-being in adult life", *Current Directions Psychological Science*, 4, 99–104.

Ryff, C.D. and Singer, B. (1998) "The contours of positive human health", *Psychological Inquiries*, 9, 1–28.

Ryff, C.D. and Singer, B. (2000) "Interpersonal flourishing: a positive health agenda for the new millennium", *Personality and Social Psychology Review*, 4, 30–44.

Ryff, C.D., Singer, B.H., Wing, E. and Love, G.D. (2001) "Elective affinities and uninvited agonies: mapping emotion with significant others onto health", in Ryff, C.D. and Singer, B.H. (eds) *Emotion, Social Relationships, and Health: Third Annual Wisconsin Symposium on Emotion*, New York: Oxford University Press.

Sacco, P. and Zamagni, S. (eds) (2002) *Complessità relazionale e comportamento economico: materiali per un nuovo paradigma di razionalità*, Bologna: Il Mulino.

Sally, D. (2000) "A general theory of sympathy, mind-reading, and social interaction, with an application to the prisoner's dilemma", *Social Science Information*, 39, 567–634.

Schabas, M. (1990) *A World Ruled by Numbers: William Stabkey Jevons and the Rise of Mathematical Economics*, Princeton: Princeton University Press.

Schelling, T. (1960) *The Strategy of Conflict*, Harvard: Harvard University Press.

Schumpeter, J.A. (1994 [1954]) *History of Economic Analysis*, New York: Oxford University Press.

Scitovsky, T. (1976) *The Joyless Economy: an Inquiry into Human Satisfaction and Consumer Dissatisfaction*, Oxford: Oxford University Press.

Scitovsky, T. (1986) *Human Desire and Economic Satisfaction: Essays on the Frontiers of Economics*, Brighton: Wheatsheaf Books.

Scitovsky, T. (1996) "My own criticism of the *Joyless economy*", *Critical Review*, 10, 595–605.

Sen, A.K. (1991) *The Standard of Living*, Cambridge: Cambridge University Press.

Sen, A.K. (1993) "Capability and well-being", in Nussbaum, M. and Sen, A. (eds) *The Quality of Life*, Oxford: Clarendon Press.

Sen, A.K. (2000) *Development as Freedom*, New York: A. Alfred Knopp.

Sen, A.K. (2002) *Rationality and Freedom*, Cambridge, MA: Belknap Press of Harvard University.

Sen, A.K. (2005) "Why Happiness is Important But Not Uniquely So". Paper presented at the workshop, "Capabilities & Happiness", Milan-Bicocca, 16–18 June.

Sidgwick, H. (1901 [1874]) *The Methods of Ethics*, London: Macmillan.

Silver, A. (1990) "Friendship in commercial society: eighteenth-century social theory and modern sociology", *American Journal of Sociology*, 95, 1474–1504.

Skinner, Q. (1978) *The Foundations of the Modern Political Thought*, Vol. 2, Cambridge: Cambridge University Press.

Skinner, Q. (1999) *Machiavelli*, Bologna: Il Mulino.

Smith, A. (1976 [1776]) *The Wealth of Nations*, Oxford: Oxford University Press.

Smith, A. (1978 [1763]) *Lectures on Jurisprudence*, The Glasgow Edition of the Work and Correspondence of Adam Smith, Indianapolis: Liberty Fund.

Smith, A. (1984 [1759]) *The Theory of Moral Sentiments*, edited by D.D. Raphael and A.L. Macfie, Indianapolis: Liberty Fund.

Sombart, W. (1950 [1913]) *Il borghese. Contributo allo storia dello spirito dell'uomo economico moderno*, Milan: Longanesi.

Sombart, W. (1967 [1902]) *Il capitalismo moderno*, Turin: Utet.

Spinoza, B. (1667) *Ethics*, Online, available at: frank.mtsu.edu/~rbombard/RB/Spinoza/ethica-front.html.

Stack, Steven and Eshleman, J. Ross (1998) "Marital status and happiness: a 17-nation study", *Journal of Marriage and the Family*, 60, 2, 527–536.

Steedman, I. (1994) "Wicksteed: economist and prophet" in Brennan, H.G. and Waterman, A.M.C. (eds) *Economics and Religion: Are They Distinct?*, Boston: Kluwer Academic Publishers.

Steedman, I. (1995) "Rationality, economic man and altruism in P.H. Wicksteed's *Common Sense of Political Economy*", in Zamagni, S. (ed.) *The Economics of Altruism*, Aldershot: Elgar.

Sudipta, K. and Khilnani, S. (eds) (2001) *Civil Society*, Cambridge: Cambridge University Press.

Sugden, R. (1991) "Rational choice: a survey of contributions from economics and philosophy", *The Economic Journal*, 101, 751–785.

Sugden, R. (1993) "Welfare, resources and capabilities: a review of inequality re-examined by Amartya Sen", *Journal of Economic Literature*, 31, 1947–1962.

Sugden, R. (2005a) "The correspondence of sentiments: an explanation of the pleasure of social interaction", in Bruni, L. and Porta, P.L. (eds) *Economics and Happiness: Framings of Analysis*, Oxford: Oxford University Press.

Sugden, R. (2005b) "Capability, Happiness and Opportunity". Paper presented at the Conference, "Capabilities & Happiness", Milan-Bicocca, 16–18 June.

Tateo, F. (1972) *L'umanesimo meridionale*, Bari: Laterza.

Thoits, Peggy A. and Hewitt, Lyndi N. (2001) "Volunteer work and well-being", *Journal of Health and Social Behavior*, 42, 2, 115–131.

Thompson, W. (1963 [1824]) *The Inquiry into the Principles of the Distribution of the Wealth most Conducive to Human Happiness*, New York: A.M. Kelley.

Todeschini, G. (2002) *I mercanti e il tempio: la società cristiana e il circolo virtuosi della ricchezza fra Medioevo ed Età Moderna*, Bologna: Il Mulino.

Todorov, T. (1998) *La vita in comune*, Milan: Nuova Pratiche Editrice.

Trinkaus, C. (1965) *Adversity's Nobleman: the Italian Humanists on Happiness*, New York: Octagon Books.

Tversky, A. and Kahneman, D. (1991) "Loss aversion in riskless choice: a reference dependent model", *Quarterly Journal of Economics*, 106, 4, 1039–1061.

Tyler, T.R. (1990) *Why People Obey the Law*, New Haven: Yale University Press.

Uhlaner, C.J. (1989) "Relational goods and participation: incorporating sociality into a theory of rational action", *Public Choice*, 62, 253–285.

Urbinati, N. (2002) *Mill on Democracy: From the Athenian Polis to Representative Government*, Chicago: Chicago University Press.

Van Praag, B. and Frijters, P. (1999) "The measurement of welfare and well-being: the Leyden approach", in Kahneman, D., Diener, E. and Schwartz, N. (eds) *Well-Being: Foundations of Hedonic Psychology*, New York: Russell Sage Foundation, pp. 413–433.

Van Praag, B.M.S. (1968) Individual Welfare Functions and Consumer Behavior: A Theory of Rational Irrationality, PhD thesis, Amsterdam: North Holland.

Van Praag, B.M.S. (1971) "The welfare function of income in Belgium: an empirical investigation", *European Economic Review*, 2, 337–369.

Van Praag, B.M.S. (2005) *Happiness Quantified – a Satisfaction Calculus Approach*, Oxford; Oxford University Press.

Van Praag, B.M.S. and Kapteyn, A. (1973) "Further evidence on the individual welfare function of income: an empirical investigation in the Netherlands", *European Economic Review*, 4, 33–62.

Van Praag, B.M.S. and van der Sar, N.L. (1988) "Household cost functions and equivalence scales", *Journal of Human Resources*, 23, 193–210.

Vasco, G.B. (1769) *La felicità pubblica considerata nei coltivatori di terre proprie*, Brescia: Rizzardi.

Veblen, T. (1899 [1998]) *The Theory of the Leisure Class*, New York: Prometheus Books.

Veenhoven, R. (1991) "Is happiness relative?", *Social Indicators Research*, 24, 1–34.

Veenhoven, R. (1993) *Happiness in Nations*, Rotterdam: RISBO, Erasmus University.

Veenhoven, R. (1994) "Is happiness a trait? Tests of the theory that a better society does not make people any happier", *Social Indicators Research*, 32, 101–160.

Veenhoven, R. (2000) *Freedom and Happiness: a Comparative Study in 44 Nations in the Early 1990s*, mimeo, Oxford University.

Veenhoven, R. (2005) "Happiness in hardship", in Bruni, L. and Porta, P.L. (eds) *Economics and Happiness: Framings of Analysis*, Oxford: Oxford University Press, forthcoming.

Venturi, F. (1962) *Illuministi italiani*, Turin: Einaudi.

Venturi, F. (1969) *Settecento riformatore*, Turin: Einaudi.

Verri, P. (1948) *Del piacere e del dolore ed altri scritti*, Milan: Feltrinelli.

Verri, P. (1963 [1763]) *Il discorso sulla felicità*, Milan: Feltrinelli.

Verri, P. (1964) *Del piacere e del dolore ed altri scritti*, edited by R. De Felice, Milan: Feltrinelli.

Vico, G.B. (1957 [1710]) *De Antiquissima Italorum Sapientia, in Tutte le opere di G.B. Vico*, Milan: Mondadori.

Vico, G.B. (1948 [1744]) *The New Science*, English translation by Thomas Goddard Bergin and Max Harold Fisch, Ithaca: Cornell University Press.

Viner, J. (1972) *The Role of Providence in the Social Order*, Philadelphia: American Philosophical Society.

Von Neumann, J. and Morgenstern, O. (1964 [1944]) *Game Theory and Economic Behaviour*, New York: John Wiley and Sons.

White, N. (1995) "Conflicting parts of happiness in Aristotle's Ethics", *Ethics*, 105, 258–283.

Wicksteed, P.H. (1884) "The marxian theory of value. Das Kapital: a criticism", *To-day*, Vol. 2 (new series), October, 388–409. Republished in Wicksteed, P.H. (1933 [1910]), *Common Sense of Political Economy*, Vol. II, London: Macmillan, 705–733.

Wicksteed, P.H. (1894) *The Co-ordination of the Laws of Distribution*, London: Macmillan.

Wicksteed, P.H. (1933 [1906]) "Review" of Pareto (1906), *Economic Journal*, XVI.

Wicksteed, P.H. (1933 [1910]) *Common Sense of Political Economy*, London: Macmillan.

Wicksteed, P.H. (1933 [1914]) "The scope and the method of Political Economy" *Economic Journal*, 24, 1–23.

Wicksteed, P.H. (2002 [1913]) *Dante and Aquinas*, Honolulu: University Press of the Pacific.

Widmar, B. (ed.) (1964) *Scrittori politici del '500 e '600*, Milan: Rizzoli.

Winch, D. (1978) *Adam Smith's Policy*, Cambridge: Cambridge University Press.

Wood, D. (2002) *Medieval Economic Thoughts*, Cambridge: Cambridge University Press.

Zamagni, S. (2005) "Happiness and individualism: a very difficult union", in Bruni, L. and Porta, P.L. (eds) *Economics and Happiness: Framings of Analysis*, Oxford: Oxford University Press.

Index

Printed in the United States
by Baker & Taylor Publisher Services